A Blackqueer Sexual Ethics

T&T CLARK ENQUIRIES IN EMBODIMENT, SEXUALITY,
AND SOCIAL ETHICS

Series editors
Monique Moultrie
Kate Ott
Darryl W. Stephens

A Blackqueer Sexual Ethics

Embodiment, Possibility, and Living Archive

Elyse Ambrose

t&tclark
LONDON • NEW YORK • OXFORD • NEW DELHI • SYDNEY

T&T CLARK
Bloomsbury Publishing Plc
50 Bedford Square, London, WC1B 3DP, UK
1385 Broadway, New York, NY 10018, USA
29 Earlsfort Terrace, Dublin 2, Ireland

BLOOMSBURY, T&T CLARK and the T&T Clark logo are
trademarks of Bloomsbury Publishing Plc

First published in Great Britain 2024

Copyright © Elyse Ambrose, 2024

Elyse Ambrose has asserted their right under the Copyright,
Designs and Patents Act, 1988, to be identified as Author of this work.

For legal purposes the Acknowledgments on pp. ix–xi constitute
an extension of this copyright page.

Cover image © Elyse Ambrose

All rights reserved. No part of this publication may be reproduced or transmitted
in any form or by any means, electronic or mechanical, including photocopying,
recording, or any information storage or retrieval system, without prior
permission in writing from the publishers.

Bloomsbury Publishing Plc does not have any control over, or responsibility for,
any third-party websites referred to or in this book. All internet addresses given
in this book were correct at the time of going to press. The author and publisher
regret any inconvenience caused if addresses have changed or sites have ceased
to exist, but can accept no responsibility for any such changes.

A catalogue record for this book is available from the British Library.

Library of Congress Cataloging-in-Publication Data
Names: Ambrose, Elyse, author.
Title: A Blackqueer sexual ethics: embodiment, possibility,
and living archive / Elyse Ambrose.
Description: London; New York: T&T Clark, 2024. |
Series: T&T Clark enquiries in embodiment, sexuality, and social ethics |
Includes bibliographical references and index.
Identifiers: LCCN 2023051120 (print) | LCCN 2023051121 (ebook) |
ISBN 9780567707925 (pb) | ISBN 9780567707932 (hb) |
ISBN 9780567707949 (epub) | ISBN 9780567707956 e(pdf)
Subjects: LCSH: African American gay people–New York (State)–New York–20th century. |
Sexual minorities, Black–History. | Sexual ethics–Religious aspects. | Sexual orientation–
Religious aspects. | Christian ethics. | Christian gay people–Religious life. | Christianity
and homosexuality. | Harlem Renaissance. | Harlem (New York, N.Y.)
Classification: LCC BR563.B53 A43 2024 (print) | LCC BR563.B53 (ebook) |
DDC 176.086/6–dc23/eng/20231222
LC record available at https://lccn.loc.gov/2023051120
LC ebook record available at https://lccn.loc.gov/2023051121

ISBN:	HB:	978-0-5677-0793-2
	PB:	978-0-5677-0792-5
	ePDF:	978-0-5677-0795-6
	eBook:	978-0-5677-0794-9

Series: T&T Clark Enquiries in Embodiment, Sexuality, and Social Ethics

Typeset by Integra Software Services Pvt. Ltd.
Printed and bound in Great Britain

To find out more about our authors and books visit www.bloomsbury.com
and sign up for our newsletters.

To Lee and others like them

CONTENTS

List of Figures viii
Acknowledgments ix

Introduction: Toward Blackqueer Possibility in/through Living Archive 1

1 Examining the Integrative in Blackqueer Harlem 27

2 Blackqueering of Ethical and Theological Discourse 63

3 Spirit in the Dark Body: Blackqueer Expressions of the Im/material 101

4 Constructing a Blackqueer Sexual Ethics 161

Epilogue 193
Bibliography 196
Index 208

FIGURES

3.1 "black queer feminist planet" (New Orleans, 2019) 108

3.2 "strength and blessing/blessed strength" (Philadelphia, 2022) 109

3.3 "black queer mystic warrior poet" (New Orleans, 2019) 110

3.4 "i am a listener, an observer" (New York City, 2019) 111

3.5 "being so that i can be in the quest of becoming" (New Jersey, 2022) 112

3.6 "black queer believer" (Atlanta, 2019) 113

3.7 "black ethical liberation humanist" (New York City, 2018) 114

3.8 "i am a gatekeeper [...] i am multiplicities" (New York City, 2019) 115

3.9 "african american gay man who still carries the energy forces, or the souls, of my people" (New York City, 2019) 116

ACKNOWLEDGMENTS

This book has become through the efforts, generosity, and overflow of kindness of many persons and organizations to whom I am deeply grateful. I need to start at this work's beginnings.

I thank the learning community at the Interdenominational Theological Center and Gammon Theological Seminary with whom I journeyed to come to a fundamental understanding of the divinity within blackness and sexuality, the sacred that surfaced at my fingertips and reverberated in my voice and pen during those years of my Master of Divinity program. I especially thank Riggins R. Earl, Temba Mafico, Beverly Wallace, Carolyn McCrary, Margaret Aymer, Lisa Allen-McLaurin, and Albert Mosley. I offer special thanks to Randall C. Bailey, Jacquelyn Grant, and Itihari Touré for your generous mentorship and support in my development as a scholar and human. Gerald I. Parks II, I remember you often and thank you for the laughs and your belief in us.

I am grateful for the intellectual and communal spaces that I first encountered during my doctoral program, which enabled me to listen to my voice and to sharpen my queries through rigor and tenderness. I express deep gratitude for each fellow, mentor, and staff person I encountered through the Women of Color Scholars Program of the General Board of Higher Education of the United Methodist Church (now the *Angella P. Current-Felder Women of Color Scholars Program*). Thank you to Rosetta E. Ross, Cristian De La Rosa, Rita Nakashima Brock, Jung Ha Kim, Allyson Collinsworth, and Marcie Bigord. I am especially grateful to Rosetta E. Ross and I am indebted to you for introducing me to the archive (even microfilm!).

Thank you, blackqueer Harlem. Thank you blackqueering and LGBTQ+-focused scholars of religion before me and those to come. Thank you to each person who allowed me the honor of photographing and interviewing you. Your wisdom and insight have forever changed me.

I am grateful for the colleagues and staff of the Coolidge Fellowship through the CrossCurrents Summer Research Colloquium/Auburn Seminary who aided my development of Chapter 2 of this project. Special thanks to K. J. Cerankowski, Cypress Reign, Marshall Green, Wriply M. Bennet, Katie Horowitz, Max Strassfeld, and Elliot Ratzman for aiding my thinking and my feeling more expansively around this work.

Thanks to the mentors and colleagues of the Yale University Sarah Pettit Doctoral Fellowship in LGBT Studies for your support with an early iteration of Chapter 4.

I am grateful to the Forum for Theological Exploration for mentorship, fellowship, and support. Thank you to Edwin David Aponte and the Louisville Institute, namely the Vocation as Theological Educator and Postdoctoral Fellowship cohort and our tireless guide, Carmen M. Nanko-Fernández. I am especially grateful to the fellows who provided invaluable advice and encouragement throughout these paths of book-making and scholarly and personal growth, during a pandemic no less! Deep gratitude to the students I encountered at Meadville Lombard Theological School, who made the time that I was not writing so fulfilling. Thank you, Pamela R. Lightsey and Elías Ortega Aponte, for the spaciousness to bring this work to life and for your encouragement.

Thank you Susan Woolever, Natalie Williams, Sung Hyun Lee, June Hee Yoon, Leah Thomas, Lisa Asedillo, and Nikki Hoskins. You all were a lifeline to me in bringing the ideas within this book to life and sustaining me in the process. Thank you for the deep, rigorous, belly-laughing, thinking, honest community, Leonard Curry, Minenhle Khumalo, and Eric A. Thomas. For the years of sharing learning space, encouragement that speaks to my bones, and imagining with, special thanks to you, Eric. Thank you to my intellectual guides at Drew University, namely Lillie Edwards and Traci C. West. Special thanks to you, Traci C. West, for your tireless support from the very beginnings of this journey.

I am grateful to the Department of Black Study and the Department for the Study of Religion at the University of California, Riverside, for their flexibility and granting me the space to create. Thank you for enabling the opportunity for me to live into my rhythms and do academia more and more differently. Deep gratitude to Vorris

Nunley, Sage Whitson, and Melissa M. Wilcox for your advocacy and model. I offer a very special thanks to my research assistant, Kori Pacyniak, for your timely and vital help on this project.

Thank you to Anna Turton and the entire team at Bloomsbury. To the editors of the Enquiries in Embodiment, Sexuality, and Social Ethics series—Monique Moultrie, Kate Ott, and Darryl Stephens—I am grateful for your confidence in this project and for your generative feedback. Special thanks to you, Kate Ott; your generosity has been invaluable. For your thoughtful editing work, thank you Raedorah Stewart.

Thank you to my LA blackqueer community for helping me reach the finish line with joy. Thank you to every scholar-friend and friend-friend for your compassion, tenderness, and encouragement. Thanks to you, Jé Hooper, for reminding me to be/that I am big. Thank you, Cynthia Hooper, for a soft place to rest and write. storäe michele, thank you for the years of holding, tending, and believing. Thank you, Allison Manuel, for your presence and every luxuriously meandering conversation. Thank you, Jorge Lockward, for reminding me of all that is important and for walking with me. For helping me open the way and being my friend from the beginnings of this, before, after, and today, thank you Eugene Allen Minson III. Thank you, Mom, Dad, Derek, Yaves, Bryson, and Mamá for your deep love. Thank you, niblings, for being you.

Jessica Susan Oler, thank you for loving me wholly and daily. Each load is made lighter with you by my side. I could not ask for more.

I offer loving gratitude to my co-sojourners along every way, my benevolent ancestors.

Introduction: Toward Blackqueer Possibility in/through Living Archive

"How does it feel to be a *possibility*?" As I sat with nearly thirty years of scholarship from black ethicists and theologians foregrounding LGBTQ+ experience in their research, with histories of the communities of black folks embodying sexual and gender nonconformity, and contemporary folks living into the fecundity of their moral imagination and faith practice in their blackqueerness, these words and worlds of possibility intumesced. I settle into this expansion invited by blackqueerness to consider another approach to exploring the experiences of systematically marginalized people and constructing liberative social and sexual ethics. This spin on the question suffused in the social sphere and recorded by W. E. B. Du Bois in *The Souls of Black Folks* (1903) refuses the alienation of problematization of blackness and queerness and grounds not on the logics of a dominating imagination, but in the vast possibilities of blackqueerness.

A Blackqueer Sexual Ethics: Embodiment, Possibility, and Living Archive serves as an invitation to one possibility of what an approach to ethics that takes seriously blackqueer experience, intellect, feeling, and moral imagination may yield.[1] What is forwarded here is not a concrete, systematic ethic but *a* possibility; therefore, I employ the language of "a blackqueer ethics" instead of a presumably singular or homogeneous *the*. There has been, will be, and ought to be a multiplicity of blackqueer ethics. A blackqueer ethics speaks to a methodological lens for doing ethics, namely for our purposes, sexual ethics. It posits values that challenge traditionalism and its disintegrative, limiting power and considers how blackqueerness and its living archives may serve as a resource for moral and ethical reflection in communities. Because community is the location for the practice of ethics, I define community not in terms of spatial proximity or shared (religious) space, but in terms of integration and intentionality—those with whom persons willingly pursue right relations in vulnerability, truth, accountability, and becoming. This book builds upon a tradition of an embodied and theoretical critique at the intersections of race, sexuality, gender, and religion through 1920s Harlem sexual and gender nonconformist communities; LGBTQ+-centered ethics and theology scholarship; and contemporary oral histories of those living into their blackqueerness and religion/spirituality simultaneously. These sites of moral reflection inspire integrative practices for doing ethics: communal belonging, individual and collective becoming, goodness, inspirited bodies/embodied spirits, and shared thriving. Emphases on both personal and social right-relatedness mark a shift from Christian sexual ethics based in rules toward a communal relations-based and transreligious approach to sexual ethics whose aim is toward the integrative, toward justice love.

Living Archive

Imagination rarely exceeds the limits of a chosen canon. The archive collected in this book aims toward disrupting, expanding, and remaking notions of canon, of archive, particularly in the location and formation of moral knowledge. I come to a blackqueer archive as a blackqueer gender-ambiguous person seeking to examine the fecundity of moral imagination and black religion through the experience of blackqueerness. The disruption and irruption, as named by Thelathia "Nikki" Young, this subjectivity represents inform my approach to ethics, one that is at once rooted in liberative values and virtues and yields expansive and open-ended ethics. My intention with this living archive is a collective invitation to tending—giving attention to, looking into and after, shifting, sitting with.

The significance of archives for my work became increasingly present during a peak of COVID-19 and in the reality and ever-present specter of black loss in the United States, when I and many others contemplated in distinct ways black and blackqueer futures. In collaboration with blackqueer femme artist, scholar, and playwright, storäe michele, I had the opportunity to think, experiment, and feel more deeply into the limits and creative potential of archives. We developed speculative fiction video archives for their film, *mama [rose.]* (2021), and laid the groundwork for our project through a Center on African American Religion, Sexual Politics, and Social Justice at Columbia University and Luce Foundation grant, wherein we tasked ourselves with collecting and artistically integrating the strategies and technologies of survival and thriving employed by blackqueer people, building upon storäe michele's framework, "a practice in black femme freedom-making."[2] Additionally, in Saidiya Hartman's *Wayward Lives, Beautiful Experiments: Intimate Histories of Social Upheaval* (2019), I saw examples of creatively and thoughtfully approaching the lives of "queer radicals" to forward their agency and to retell (and in her words, to redress) histories and their erasures.[3] At the same time, I was exploring speculative futures and the transdisciplinary, nontraditional, queer potential of archives through the works of Alexis Pauline Gumbs in *M Archives: After the End of the World* (2018) and "Evidence," her "visionary fiction" piece in *Octavia's Brood: Science Fiction Stories from Social Justice Movements* (2015).[4] Both storäe michele and Gumbs explicitly and creatively imbue archives (particularly those of black femmes and women) with aliveness. storäe michele, Hartman, and Gumbs each inspire me to consider what it might look like to trouble the limits of blackqueer archives, to see them as fluid, growing, here and there, surmised, now, as distant as a private institution's collections and as accessible as an elder's photo album, like a breathing, growing and contracting, complex entity—living.[5]

Blackqueer Methods

A blackqueer ethics is integrative, transdisciplinary, transreligious. It aims toward right relationship with self and others and is rooted in the experiences of persons living (in[to]) blackqueerness. Integrative reflects a commitment to wholeness of the self and community that refuses to discard any of its parts. It is allowing together, even assuming together, black and queer, body and spirit, sacred and secular, collapsing the delineations between them and expanding their meanings as they are placed in nonoppositional relationship to one another. Integrative speaks to an entanglement with all that it is to be human and, in particular, a full expression of sexuality without a morally dichotomous relationship to desire, power, the body, or difference; sexuality is of the self and as necessary to wholeness as any other aspect. Additionally, sexuality as relational is communal and, therefore, a vital aspect of right relationship. Integrative speaks to relating in justice love.[6] I offer *integrative values* as a constructive possibility in envisioning blackqueer sexual ethics, and an alternative to the disintegrative principles and practices that often fracture self- and communal-relating, such as racism, heteropatriarchy, gender binarism, disembodiment, and their accompanying ethical proscriptions. *Disintegrative values* are often found in moral thought guided by traditionalism, a term that does not seek to problematize tradition in itself, but rather, the long-standing, fixed commitment in Christian morality and academia to "business"—that is, imperialist white supremacist capitalist heteropatriarchy—"as usual."[7] Integrative, as a descriptor and not a state, speaks to a process rather than an end, the continual reworking that sexual, or any, ethics requires.

In its commitment to right relations and communality, drawing from connections to its shared womanist, black feminist, and liberative values, a blackqueer ethics concerns the well-being and integrative wholeness of black people as a community, as collective selves. A focus on communality marks a blackqueer ethics as relations-based and not rules-based, to actively refuse, as liberative Christian ethicist Marvin M. Ellison names it, "a rule-based sexual morality [that] has been rigid, legalistic, and punitive, relying on fear and shame to keep people compliant and on the 'straight and narrow.'"[8] Communal right-relatedness does not manifest in the face of the demand to be compliant or to bear fear, shame, and punishment. Instead, it exists where right relationship, that is, justice love, is held as a virtue. I propose an approach to sexual ethics that is not at all tied to sex acts—a set of do's and don'ts. Instead of assessing *what* one is doing, it assesses *how* one is doing—what values inform the relational posture that undergirds any particular sex act. More broadly, this is to say, sexual ethics are always communal ethics. On this wise, I employ the framing communal-sexual ethics.

A transdisciplinary approach is necessary to bring together, analyze, and build from a living archive of blackqueerness. Considerations of ethics grounded in blackness and queerness have developed since the turn of the century considering questions of embodiment, cultural artifacts, liminality, family, and justice and have looked to performance studies, LGBTQ+ artistic productions, and auto/ethnography as ways of getting at ethical considerations through this subjective lens. Because black liberation theologies addressing lesbian, gay, bisexual, queer, and trans life frequently have within them an ethical inquiry (i.e., "In light of who God is, who/how ought we be?") and accompanying ethical claims, theological resources are included with ethics scholarship to capture a fuller history of black LGBTQ+-focused scholarship. I also draw from performance studies, particularly in examining sexual and gender nonconformist communities in 1920s Harlem, in addition to black studies and black religious studies. Such interlocutors aid me in approaching the archive with attentiveness to the unique ways that gender, sexuality, and race inform lived experience and may enliven disciplinary discourse.

Christian ethics and theology make up much of the scholarship in this book that directly addresses religion. Because many blackqueer and black people hold commitments to Christian religion or are informed by it through familial, cultural, social, aesthetic, or proximate means and because of how Christianity shapes social discourse in the United States, it is important to interrogate Christian sexual ethics and their, at times, disintegrative values as a problem that I argue is countered by blackqueer possibility. In speaking of black queer theology, Amaryah Shaye Armstrong states:

> ... maintaining the boundaries of orthodox Christian claims is a project that is historically tied up with the maintenance of an anti-black Christian identity and its imagination of the world as governed by white patriarchal authority [...] Moreover, the task must be to continue to displace Christian theology and its habits and practices of thought as the guiding norm for doing black queer theology.[9]

Likewise, this work seeks to displace the existent anti-black, white patriarchal, and Christian-centric habits and practices in (sexual) ethics, alongside scholars like Roger A. Sneed who takes a humanist approach, Thelathia "Nikki" Young a philosophical one, and Pamela Ayo Yetunde whose hermeneutic is Buddhist.

Further, in the case of the oral histories of contemporary practitioners of religion and ethics, we see examples of a use, or integration, of religion and of varying, multiple spiritualities and traditions where it is helpful, as well as willingness to sever ties where religion is unhelpful to life and wholeness. Lived religion, evidenced in such practices, proves a key source for translating moral wisdom. The oral histories integrate rituals like ancestral veneration, New Age practices, and the sacred nonreligious that are not necessarily theocentric or tied to a singular religion. Further, moral imagination does not require a deity as blackqueer Harlem communities and the oral histories reflect. A blackqueer ethics is not rooted in any religious tradition, but finds its foundation in particular communal praxes, in relating, in the unfixed, living archive, and in the processes of communities revisiting and reworking ethics with integration/wholeness as a value. It is decidedly transreligious—*trans*—meaning across religions, as well as over and beyond them.[10] Blackqueer living archives demand such an approach.

Gathering pieces of a blackqueer archive to inform a communal-sexual ethics lens took me directly to 1920s Harlem, but not to the famed individuals—writers, poets, entertainers—that are often associated with a queer Renaissance past, but to the everyday communities in Harlem (some of which shaped these well-known figures), for as Saidiya Hartman names, "Harlem was surely as queer as it was black."[11] Further, thinking transreligiously, I wondered about ethics *beyond* (sometimes counter to) religion and what sources might inform such an approach. If histories and ethical resources only drew from conceptions of social good in Harlem among religious or even community organizations and leaders (e.g., the Harlem YWCA and Cecelia Cabaniss Saunders or Abyssinian Baptist Church and Adam Clayton Powell, Sr.), one might miss the profound moral practices and imaginations in the quotidian and among those whom many leaders of such organizations would have considered to be immoral. In her critique of racism within Christian ethics that places Reinhold Neibuhr's texts in conversation with black women activists in 1930s and

1940s Harlem, *Disruptive Christian Ethics: When Racism and Women's Lives Matter* (2006), Traci C. West argues, "When we [place only important white thinkers at the center of our narratives of history and moral innovation], it conceals the multiple actors and innovators in the moral dramas of history, and reinforces the supremacy of whites in our understanding of how important moral knowledge is generated."[12] Likewise, it is true, when we ground moral and ethical inquiry in heteropatriarchal logics or even when we allow a sacred-secular binary to guide such inquiries, they function in the service of a reification of established hegemonic norms, not a subversive alternative resource to what has been—a resource that could aid in responding ethically and differently to the present moment.[13]

As noted above, the work of exploring through archives is often the work of meeting and attempting to engage the gaps responsibly. Various scholars of the last two decades in queer studies have noted the challenge of locating and documenting queer archives, that there is a quality of "trace and absent-presence" that accompanies describing queer life through archives.[14] The lived experiences I foreground from 1920s Harlem sometimes reflect a "thick imagining" of the lost histories, as in the case of the effects of the blues environments and Hamilton Lodge Balls.[15] For instance, while the proliferation of the blues in Harlem and the droves of attendees to the Balls are facts, the ephemera of these black nonconformist spaces is often "inadequate to the task of documentation."[16] Therefore, with the evidence we have—memories of those present, an understanding of how queer counterpublics function, cultural histories of Harlem as a socially and politically subversive space— my inclusion of gender and sexual nonconformist communities in 1920s Harlem seeks to "tell impossible stories" of blackqueer life to assert their past and ever-imminent possibilities.[17]

Black LGBTQ+-focused scholarship in ethics and theology has introduced readers to a discourse grounded in marginalized sexual, gender, and racial subjectivities simultaneously. This pushes the limits of Christian sexual ethics and reorients the fields' values through five themes I identify that have emerged since the early 1990s: inclusion, subjectivity and identity, resistance and difference, embodiment, and power. Blackqueering discourse seeks to affirm the goodness by way of being-ness of those who are marginalized sexually (with room for continued growth regarding those of marginalized gender identities) and orients its approaches to sexuality toward being in a just relationship to power, to the body, and to one another. It aims toward integrating the fullness of what it is to be human through honoring the spirits and bodies of all black persons and toward practicing being community—struggling against oppressions, while locating and celebrating communal goodness for the well-being of the collective.

More specifically, the scholarly voices of black queer ethicists, womanists, and black feminists contribute to nuancing our understandings of sexual identities in religious scholarship and they are of prime importance in understanding how and where a blackqueer ethics enters. I see the scholarship of black queer ethicist Thelathia "Nikki" Young, quare ethicist Jennifer S. Leath, and womanist theologian Pamela R. Lightsey who address communal flourishing and thriving of black queer/LGBTQ+ people as foundational to the ethics I propose here. Their scholarship encompasses more than the problems of heterosexism and homophobia to incorporate the good that black queer/LGBTQ+ people and experiences propose for ethics and theology, their communities, and the broader social world. Each scholar understands their subjects as an integral part of a communal whole and provides a vital foundation for considering how persons might best relate to others in light of (not in the erasure of) their sexual and gender self-understandings.

Uniquely, Leath reflects a relational imperative in self-naming and thinking black and Afro-Diasporic, queer, and justice together by invoking "quare." Leath asserts a blackness and queerness that does not have the trouble of stumbling over the whiteness of queerness and the heterosexism that is at times associated with blackness. Quaring is an act of and toward justice, according to Leath, offering new visions and "troubling epistemological and ontological certainties or arrogances."[18] While quare is not a linguistic or theoretical move that I make, the step quare takes deeply informs my framing of blackqueerness wherein the two terms are mutually illuminative and enmeshed with justice-seeking. Leath further elaborates the interwovenness of blackness and queerness in this way: "'queer' [...] does not supplant racial discourse, [though] we might strategically and occasionally conceive of it as another black—or (alternatively) a blackness. Similarly, black might be conceived of as another queer—or a queerness."[19] Leath invites an inhabiting of the spaciousness that both positionalities create together. Such assertions of blackness as a queerness and with queerness, like Young's approach, offer a counternarrative to queer theory's deconstruction of identity and the postmodernist critique that claims the unintelligibility of group identity.

Lightsey argues from the perspective of the gifts of LGBTQ sexual expression,[20] a concept that informs the point of view of my model. As Lightsey turns to terms like "bhomophobia" to highlight black communities' disintegrative values enacting upon sexual selves,[21] I want to ground my scholarly inquiry in the integrative gifts offered through an ethics rooted in blackqueerness that decenters questions of heterosexism and homophobia. On this wise, Young informs my method with her emphasis on black queer communal thriving. Young theorizes relationality among queer folks as collective moral agents and builds upon West's disruptive Christian ethics with her disruption-irruption paradigm, creative resistance, and subversive-generative imagination that speaks not only to contesting and challenging, but dismantling and creating toward possibility.[22] In like manner, I look to blackqueer people—their ways of being and becoming, strategies of resistance, experiences, and ideas of the good—as insufficiently explored sources of knowledge about moral agency that is needed for broadening a vision of liberative community and integrative gender and sexual existence across communities.

As a final site of moral imagination in this blackqueer archive, I turn to oral histories with accompanying images of contemporary blackqueer religious and/or spiritual practitioners. I came to each subject seeking to co-create a photographic and sound record of material aliveness through ritual, meditative practices, and religious devotion, in order to create space for articulation of the spirit that moves in and through blackqueer bodies. This first manifested as the photo-sonic (photography and sound as artistic media) exhibition, *Spirit in the Dark Body: Black Queer Expressions of the Im/material* (2019). I collaborated with each subject regarding their visual representation, to reflect how they saw themselves as black and queer folks doing spirituality and/or religion, and subsequently, moral imagining. My aim as an artist and scholar was to create space for the expansiveness, ingenuity, and strategies toward thriving in blackqueerness. I held in mind the black LGBTQ+ people that I ministered to as a Christian pastor in the years prior to my leaving Christianity who, with the aforementioned subjects, disrupt the idea of blackqueerness as disinherited and disassociated with the religious, with spirit—that blackqueer folx and their expression are not immaterial or meaningless. They matter. The aim was also to explore the ways that persons, in their blackqueerness, have transgressed prescribed boundaries to create an engagement with immateriality (or that which is not material, is transcendent) all their own that blurs dichotomies like body or spirit, transcendent and imminent, right or wrong. Working with these subjects, mostly while also sifting through black LGBTQ+-focused ethical and theological voices, and Harlem's sexual and gender nonconformist past further inspired and expanded my grounding in the possibilities of blackqueer moral imagination for sexual ethics and its potential impact on all who do sexual ethics. When an ethic is rooted in a particular marginalized community's experience, it offers valuable principles toward informed praxes for the thriving of entire communities. Such an approach to ethics breaks down othering and hegemonic delineations; it enables communal reflections from all parties as a resource for human thriving and just relations. A blackqueer ethics is grounded in the experiences of blackqueer people, while creating an opening to communities' transformative potential in the broader society and enabling those who benefit from harmful ethics "to see how injustice is present in their own experience and diminishes their humanity."[23]

Disintegrative Paradigms, Integrative Interventions

Part of the challenge that a blackqueer ethics seeks to address within (Christian) sexual ethics, as well as lived religion, is what I refer to as disintegrative values.[24] Communities, of faith and otherwise, that value the integrative seek to embody a sense of relationality and mutuality that honors each person and holistically, peaceably, supports community members in the journey toward some collectively desired process and aim.[25] Others forward disintegrative values that prevent vulnerability and mutuality, space for self-discovery and growth, and authenticity that makes for communality. For those who ascribe to the Christian faith and believe in a God whose ultimate desire for humanity is love of the self, God, nature, and one another, disintegrative selves and communities contradict the reconciled wholeness that love seeks to enable. The sexually disintegrative and integrative warrant exploration in the formulation of a liberative transreligious and communal-sexual ethics with expansiveness and wholeness, like that proposed by blackqueerness, as its virtues.

The practice of disintegrative values does not solely take place within the realm of sexuality, but sexual disintegration has implications for the whole.[26] Drawing from Christian ethicist James B. Nelson, I understand sexuality to be "who we are as body-selves who experience the emotional, cognitive, physical, and spiritual need for intimate communion—human and divine."[27] Sexuality is about relationality. I note that a sexual ethic and ways of being in relation to one's sexuality can be integrative in some ways and disintegrative in others, can change from moment to moment, and is lived along a spectrum. I find the spectrum of categorizations useful for envisioning blackqueer sexual ethics.

Disintegrative values exist where ethical norms create fissures in individual and communal wholeness and wellness. Disintegrative connotes states of fragmentation and the subsequent actions that may result from living in(to) such states. These values may be described as reflecting disjuncture, a sense of knowing that occurs within the body and mind alongside belief that does not allow the free existence of this knowing. Like an incomplete puzzle, pieces of the self or community may be missing or broken beyond recognition, lost, or discarded. We can observe that disintegrative ways of being and doing must be taken seriously in communal moral life, as they can lead to shame, unhappiness, depression, or self-harm.[28] They may lead to actions that harm others, such as dishonesty toward partners or enacting violence against those who reflect the integrative values one secretly desires to embody. In disintegrative existence, one's sexual and gender journey is not one of exploration, but of proscribed, dogmatic limitations. Often, established knowledge, no matter how disintegrating, is accepted as true because it reflects established familial, cultural, social, and religious norms. Persons are often wedded to the disintegrative narrative even when it is not beneficial to their being and becoming or that of their communities.

Disintegrative practices take place when communities hold disintegrative values. Communities are especially significant because of the meaning-making power they hold. A community holds the power to shape knowledge and subjugate knowledge, to confer social rewards where the desired, normative behaviors are practiced and to withhold rewards. In a community that practices disintegrative values, often there is little space for new knowledge or for authentic flourishing. Identities are perceived as static, and dynamism tends to warrant subduing and "fixing" via the prescribed rules. Language tends to be constricting and exploration limited as the community seeks to establish itself through the status quo. Such environments enforce the denial of an evolving sense of self and teach repression as the faithful response to desire, pleasure, and identities and expressions beyond the dominating norm. The resulting rigidity leads to a reluctance to revisit understandings of sexuality and gender that have proven harmful. Disintegrative patterns are identifiable wherever one receives codified proscriptions that limit authenticity of expression, and the community utilizes coercive power to force conformity so that a sense of uniformity may be maintained. It is not merely that the community holds ethical standards; this is needful for communities that intend to act in accordance with what they believe to be good and just. It is, rather, that the community has an ideal (that frequently upholds hegemonic norms) and will not suffer deviation, transformation, dynamism, or flexibility, which can lead to the community's fracturing and its loss of a thriving diversity that makes it whole.

On the other hand, integrative values can reflect a sense of accord, growth, and healing. Individuals who seek to embody integrative values can experience an internal sense of well-being resulting from one's actions aligning with one's sense of what should be; that is, when one's *doing* aligns with one's *being* and *becoming*. Living into an integrative existence does not indicate an undisturbed state. Still, buttressing integrative values with a supporting ethical practice can yield a liberative reality that may serve as a base to which one may return when disintegrative ways of being loom. Integrative existence attends to disintegrative effects on the self and within society present through systems of heterosexism, sexism, cis-sexism, classism, and racism. Fluidity in expression (including sexual and gender), rather than fixity, is embraced rather than curtailed. Further, a hallmark of integrative practices is the willingness to change without shame. What is discovered through justice love-rooted exploration is not resisted or forbidden but incorporated as part of journeys toward individual and collective becoming. The self that strives toward integrative values can explore their own self-understanding as a vital part of a dynamic and transformative community, which depends on every member's practice toward integrative ways of being for the sake of its communal wellbeing. This can lead to a more just society as integrative values are pursued by inspired communities.

While communities strive to hold integrative values, these communities are not purist or self-righteous, as trial and error are as natural to the community's existence as they are to the community's flourishing. Such communities are seeking communities, willing to transform and expand their language, boundaries, and vision for humanity as they discover more of who they are and what is just. Subsequently, space is created for authentic becoming, while the community demonstrates accountability to collective processes and aims. Integrative values do not connote a sense of unity and togetherness at any cost. Communities that devalue integrative values often prioritize unity above the honoring of each individual member and, in the process, the vulnerable are harmed. Where there is a commitment to integrative values, the virtue is not unity, particularly where staying together would cause harm. Communities that seek integrative existence have the capacity to recreate themselves and redraw their lines of commitment to ensure a faithful reflection of their values. Here, bodies and difference are celebrated, and the community learns from the moral agency and praxes at the margins.

At various times throughout Christian history and contemporarily, sexual ethics espoused within Christian spaces and academic discourse have not reflected individual and communal integrative values, often curbing the subversive, disparate, and perceptibly aberrant in favor of heteronormativity and homonormativity.[29] Christian traditions, from their ancient expressions to modern traditions, have often codified disintegrative sexual ethics as sacred through its doctrine, official statements, sermons, and its social and supposed divine rewards conferred upon those who undertake this socialization into Christian piety. Western Christian history offers some indication of how disintegrative values have gained such a firm footing in the Christian tradition through its suppression of desire and pleasure, its alienation from the body, its focus on the sin of sex acts rather than the good of its pleasures, its rigid commitment to self-denial as a primary paradigm of sexual goodness, as well as its subjugation and violation of the bodies/sexual selves of black, Indigenous, Asian, and Latine people namely throughout the Americas.

Formative LGBTQ+-focused Ethical and Theological Perspectives

To respond effectively to the call toward integrative values that yield justice love, Christian discourse must rethink its approaches to formulating ethics. Christian traditions have often worked against societal progress toward just, equitable, affirming, exploratory, and expansive relations to gender and sexual selves. On the other hand, scientific developments and marginalized people's experiences, for example, have served as key interventions in formulating more relevant, useable ethics. (Christian) sexual ethics as an academic discipline is sharpened by the incorporation of other disciplines dedicated to exploring and interrogating gender and sexuality because of the ways rigid ideals related to gender and sexuality have dominated Christian discourse (and often, public discourse in the United States influenced by Christianity, namely conservative iterations). For this reason, this book depends on the work of scholars from various disciplines who engage in studies of gender and sexuality, and the experiences of persons living gender and sexual difference.

Liberative—namely, womanist, black feminist, and feminist—ethicists and theologians have contributed invaluably to the construction of Christian sexual ethics and theological perspectives that provide alternatives to patriarchal traditions, while countering racism and anti-blackness, misogyny, heterosexism, and homophobia. Many womanists have already laid the groundwork for a race- and gender-conscious attentiveness to embodied experience but have infrequently taken up Renee L. Hill's decades-past, pivotal critique. Hill, in "'Who Are We for Each Other'?: Sexism, Sexuality, and Womanist Theology" (1993), provided an early challenge to womanists who claimed commitment to black women's experience but neglected black lesbians' subjectivity. Hill conceives of black lesbians as theological and ethical agents and emphasizes the kinship and communality that women of all sexual orientations can share. She and Elias Farajajé-Jones (later, Ibrahim Abdurrahman Farajajé) offer first promptings toward womanist and black theologies to take seriously the presence of and the challenges experienced by lesbian, gay, bisexual, transgender, and queer people, notably those with HIV/AIDS, as theological, ethical, and communal matters. Distinctly, Farajajé's "in-the-life theology of liberation [...] grows out of the experiences, lives, and struggles against oppression and dehumanization of those in-the-life."[30] His liberative, intersectional lens, as well as the embodied nature of his analysis, alongside Hill's critique and vision, inform my own understanding of the integrative and disintegrative.

Womanist theologian Kelly Brown Douglas was among the first to respond extensively to Hill's challenge by giving attention to the experiences of black lesbians and gay men within "the Black Church" with her *Sexuality and the Black Church: A Womanist Perspective* (1999).[31] Douglas frames black sexuality as acted upon and subsequently shaped by "white culture" in the religious and social imagination. It is worth noting, conversely, later scholarship (including my own) shifts toward the good of black LGBTQ+ sexualities that subvert black sexual politics of respectability, patriarchy, and heteronormativity, centering black queer politics rather than the effects of whiteness. Douglas's work follows Hill's and Farajajé's pioneering contributions as it calls black institutions to task for their neglect of gay and lesbian persons and their concerns and counts black "homosexuals" as integral to black community and black theologies. In like manner and consistently throughout the 1990s, black pastoral theologian Horace L. Griffin assesses the internal harm of the institutional demonization of gay and lesbian persons, and challenges black heterosexuals to live into the call of black liberation theology to liberate the oppressed among the black community. Key contributions from Roger A. Sneed forward a black gay and queer subjectivity that refuses victimhood and embraces living into subversive existence and strategies that do not rely upon an oppositional relationship to heterosexuality or even a God.[32]

The experiences of marginalized peoples as ethical and theological resources rely upon additional liberative and feminist Christian ethics interlocutors. My use of Beverly Harrison and Marvin M. Ellison's concept of right-relatedness in sexual ethics enables scrutiny of the power dynamics at play in sexual ethics historically.[33] It also aids in orienting the ethic I construct toward community and relationality, rather than an individual's sex acts and gender expressions. More broadly, early (white) feminist emphases on equality of the sexes and the socially constructed understandings of gender, as well as the conception of healthy relationships as those reflecting relational reciprocity, equity, and mutuality, challenge the conceptions of gender shaped by traditionalism. They raise questions about the authority of sources for Christian sexual ethics and consider the communal implications of sexuality for responsibility, accountability, and practices of continual ethical reflection. It is the experiences of white cis-gender women that largely direct Christian sexual and gender disciplinary discourse and create a void in dialogue about communality and the effects of marginalization in misshaping a just sexual ethics. While Ellison names racism frequently as a tool of sexual injustice within "racist patriarchal Christianity,"[34] there is an inattentiveness to the implications of race in formulating a sexual ethic and a lack of particularity in elucidating the potentiality of justice love among black, as well as Latine, Asian, and Indigenous people. Additionally, despite some scholars' inclusion of lesbian and gay people, many ground their inquiries in narrow conceptions of family and procreative norms. Formative liberative sources largely construct ethics within the realms of gender conformity and normativity. Though studies of gender and sexuality in ethics and theology have developed considerably since the 1960s and continue to evolve, the shortcoming is worth mentioning due to the myriad gay, lesbian, bisexual, queer, gender nonconformist and transgender persons, organizations, and movements openly and prominently present in the United States society since the 1960s who could have served as valuable resources for thinking gender and sexuality in theory and in practice.[35]

 It is also necessary to name Christian theologian Patrick S. Cheng and liberative ethicist Miguel A. De La Torre for their comprehensive critiques of white-centeredness in shaping the ethics and theologies that engage non-normative sexuality. Cheng theorizes with lesbian, gay, bisexual, transgender, intersex, and queer persons in mind, particularly as these intersect with race/ethnicity (i.e., black, Asian, Latine, and Indigenous). In "Reclaiming Our Traditions, Rituals, and Spaces: Spirituality and the Queer Asian Pacific American Experience" (2006), Cheng calls for a recovery of spiritual identity and expressions among Queer Asian Pacific American (QAPA) people. He briefly defines some common experiences of QAPA communities, which he states might also be applied to other queer people of color in the United States. He argues for indwelling tradition, ritual, and space for QAPA's personal sense of wholeness, which Christianity often cannot provide. Cheng takes this further in his 2013 book *Rainbow Theology: Bridging Race, Sexuality, and Spirit* (2013). He notes, "Rainbow theology is not just about LGBTIQ people of color, but it is a 'subjectless critique' that challenges all theologies to rethink the relationships between race, sexuality, and spirituality."[36] Using the rainbow motif, he chooses the themes of multiplicity ("co-existing and overlapping identities"), middle spaces (never quite being "at home"), and mediation (holding identities and ideas together, between their racial community and LGBTIQ community) to illumine the experiences of queer people of color. This is a paradigm shift, argues Cheng, from "monochromatic theology" that is the usual.

De La Torre proposes a sexual ethic centered in orthopraxis, and more specifically orthoeros—"correct erotic sex"[37] in his book, *A Lily among Thorns: Imagining a New Christian Sexuality* (2007). Mutuality and relationality are key, namely in his conception of orthoeros, "a way of being" that exists in "a familial relationship of love and commitment, vigilant against any suffering of others due to that relationship," with a focus on "strengthening, securing, and supporting a mutually giving and vulnerable familial relationship."[38] Such an ethic would not exclude same-sex relationships. De La Torre proposes a liberative reading of scripture that suits this end in his chapter, "Same Sex Relationships." While his analysis of scripture was not reflective of having engaged contemporary ethical, biblical, or theological scholarship referencing LGBTQ+ people, De La Torre does note the many factors that impact attitudes toward scripture and the selectivity of interpretations with a heteronormative bent.[39] He also presents the social implications of such attitudes, asserting, "When the interpretation fosters oppressive structures, then agreeing to disagree can never be an option."[40] De La Torre ultimately fosters an orthoeros that holds people of all sexualities to the same ethical standard—to love God and neighbor. De La Torre continues his critique of white supremacy and racism enacted upon "dark bodies" and of masculinity in *Liberating Sexuality: Justice Between the Sheets* (2016) wherein he offers an apology letter to "homosexuals," a confession of his former life as a "gay-bashing *macho*," and repentance in the form of "alternative interpretations" of "clobber texts."[41]

The problem of whiteness and anti-blackness in Christian sexual ethics is especially challenging because of the hyper-focus on black bodies in the white fantastic hegemonic imagination, as Emilie M. Townes names it, and racism and anti-blackness in disciplinary discourse.[42] Black bodies have always mattered in the United States as a site of contestation, violence, hypersexualization, and exploitation that has worked to disintegrate black individuals and communities, as well as those proximate to blackness. Likewise, within the bastions of scholarly meaning-making and intellectual exploration, and in spaces that claim to desire justice and to honor the sacredness of bodies, anti-blackness prevails. Still, beyond the harm, black bodies matter as sites of creativity, resistance, thriving, and moral fecundity that have been underexamined as sites of ethical knowledge, particularly those black bodies that are further de-moralized by their queerness. These absences speak to the need for a blackqueer sexual ethics that values the experiences of blackqueer people and gathers the effects of fragmentation toward a more integrative ethic.

Tending the Archive: Overview of Chapters

A Blackqueer Sexual Ethics formulates an archive of blackqueerness in order to create an opening toward a communal relations-based transreligious sexual ethics. In seeking a setting in which I might identify the communal values to inform an integrative ethic, I look to 1920s black Harlem and its gender and sexual nonconformists. The subversive spaces of blues environments, rent parties, and the Hamilton Lodge Balls serve as sites of moral imagination and moral knowledge in Chapter 1, "Examining the Integrative in Blackqueer Harlem." In this chapter, I introduce the reader to a transdisciplinary method that draws from queer theory and LGBTQ+-focused performance studies, alongside primary sources (e.g., blues lyrics, black Harlem newspaper clippings, historical interviews) to presence the spirit of the era.[43] Focusing on communality, I decenter the usual iconic Harlem Renaissance political and artistic leadership, to be informed by everyday blackqueerness. Shaped by the repressive race, gender, sexuality, and class forces surrounding them, black sexual and gender nonconformists of Harlem formed counterpublics to the publics of black Harlem, as well as the wider New York City—both with which blackqueer communities often found themselves at odds. In such communal spaces, black gender and sexual nonconformists pursued an alternative vision of the good, while participating in their own self-making, embracing their pleasures, refusing respectability politics, and creating possibility. The chapter provides a deeper look into integrative values, which are not drawn from a utopic blackqueer Harlem, but in their queer failure and complexity, they inspire liberative praxes for a blackqueer ethics.

"Blackqueering of Ethical and Theological Discourse" introduces the reader to black LGBTQ+-focused discourse and scholars' transformative approaches to ethics and theology that resolutely foregrounds the significance of LGBTQ+ experience, cultural productions, moral imagination, and life. I explore the five themes that have shaped these interventions since the early 1990s: inclusion, subjectivity and identity, resistance and difference, embodiment, and power. The chapter features a diversity of black scholarship, including from groundbreaking theologians Ibrahim Abdurrahman Farajajé and Renee L. Hill and their promptings toward unapologetic black lesbian, gay, bisexual, transgender, and queer subjectivities in theology. I follow the genealogy toward later apologetic calls for inclusion and, most recently, queer resistances and black queer and quare ethics. Through a thematic analysis, this chapter offers a critical overview of signal contributions to black LGBTQ+ discourse in ethics and theology, which provide foundations upon which I build and depart for the integrative, communality-based blackqueer ethics proposed in Chapter 4.

Chapter 3, "Spirit in the Dark Body: Blackqueer Expressions of the Im/material," is a visual and narrative expression of the integration, communality, and rootedness in blackqueerness reflected in my proposed ethic. As the integrative is concerned with wholeness, the subjects are presenced through minimally edited words and photographic representation of each person elaborating their living relationship to spirituality/religion in their blackqueerness. The oral histories were collected over the course of a year and a half from persons in the United States who identify as black and queer, and who claim various genders. They are persons with whom I am in or became in community, directly and indirectly, who practice and live into integrative embodiments as persons black, queer, and in spirit—whatever that may mean to the subject. The aim is to be inspired and challenged by the ways life, in its blackqueerness, animates, naming itself for itself without interpretive analysis that may universalize and normativize. It is a multivocal, multivalent oral history that serves as an opening to the practice of embodying a practice of ethics as one's blackqueer self.

Finally, inspired by the moral imagination of those, past and present, who have fashioned thriving beyond Christian traditionalism and a liberative tradition that shapes a blackqueering critical discourse, Chapter 4, "Constructing a Blackqueer Sexual Ethics," offers an approach to sexual ethics rooted in various modes of blackqueerness. I offer communal belonging, individual and collective becoming, goodness, embodied spirits/inspirited bodies, and shared thriving as integrative values that inform the theory of a blackqueer ethics while, most importantly, inviting communities to the communal praxis of doing ethics. This transreligious approach to sexual ethics—which necessarily transcends/deconstructs the limits of an explicitly Christian ethic—reflects the liberative aims toward integrative communality and right relating through justice love that root a blackqueer sexual ethics.

Notes

1 I use "blackqueer" to signal my thinking and feeling this subjectivity as one. It negates oppositionality between the two and acknowledges the inseparability. For my part, I am speaking to integration, a bringing together of what was made to feel like disparate parts in the public imagination/white supremacist heteronormative logics. I am attempting to presence the fullness of black (however complex that may be) and the fullness of queer (however complex that may be). Both positionalities and experiences

are expansive as they are mutually illuminative. Blackqueer/
blackqueerness is a positionality, a politic, a methodological lens.
I mean a politic and positionality that allows for the multiplicity
and wideness of sexual and gender (and more) expression, and that
subverts both heteronormativity and homonormativity. Because
of the multiplicitous and spacious nature of queerness, I find it
hard to conceive of it without gender, specifically trans genders
(e.g., transgender, nonbinary, agender). I also feel the caution not
to conflate gender and sexuality in a way that transness is lost
in queerness. It is also the case that trans life, experiences, and
approaches require a more expansive, in-depth treatment than
what is offered here. Throughout this book, I intentionally employ
blackqueer, black queer, and LGBTQ(+) not as an effort toward
gatekeeping blackqueerness, but to mark a distinction in process and
ends, and to maintain the integrity of scholars' voices. Queerness
is radical and oppositional to normativity. This may not have been
the aim of some scholars. Particularly in Chapter 2, I speak to a
process of "blackqueering." "Blackqueer" is found and described
in the scholarship of Ashon T. Crawley whose work (along with
that of Fred Moten) has inspired this immediate foregrounding of
what is meant by "blackqueer." For example, "Blackqueer Aesthesis:
Sexuality and the Rumor and Gossip of Black Gospel," in *Race and
Displacement Nation, Migration, and Identity in the Twenty-First
Century*, ed. Maha Marouan and Merinda Simmons (Tuscaloosa,
University of Alabama Press, 2013), 27–42. In the disciplines of
ethics, inquiries at the intersection of blackness and queerness have
been foundationally shaped by Thelathia "Nikki" Young's black
queer ethics and Jennifer Leath's quare/quaring (building upon E.
Patrick Johnson's formulation of the term).

2   storäe michele, "Freedom-Making as Praxis," accessed March 1,
2021, https://www.practicefreedommaking.com/.

3   Saidiya Hartman, *Wayward Lives, Beautiful Experiments: Intimate
Histories of Social Upheaval* (New York: W. W. Norton, 2019), 31.

4   Walidah Imarisha, who co-edited *Octavia's Brood: Science Fiction
Stories from Social Justice Movements* with adrienne maree brown,
speaks of the short stories in the volume this way: "'Visionary
fiction' is a term we developed to distinguish science fiction that has
relevance toward building new, freer worlds from the mainstream
strain of science fiction, which most often reinforces dominant
narratives of power." Walidah Imarisha and adrienne maree
brown, *Octavia's Brood: Science Fiction Stories from Social Justice
Movements*, ed. Walidah Imarisha and adrienne maree brown
(Oakland: AK /IAS, 2015), 4.

5   I distinguish my use of "living archive" from the innovative, interactive ways it is proposed by various scholars attempting to transform how we view archives. I do, however, note our shared interest at the convergence of the historical with the contemporary to breathe life into archives. See, for example, Tamara, "A Living, Breathing Revolution: How Libraries Can Use 'Living Archives' to Support, Engage, and Document Social Movements," *IFLA Journal* 40 (2014): 5–11.

6   I build upon Marvin Ellison's understanding of justice love, which leans into the relationality of the sexual self and is attentive to one's relationship to their own bodies, as well as to the relationship of multiple bodies in society. He argues, in the embodying of justice love, that we move toward "an intimate co-mingling of our longing for personal well-being in our bodies and right-relatedness with others throughout the social order." Marvin M. Ellison, *Erotic Justice: A Liberating Ethic of Sexuality* (Louisville: Westminster John Knox, 1996), 115.

7   For more on "imperialist white supremacist capitalist patriarchy," see bell hooks, *Belonging: A Culture of Place* (New York: Routledge, 2009).

8   Marvin M. Ellison, *Making Love Just: Sexual Ethics for Perplexing Times* (Minneapolis: Fortress 2012), 4.

9   Amaryah Shaye Armstrong, "Thinking Practice: Method, Pedagogy, Power and the Question of a Black Queer Theology," *Modern Believing* 60, no. 1 (2019): 11.

10 Theologians have been considering a transreligious turn in recent years, albeit differently (that is, turning to religious universalism and pluralism) than I have proposed here. See Roland Farber, *The Ocean of God: On the Transreligious Futures of Religion* (New York: Anthem 2019) and Jerry L. Martin, ed., *Theology without Walls: The Transreligious Imperative* (New York: Routledge, 2020). A similar framing, in this case "spiritual fluidity," is found in Duane R. Bidwell, *When One Religion Isn't Enough: The Lives of Spiritually Fluid People* (Boston: Beacon 2018).

11 Hartman, *Wayward Lives*, 304.

12 Traci C. West, *Disruptive Christian Ethics: When Racism and Women's Lives Matter* (Louisville: Westminster John Knox 2006), 9.

13 In *Queer Religiosities: An Introduction to Queer and Transgender Studies in Religion* (2021), Melissa M. Wilcox prompts a consideration of how queer and trans religious practices might transform religious studies as a discipline, and references Paul

Gorrell's framing of gay men's circuit parties as a religious experience. I am curious to think further about the communal ritual of convening to celebrate gender subversion in a Hamilton Lodge Ball or of how the ecstasy of, for a moment, transcending constrictive norms of sexual expression under the influence of blues music might signal a kind of religious experience that is not explored here, but if "religion is one of the queerest things about being human," this seems another compelling lens to bring to 1920s blackqueer Harlem. Melissa M. Wilcox, *Queer Religiosities: An Introduction to Queer and Transgender Studies in Religion* (Lanham: Rowman & Littlefield, 2021), 108–9.

14 Vanessa Agard-Jones, "What the Sands Remember," *GLQ: A Journal of Lesbian and Gay Studies* 18, nos. 2–3 (2012): 328.

15 Bruce Dorsey, "'Making Men What They Should Be': Male Same-Sex Intimacy and Evangelical Religion in Early Nineteenth-Century New England," *Journal of the History of Sexuality* 24, no. 3 (September 2015): 346. The quote is a reference from essayist and critic, Phillip Lopate.

16 Ann Cvetkovich, *An Archive of Feelings: Trauma, Sexuality, and Lesbian Public Cultures* (Durham: Duke University Press, 2003), 9.

17 Saidiya Hartman, "Venus in Two Acts," *Small Axe* 12, no. 2 (June 2008): 10.

18 Jennifer S. Leath, "Is Queer the New Black?" *Harvard Divinity Bulletin* 43, nos. 3 and 4 (Summer/Autumn 2015), https://bulletin.hds.harvard.edu/articles/summerautumn2015/queer-new-black.

19 Leath, "Is Queer the New Black?"

20 Pamela R. Lightsey, *Our Lives Matter: A Womanist Queer Theology* (Eugene: Wipf and Stock, 2015), 6–7.

21 Pamela R. Lightsey, "Inner Dictum: A Womanist Reflection from the Queer Realm," *Black Theology* 10, no. 3 (November 2011): 339–49.

22 Young, *Black Queer Ethics*, 9, 58.

23 Emilie M. Townes, *Womanist Ethics and the Cultural Production of Evil* (New York: Palgrave Macmillan, 2006), 11.

24 For more on the contours of Christian sexual ethics as an academic discourse, see Kate M. Ott, "Introduction," in *Sex, Tech, and Faith: Ethics for a Digital Age* (Grand Rapids: Wm. B. Eerdmans 2022).

25 As named briefly above, my use of the term "community" most frequently refers to communities as organized bodies of people pursuing right-relatedness. The communities' members are informed

by one another and grant one another permission to explore, challenge, or reify norms. I have in mind not an institutional setting, but a people.

26 While the focus of this book and its ethic is sexual, implications for gender are also explored and necessarily that which makes up an integrative existence—any aspects of humanness that inform this self. I do not conflate gender and sexuality; I recognize the ways one's gender becomes a significant part of one's embodiment of a sexual self.

27 James B. Nelson, *Embodiment: An Approach to Sexuality and Christian Theology* (Minneapolis: Fortress 1978), 18.

28 For example, the Religious Institute, quoting from the publication "Faith Matters: Teenagers, Religion, and Sexuality" (2003), indicates the difference that integrative and disintegrative communality makes for LGBT youth: "Those [youth] who were able to be open in their faith-based communities were also less likely to have considered suicide than other non-heterosexual teens. Those who are in faith-based institutions where there are negative views toward homosexuality and bisexuality rarely are open about their orientation. Those teens live with a very painful silence." "Fact Sheet on LGBT Youth," Religious Institute, accessed May 8, 2019, http://religiousinstitute.org/resources/fact—sheet-lgbt-youth/.

29 Homonormativity may be defined as normative ideas that shape an ideal imaginary as it relates to lesbian and gay identity. The ideal imaginary mirrors heteronormativity (including its whiteness, reproductive impulse, gender roles, able-bodiedness, and socioeconomic status), but within "homosexual" relationships. Social and cultural theorist Lisa Duggan defines homonormativity as "a politics that does not contest dominant heteronormative assumptions and institutions, but upholds and sustains them, while promising the possibility of a demobilized gay constituency and a privatized, depoliticized gay culture anchored in domesticity and consumption." Lisa Duggan, *The Twilight of Equality?: Neoliberalism, Cultural Politics, and the Attack on Democracy* (Boston: Beacon 2003), 50.

30 Elias Farajajé-Jones, "Breaking the Silence: Towards an In-the-Life Theology," in *Black Theology: A Documentary History* (Volume Two: 1980–92), ed. James H. Cone and Gayraud S. Wilmore (Maryknoll: Orbis 1993), 140. "In-the-life" is a term that has long been used by African Americans "to connote a broad spectrum of identities and behaviors," generally non-normative, related to their sexuality.

31 See Kelly Brown Douglas, "Homophobia and Heterosexism in the Black Church and Community," in *Sexuality and the Black Church: A Womanist Perspective* (Maryknoll: Orbis, 1999), 87–108.
32 See Roger A. Sneed, *Representations of Homosexuality: Black Liberation Theology and Cultural Criticism* (New York: Palgrave Macmillan, 2010).
33 Ellison, *Erotic Justice*, 3.
34 Ellison, *Erotic Justice*, 114.
35 Ellison's later work takes a more critical view toward relational normativity, with considerable room for exploration as it relates to transgender identities. See Marvin M. Ellison, *Making Love Just: Sexual Ethics for Perplexing Times* (Minneapolis: Fortress 2012), in addition to his various edited volumes. Additionally, for an example of countering such theologies and ethics referenced in this paragraph, see Marcella Althaus-Reid, *The Queer God*, (New York: Taylor & Francis, 2003).
36 Patrick S. Cheng, Rainbow Theology: Bridging Race, Sexuality and Spirit (New York: Seabury, 2013).
37 Miguel A. De La Torre, "Same Sex Relationships," in *A Lily among Thorns: Imagining a New Christian Sexuality* (San Francisco: Jossey-Bass, 2007), 73.
38 De La Torre, "Same Sex Relationships," 75.
39 In one example, De La Torre proposes that "the original intent of the biblical authors" can be ascertained, and that "conservatives" have come to the wrong meaning. This contrasts with New Testament scholar Dale Martin who finds the intent is impossible to ascertain and that all interpreters are ultimately imposing meaning. See De La Torre, "Same Sex Relationships," 139, 140.
40 De La Torre, "Same Sex Relationships," 142.
41 See Miguel A. De La Torre, "When the Bible Is Used for Hate," "Confessions of a Latino Macho: From Gay Basher to Gay Ally," and "The Bible: What Our Family Album has to Say," in *Liberating Sexuality: Justice between the Sheets* (Saint Louis: Chalice 2016).
42 Townes, *Womanist Ethics and the Cultural Production of Evil*, 17.
43 Throughout this text, I employ the terms "presence" and "presencing" as verbs. This is intended to reflect the hereness, the aliveness, and the embodiedness of blackqueerness.

1

Examining the Integrative in Blackqueer Harlem

The integrative communality of a blackqueer ethics offers a striving toward both wholeness and right-relating that counter the anti-black racism, cis-centrism, and heterosexism of disintegrative sexual ethics. In critically reflecting on right relating that serves blackqueer life, blackqueer community serves as a salient resource for expansive, otherwise moral imagination. Further, through listening to such voices as a methodological commitment within liberative sexual ethics, a blackqueer ethics provides support for the exploration of the integrative as a useful means of constructing approaches to thriving and flourishing through a communal-sexual ethic. This chapter examines integrative values through the experiences of blackqueer communities in 1920s Harlem.

I locate this integrative communal-sexual ethic among those deemed abject by hegemonic standards of normativity, among the experiences of those pushed to the margins. Thelathia "Nikki" Young posits, "The irruption of black queers as moral agents not only troubles the category of 'moral' (since the intersection of racial and sexual subjugation has generally rendered the black queer subject as morally reprobate), but it also provides us a new moral lens through which to critique norms."[1] They are norms related to family for Young's inquiry and norms related to community for the inquiry forwarded here. Critiquing dominant norms and doing ethics with a blackqueer moral lens create space for liberative strategies of well-being and resistance while disrupting constructions of morality that have long caused harm to gender, sexual, and racial nonconformists. Further, utilizing blackqueer Harlem as both an instance of integrative values at work and to "inform and alter" sexual ethics serves as a challenge to both Christian and scholarly white supremacy.[2] This is a strategic discursive, political, and moral move intended to call forth the value of blackqueer life, and to uncover the disintegrative values that are found in Christianity's dominant sexual ethical frameworks. As feminist Christian ethicist Beverly Harrison affirms, "It is by listening to those voices that are not being heard that we begin to see what moral complacency and conventional wisdom cannot yet see."[3]

Thus, as I consider how to do a blackqueer sexual ethics, I ask the reader to consider the following: What does it *mean* to theorize ethics from among those deemed immoral by the traditionalism of Christian ethical framings and those largely absent from liberative ethical conceptualizations? I intend to signify *meaning* as in the meaning that is made when communities are deepened, expanded, and troubled; when personal piety is not made the *telos*, but rather, processes toward communal wholeness are prioritized. I wonder about the meanings to be revealed when whiteness and sexual and gender conformity are ungrounded as moral ideals.

Blackqueer Harlem in the 1920s serves as an unstable (queer) site of meaning-making through moral inquiry. The space was not an ethical utopia and need not be to reflect integrative values and communal, redefined meanings of the good. Harlem's black gender and sexual nonconformists—blackqueer communities—pursued subversive moral visions, while participating in their own self-making, embracing their pleasures, refusing respectability politics, and living into their possibility; herein lies their blackqueerness.[4] This chapter attends to spaces of blackqueerness in Harlem—blues environments, rent parties, and Hamilton Lodge Balls—to identify the ways they topple hegemonic norms. As a space often at cross-purposes with the prevalent agenda of black Harlem's leaders, blackqueer Harlem, as a counterpublic, created a differing set of values and ways of being community that yielded an ethos of integration toward sexuality and gender.[5] Integrative space for the "bulldykers" and "fairies," "sissies" and women who "talk to the gals just like any old man" made up blackqueer Harlem.

A counterpublic often acts in a disparate relationship with the public with which it associates and finds within itself divergent conceptions of its lived reality and ways of relating to its members.[6] This relationship creates possibility that may be unwelcome or impossible within the larger public but has the capacity to create a more welcome home for gender and sexual difference. Queer theorist Michael Warner, like black feminist political scientist Cathy J. Cohen, argues that it is exactly the "indecorousness" or "deviance" that gives the space its power.[7] With a counter-locus of power and lesser discursive restraints, blackqueer Harlem reflects how increased agency, imagination, and embodied resistances offer opportunity to radically challenge the status quo, and for that challenge to establish the space as viable for constructive blackqueer possibility.[8] The set apart spaces of blues environments, rent parties, and the Hamilton Lodge Balls reflect the everydayness of blackqueer Harlemites' refusals of conventionality, a strategy that was less a formal social change campaign, and more quotidian in its subversion and subsequent transformation of the public.[9] Because these blackqueer stories are often marginalized in histories of black or Renaissance Harlem and in histories of gender and sexual nonconformity in the United States, weaving together these discarded fragments, or microhistories, into a cohesive contribution to a blackqueer archive is an essential task of this chapter.

Performance theorist Shane Vogel notes, "Historians have excavated 1920s Harlem as a space of gay and lesbian subcultural formation, tracing the extensive social networks of drag ball, 'pansy parades,' buffet flats, and rent parties that provided [...] spectacles of racialized sexual deviance and knowledge production."[10] I argue for the significance of perceiving blackqueerness in Harlem beyond the spectacle so frequently inscribed upon blackqueer bodies—wherein expression is perceived as a consumable performance for an external, often white, gaze—and for its unconventionality, which casts another vision for thinking and doing sexual ethics. The spaces reveal integrative strategies and ways of being blackqueer community with the understanding that the spaces communities create are not knowable apart from the community members that make the space. To speak of a space is to speak of the community that, through its power, names and makes itself, even "from scratch."[11]

I will first elaborate the meta-setting of 1920s black Harlem, of which blackqueer Harlem was an integral part. I offer an overview of sociopolitical factors that converged in Harlem to make it such a significant setting for black people in the United States. I examine three primary settings in which blackqueer people created community, while formulating creative responses to the conditions imposed upon them, and with which they interacted to create possibility for themselves. I utilize a transdisciplinary method that draws from queer theory, cultural studies, African American histories, and queer-focused performance studies, alongside primary sources (e.g., blues lyrics, black Harlem newspaper clippings, historical interviews) to embody the spirit of the era. Through this approach, I decenter the well-known Harlem Renaissance political and artistic leadership with everyday, communal blackqueerness. The chapter provides a deeper look into integrative values from a blackqueer Harlem that in its "failure," imaginative world-making, and complexity hint toward a liberative praxis for blackqueer ethics today.[12]

Harlem: The Making of a "Black Mecca"

By the 1920s, Harlem became a bastion of black social activism and political leadership, a center for the creation of black intellectual, cultural, and artistic expression, and a burgeoning "Black Mecca."[13] At the same time, Harlem also became a prime space for blackqueer becoming—pushing the boundaries of gender and sexuality in subtle and not so subtle ways. The vitality of the political and intellectual movements that arose in Harlem nurtured an ethos for communality that actively challenged racial, economic, gender, and sexual norms.

Black Harlemites' activism, leadership, and communality deepened alongside various limiting sociopolitical and economic factors. According to historian Jill Watts, "despite the booming war industry and the glitter of Harlem, the vast majority of blacks in Harlem lived in destitution."[14] Still, they created and established multiple means of addressing the racism and economic disparity that challenged their community, while wielding their social and political agency. Even aspects of what some considered the "private life" (including, but not limited to, sex and sexuality) would not escape change's pull. For many in Harlem, the 1920s became an era of living and organizing in creative and tested ways, which established the neighborhood as a renowned center for civic and social modes of black resistance to and survival within and despite disenfranchisement.

The Harlem of the 1920s and 1930s saw an explosion in its black population, though such growth began to foment since the turn of the century. Exploitation in the housing market and violent racial clashes (among civilians and with police) during the race riots of 1900[15] and 1905[16] led black inhabitants of Manhattan to move uptown, from the Tenderloin and San Juan Hill areas below Central Park, concentrating in a new, relatively small area north of the park. This relocation resulted in many primarily Italian and Jewish Harlemites, including prominent families of white legislators, businessmen, and other well-to-do families, leaving Harlem behind.[17] Further, what began as a plan to create more rental property for white people was foiled by the neighborhood's inaccessibility to public transportation. In the excess of housing, black real-estate businessman Phillip Payton seized upon the opportunity by industriously approaching white landlords and suggesting that they rent to black tenants, and later founded the Afro-American Renting Company so that black people who would ordinarily experience discrimination would have opportunity at leasing.[18] Journalist and biographer Jervis Anderson notes the large scale of the geographical northward mobility of black people, as individuals, communities, and institutions:

> Between 1911 and 1922, almost all the major Black churches moved to Harlem. So did social and theatrical clubs; college fraternities and sororities; the Black Y.M.C.A. and Y.W.C.A.; Black Democratic and Republican politicians and their clubhouses; and Black branches of such fraternal organizations as the Masons, the Elks, the Pythians, and the Oddfellows [...] The National Association for the Advancement of Colored People, the National Urban League, and Socialist and Black nationalist organizations opened offices in Harlem.[19]

With the addition of distinguished black intellectuals, entertainers, and artists, a strong black press, a host of middle-class professionals and persons of lesser economic means, what some former white residents of Harlem called the "Negro 'invasion'" was fully underway.[20]

The move to Harlem also had national motivations. Within the broader context of the United States, limited European immigration due to the First World War and industrialization led to a migration of black people to the urban north. Many traveled from the south in pursuit of economic opportunity and in flight from Jim Crow discrimination with the looming terror of lynching to cities like New York City, Detroit, Chicago, Milwaukee, Buffalo, Pittsburgh, and Philadelphia.[21] Black immigrants also came in droves from the Caribbean. From 1910 to 1920, New York alone saw a 66.3 percent increase in its black population.[22] As black people concentrated in Harlem, they organized and employed strategies of racial uplift and economic self-sufficiency for black empowerment.

The clash of racism and the withholding of resources in various arenas of black American life (e.g., education, employment, housing, healthcare) with a growing practice of black American political and social power yielded an explosion of activism.[23] According to historian Julie A. Gallagher, "Depression-era and later wartime struggles for safe and affordable housing, decent jobs, community safety, and political leadership in cities like Detroit, Chicago, Philadelphia, and most dramatically in Harlem, were foundational elements in what has become known as the Northern civil rights movement."[24] Harlem's leaders made a distinct contribution to movements for black civil rights in the north. It was exemplified by the presence of intellectual, political, and institutional forces for change, such as the YWCA with Cecelia Cabaniss Saunders; the UNIA with Marcus Garvey, Amy Ashwood Garvey, and Amy Jacques Garvey; the NAACP with W. E. B. Du Bois; and Abyssinian Baptist Church with Adam Clayton Powell, Sr. Such community-based and institutional sources of change aided in generating a vital cultural ethos unmatched in nearly any other city in the United States during the era. Effective organizing and impactful leadership made inroads as black folks studied, strategized, and struggled to make their neighborhoods and homes one where race and economics were not barriers, but markers of dignity and self-sufficiency.

For many who chose and/or earned the mantle of black leadership during the 1920s in Harlem, racial uplift through respectability was a key strategy, particularly as it related to prescribed notions of morality. This moral agenda was concentrated predominantly in the realm of sexuality and gender. Many black preachers sought to spread their brand of piety throughout Harlem, as did the women's organizations and Harlem's black intelligentsia, each of whom possessed hopes of earning rights and dignity through the modification of black people's behavior. Performance theorist James F. Wilson notes that throughout the latter 1920s, "black clergy and bourgeoisie" of Harlem made a concerted effort to rid their neighborhood of so-called "filth," alongside the police, mayor, and governor of New York, targeting the theaters, nightclubs, and speakeasies where "impropriety" made itself at home.[25] Often, impropriety meant nonconformity.

In a stark example, one of Harlem's leading pastors, Powell, Sr. of Abyssinian Baptist Church, crusaded against what he castigated as the degenerate behaviors of gender and sexual nonconformists and the sullied deeds that took place in buffet flats throughout Harlem.[26] In a 1929 issue of *The New York Age*, the headline read "Dr. A.C. Powell Scores Pulpit Evils," with a subheading "In Sermon Sunday Morning, Dr. A. Clayton Powell Denounces Degeneracy and Sex-Perverts." While preaching to thousands of members of Abyssinian Baptist Church, he criticized preachers across the nation practicing "vicious immoralities" beyond, but to include, sexual vice and specifically preached about women among whom "homo-sexuality [*sic*] and sex-perversion [...] has grown into one of the most horrible, debasing, alarming and damning vices of present day civilization."[27] The following week in response to Powell's sermon, again on its cover, the newspaper printed several commendations (namely, from men) by clergy, laity of the Baptist tradition, and the editor of the newspaper, and claimed to receive "hundreds of personal expressions" of approval.[28] Wilson notes that the next week, Powell preached on the danger of vice that causes "men to leave their wives for other men, and women to leave their husbands for other women, and girls to mate with girls instead of marrying," though it is not clear what he thought of boys' homoerotic behavior with one another. Such ideas about the threat to the black heterosexual, patriarchal family were further reinforced in the popular culture.[29] For instance, the Prohibition Era with its values of pious temperance and socioreligious moralism aimed to shun sensual vice (e.g., booze drinking, dancing), which both black and white critics frequently located in black spaces like jazz and blues halls. These calls took on new life alongside the desire among some black people to appear exceptionally moral in efforts to uplift the race, akin to the aforementioned respectability. Exceptional morality, it was thought, would lead to black people being seen as fully human, as worthy of the rights and benefits bestowed upon white people, an approach that presumed a logic and a meritocratic structure to the racial hierarchy where there was none.

Additional strategies of uplift developed during this period. African American religious studies scholar Wallace D. Best identifies in New York City, and vibrantly in Harlem, "a liberal theology rooted in rationalism, biblical criticism, the historical method, and a religious culture given to issues of social concern."[30] Prominent black Harlem churches like St. Philip's Protestant Episcopal Church, Salem Methodist Episcopal Church, Abyssinian Baptist Church, Metropolitan Baptist Church, Mother AME Zion Church, and Harlem Community Church (led by Rev. Ethelred Brown, a socialist and groundbreaking figure in Black Universalism and humanism), pursued social justice in response to the material needs of their communities.[31] The Social Gospel Movement—a movement centered in Christian commitments to social and material change, as opposed to merely individual, soul salvation—was forwarded in Harlem through ministers such as Revs. Reverdy Ransom and Powell, Sr., challenging the commonly held notion of primarily white Social Gospel roots.[32] In particular, St. Philip's Protestant Episcopal Church served as a poignant example of a socially engaged church, and one with significant resources to be especially impactful. Its pastor during the 1920s, Rev. Hutchens Chew Bishop, partnered with the NAACP and the National League for the Protection of Colored Women, in addition to having established a social work department at his church in 1924, led by a social worker, Mabel Bickford Jenkins.[33] Though most of the churches in under-resourced areas lacked the means to continually provide for Harlemites in need of food or access to employment,[34] a variety of churches—from storefronts to "middle-class mainstream black churches"—organized for socioeconomic advancement.[35] In a space like Harlem, a church that ignored the material needs of its parishioners risked irrelevance, particularly among its critics.

James Weldon Johnson in his 1934 book *Negro Americans, What Now?* describes the outcry, of some intellectuals and later those in the throes of the Depression, to the churches led by and supported by Harlem's black populace. He states, "The church must as nearly as it can abolish hypnotic religion, that religion which excites visions of the delights of life in the world to come, while it gives us no insight into the conditions we encounter in the world in which we now live."[36] The critique was of an otherworldly religion unconcerned with (by way of inactivity) or impotent in confronting the hardships experienced by the masses of black people—particularly religious adherents. It is worth noting that like critiques also preceded the Depression era and developed distinctly in a greatly under-resourced black Harlem, with churches that rose in economic and social prominence among people whose need often exceeded the reach of the Social Gospel.

At the same time, varying religious sects arose, Christian and otherwise, which could offer a response to the critique of ineffectual (Christian) religion. Historian Robert Weisbrot noted most sects flourished during the post-First World War years because of the resurgence of racism and subsequent ghettoization of cities.[37] These religious sects offered space for seekers who found traditional modes irrelevant or inadequate to meet their needs, material and spiritual. Father Divine through his Peace Missions led such a movement that focused on material wellness for adherents and, to a considerable degree, for the leaders themselves.[38] Additionally, some West Indian working-class people, namely women, found their footing among Harlem's black Jewish congregations.[39] While historian David Levering Lewis pejoratively identified them as a cult that "attracted the socially marginal and spiritually dispossessed," and referred to one community as having "horrified Harlem"[40] by their very presence, historian Roberta S. Gold painted a different picture of the black people identifying themselves as Jews. The Black Jews ultimately posed a challenge to the social, religious, economic, and racial establishment, claiming for themselves a history and contemporary identity considered not their own in the social imagination, and met one another's needs in community. Such examples signal the multiplicity of black religion in Harlem and the need black Harlemites felt to enact various responses to the dire conditions in their community.

While the aim, for many religious leaders and communities, as well as other black uplift institutions, was to gain the rights entitled to citizens, in this process many black people were sacrificed, publicly reproved, and excoriated for the sake of the race. As political scientist Fredrick C. Harris affirms, "For more than half of the twentieth century, the concept of the 'Talented Tenth' commanded black elites to 'lift as we climb', or to prove to white America that blacks were worthy of full citizenship rights by getting the untalented nine-tenths to rid themselves of bad customs and habits."[41] What qualified as "bad customs and habits" often left blackqueer Harlemites as outsiders—communally and morally.

For those on the margins of gender and sexual norms, the multiplicity of Harlem as a space of communal uplift, activism, and leadership acted both in their favor and as a limitation. For blackqueer people facing racism and economic disparity, in need of everyday welfare and community, the support that could be found in many institutions of black Harlem was a gain. Yet, socially subversive persons often did not serve the aims of the black elite and middle class, allegedly acting as a foil to their advancement strategies.[42] It was rare, even in light of the challenges blackqueer Harlemites posed to heteronormativity and patriarchy, for anyone to identify as explicitly non-heterosexual,[43] and many lived "underground" where they were less identifiable "behind veils of respectability and within the ghettos of large urban centers."[44] Yet, in their own spaces, sometimes with boldness and at other times plagued by shame (and likely sometimes feeling both ways and others in between), sexual and gender nonconformists through their ways of being and becoming countered disintegrative norms and offered themselves "something else."[45]

Blackqueer Counterpublics: Liberative Praxis, Sexual Subversion, and Gender Nonconformity

What we remember and how we remember matter; that is, memory is a moral act.[46] Microhistories of blackqueer Harlem as a counterpublic—a space of marginality and another kind of meaning-making—contribute to my own constructive, liberative understandings of a blackqueer ethics. Exploring the microhistories of blackqueer Harlem's spaces created through the music of blues women, their rent parties, and the Hamilton Lodge Balls—the oft-ignored contributions that blackqueer people made to the thriving and becoming of Harlem as a powerful social and cultural force—adds greater dimension not only to the historical remembrance and impact of 1920s Harlem, but to our contemporary moral imagination. Womanist ethicist Emilie M. Townes notes, microhistories (1) create counter-memory which "[forces] a reconsideration of flawed (incomplete or vastly circumscribed) histories," and (2) subvert the dominant narrative.[47] Microhistories may also offer evidence for the ways blackqueer Harlem became a powerful social and cultural force with and for itself and in the wider public. Blackqueer gender and sexual microhistories provide examples of resistance and visibility that have been decentered in the meta-history of Harlem's black modernism, "Harlem Renaissance," and the retelling of the era of "the New Negro." These microhistories are key factors to understanding the subversive potential of blackqueer Harlem and they expand the archive—that is, what we have the opportunity to know and remember—of blackqueer communality in 1920s Harlem.

This community practiced ways of being sexual and gendered people that confronted established norms of patriarchy and heteronormativity, as well as the shamefulness ascribed to black sexuality by whiteness. In challenging normativity and orienting themselves toward community-making, these black gender and sexual nonconformists confronted racism and economic stratification, as well as sexism and heterosexism. Their practices affirmed their gendered and sexual existence in their black bodies. With their music of choice, the blues, they transgressed the boundaries of "respectable" communal space and gender roles by celebrating sex, bodies, same-gender desire, and other aspects of romantic relationship typically relegated to private space. Their rent parties served the purpose of meeting basic needs as black bodies came together out of economic and relational necessity and, in the process, made space for themselves and their expansive desires. And, at the Hamilton Lodge Ball, contestants performed and thousands from around the world celebrated blackqueerness. These three counterpublics meant that everyday persons embodying similar expressions could have examples from among themselves toward which they might aspire and models for challenging the public's dominant, normativizing logics and structures.

Members of Harlem's black literati and entertainers, like Richard Bruce Nugent, Zora Neale Hurston, and Gladys Bentley, serve as well-known examples of the significance of gender and sexual nonconformists to the fabric of black Harlem (even if the details and parties exist in varying levels of secrecy, discretion, and fabulation). Yet, this chapter looks to the communal settings created and inhabited by the everyday population of Harlem, with particular attention to those who lived at less socially acceptable interstices for this ethic rooted in community. As previously mentioned, to speak of the communities is to speak of the people who make up the communities, and vice versa. This focus does not discount the struggles or contributions of more well-known individuals, nor does it exclude them from these spaces of which they were no doubt a part. However, in formulating an ethic that gives primacy to communities and builds upon integrative values toward communal thriving, we look to blackqueerness in the quotidian. These spaces provide for us a starting point for reflection toward an ethic grounded in marginalized experiences and are inclusive of the entire self in processes of communal becoming.

Blues Environments

In 1920s Harlem, the blues provided a soundtrack for black life, describing the heartache and harmony of love and lust, the hardship of economic uncertainty, and the many facets that made up black existence. What came to be known as the "classical blues" found its way to the cities of the north from the country towns of the south.[48] It gave voice to an ambiguous post-emancipation experience fraught with the challenges of being newly free and the responsibility of agency, namely of the sexual kind.[49] Like never before, many black people in the United States were able to articulate a "freely chosen sexual love [that became] a mediator between historical disappointment and the new social realities of an evolving African-American community" through the blues.[50] The blues signify a deep claiming of the black body made abject in the United States, and a sexuality that had long been used to serve others. As Angela Y. Davis notes:

> It was the status of their personal relationships that was revolutionized [...] Sexuality thus was one of the most tangible

domains in which emancipation was acted upon and through which meanings were expressed. Sovereignty in sexual matters marked an important divide between life during slavery and life after emancipation.[51]

For people who were stripped of the chance to choose their sexual practices, the blues was more than music. Instead, it became a means of asserting bodily autonomy and personal dignity.

Sexual and gender nonconformists could find themselves in the words sang by Gertrude "Ma" Rainey, Lucille Bogan, Bessie Smith, Ida Cox, Ethel Waters, and other blues women. While men also sang the blues, the contributions of women, for the ways they transcended gender and sexual norms in song and often in their sexual and gender performance, are more significant for this chapter. Though the blues was a product of black southern culture,[52] it is explored here to convey how blues environments created new discourses in word and body in Harlem that aided in generating a significant paradigm shift in gender and sexual expression. Blues environments served as spaces of participation in another kind of possibility, signaling a subversive model of sexual and gender becoming. While some songs may have reflected hegemonic values, in engaging the music and performance of black blues women, one finds it need not be morally pure to be morally fecund. The significance of these lyrics, music, and performance within their contexts was their capacity to grant permission of expression to blackqueer Harlemites as they located their own experiences and desires through the blues that pulsed through their prized spaces.

The blues have been framed as both a compliment and a threat to black religious (namely, Christian) life. For black theologian James H. Cone, the blues represent an important connection to the spirituals, songs that were both a product of enslavement and emancipation. The spirituals, known for their deep engagement with experiences of suffering, deliverance, retribution, and triumph, boldly codified in song truths of black American experiences in the Deep South, much like the blues. Though, according to womanist theologian Kelly Brown Douglas, the blues were perceived as "the Devil's music" and the spirituals as belonging to God within the Black Church, the delineation between the two genres, as she argued, was not quite as rigid among lay practitioners of the faith as by faith leaders instructing parishioners.[53] Cone's

The Spirituals and the Blues: An Interpretation (1972) notes the ways both genres blurred the supposed line between the sacred and secular to affirm the veracity of black suffering and black hope. On the other hand, historian Lawrence W. Levine and Davis note the threat caused by the blues to the religious sphere: without religion, it distinctively created space for the release of burdens and "drew upon and incorporated sacred consciousness," namely through women's voices as they "summoned sacred responses to their messages about sexuality."[54] Bessie Smith's 1923 hit, "Tain't Nobody's Bizz-ness if I Do," contributes to the debate adeptly as she proclaims, "If I go to church on Sunday/Then just shimmy down on Monday/ 'Tain't nobody's biz-ness if I do, if I do." The blues offered opportunity to be freed in the body and in one's self-expression from repressive religious and social norms, and as a result of the expression, to be no less wholly human. Both the blues and its invitations to freedom countered strategies of black racial uplift and classist norms,[55] and what Douglas called a black Christian "narrative of civility." A particular politic of respectability employed by the Black Church, the narrative of civility sought to establish black people as morally sound and acceptable to white people by sacrificing black bodies in the process of exalting a "body-denying ethic" and "the whiteness of God."[56] The blues and their environments countered a wave of intracultural anti-blackness within religious and social spheres by asserting the body, inseparable from and expressive of its blackness, as radically present and valued.

Because of the gravitas of the blues as a musical genre and as a vital part of the Prohibition Era black northern city experience (as well as the southern black experience), the intracommunal contentions related to class, culture, and race became uniquely apparent. Some black people found the need to disassociate with the blues, as well as jazz, to avoid "[perpetuating] the idea prevalent among whites that blacks were lascivious and primitive."[57] This disavowal was especially predominant among Christians, the middle class, and black intelligentsia; during the years of the Harlem Renaissance, some artists and intellectuals sought to establish a black aesthetic to the exclusion of the blues.[58] One notable instance is that of W. E. B. Du Bois, who struggled to offer credence to the blues and other black musical expressions found in speakeasies, while forwarding instead the literature and spirituals of the era as paradigmatic of black arts.⁵⁹ In such ways, blues were labeled as "lower" or working class, even while it intervened to influence the culture and consciousness of Harlem and other major cities in the United States.

Davis argues this socioeconomic point further by looking to three blues women—Rainey, Smith, and Billie Holiday—for the ways that they signaled feminist consciousness among working-class women.⁶⁰ For example, Smith was known for having performed in the same manner no matter the race of the audience, never changing her impassioned delivery or her public airing of "private" matters.⁶¹ Additionally, the blues, and particularly blues women, reminded black people who had perceived themselves as having some economic status of a prior financial existence "they wanted to forget."⁶² The controversy surrounding the blues highlighted a tension between black middle-class and working-class, black Christians and the supposed "irreligious" blues folks, northerners and southern migrants, sexual and gender conformists and nonconformists.

The influence of the blues was felt through the gender, sexual, and musical performance of blues women. Gladys Bentley and Ethel Waters provided well-known examples of blues women who dressed in masculine attire, while Bentley, Waters, Bogan (also known under the recording name, Bessie Jackson), Smith, and Rainey all possessed a reputation for engaging in same-gender relationships.⁶³ The blues women sang boldly of sexual pleasure, non-monogamous relationships, gender subversion, desire for men and women, and even domestic violence,⁶⁴ and subsequently "introduced a new, different model of black women—more assertive, sexy, sexually aware, independent, realistic, complex, alive."⁶⁵ Through their example, aesthetic, and artistry, they created and enabled blues environments to produce an air of freedom of expression wherein sexual and gender norms could be toppled and sociocultural respectability transgressed.

The songs of the blues women, which often filled the aural space of rent parties, house parties, buffet flats, speakeasies, and other transgressive locations, served as representations of and invitations to encounter blackqueerness through sexual and gender nonconformity. For example, in the well-known "Prove It on Me Blues" (1928), written and sang most notably by Rainey, she sang,

> I looked up, to my surprise
> The gal I was with was gone
> Where she went, I don't know
> I mean to follow everywhere she goes
> [...]
> Went out last night with a crowd of my friends
> They must've been women, 'cause I don't like no men
> It's true I wear a collar and a tie
> [...]
> Wear my clothes just like a fan
> Talk to the gals just like any old man
> 'Cause they say I do it, ain't nobody caught me
> Sure got to prove it on me

This song provided one of the clearest examples of same-gender attraction, as well as gender subversion in the blues genre. After speaking of her desire for a woman, Rainey slyly boasts of her capacity to challenge constructions of masculinity by embodying it ("I wear a collar and a tie [...] Talk to the gals just like any old man") and by rejecting its normative bearers ("'cause I don't like no men"). Refusing to be made a spectacle in conformist spheres, Rainey teases, "ain't nobody caught me, sure got to prove it on me." For people in Harlem's blues counterpublics who were hidden in plain sight as they expressed their nonconformity, such lyrics could reflect shared practices and intracultural language that strengthened communality among nonconformists.

In another example of gender and sexual subversion sang by Rainey and composed by Thomas Dorsey (who later became known as "the father of Gospel music"), "Sissy Blues" (1926) proclaimed,

> Woke and found my man in a sissy's arms
> "Hello, Central, it's 'bout to run me wild
> Can I get that number, or will I have to wait a while?"
> [...]
> Some are young, some are old
> My man says sissy's got good jelly roll
> [...]
> My man's got a sissy, his name is Miss Kate

He shook that thang like jelly on a plate
[...]
Now all the peoples ask me why I'm all alone
A sissy shook that thing and took my man from home

"Sissy" in this song, without qualifiers or additional commentary that framed the person as abject or rare, seemed to reflect the normalcy of the presence of feminine men in certain social circles. For the writer, the use seemed to carry a shared, nonpejorative understanding of the term, "sissy." Rainey's tone throughout the song reflects the hurt of having been left, not necessarily that her "man" has "got a sissy." One might understand masculine women and feminine men as commonplace and figures who found belonging as they contributed to making spaces of sexual and gender nonconformity.

Lastly, Rainey's "Ma Rainey's Black Bottom" presented a view of someone that stood in contrast to the modesty desired by black elites in Harlem and that was imposed most frequently upon women's bodies of the era. Rainey took on the voice of a genderless speaker seeking to see Rainey's "black bottom."

Want to see the dance you call your big black bottom
That puts you in a trance
All the boys in the neighborhood
They say your black bottom is really good
Come on and show me your black bottom
I want to learn that dance

With this double entendre, Ma Rainey and her listeners reclaimed and proclaimed the sensual presence of their bodies and rejected limiting norms of body policing.[66]

Conversely, in a song composed and sang by Bessie Smith, "Foolish Man Blues" (1927),

Men sure deceitful, they getting worse every day
Lord, men sure deceitful, they getting worse every day
Actin' like a bunch o' women
They just gabbin', gabbin', gabbin' away

> There's two things got me puzzled
> There's two things I can't understand
> There's two things got me puzzled
> here's two things I can't understand
> That's a mannish actin' woman
> an ' skippin' twistin' woman-actin' man

In the song, Smith went on to say, "I used to love that man," presumably her "crooked" and "evil" former lover who consistently broke her heart. This provides a framing for the song that decries "foolish men." Smith's pining for the normative in this song continues as she curiously frames a "mannish actin' woman" and a "skippin,' twistin', woman-actin' man" as unintelligible to her. This is curious coming from Smith who, with her mentor, Rainey, and other blues women, could have been perceived as "mannish." It is not clear whether these lyrics reflect a commitment to rigid gender roles or ashamedness of gender nonconformity, a feeling in reference to a particular man, or a simple desire to sing a song that may have found resonance in a wider public. While the lyrics reify the presence of gender queerness, Smith offered here an uncharacteristic intolerance for gender variance.

On the other hand, Smith often exemplified gender role subversion (namely submissive, sexually modest roles of women), and particularly so in "I'm Wild about that Thing" (1929), composed by Spencer Williams.

> Do it easy, honey, don't get rough
> From you, papa, I can't get enough
> I'm wild about that thing
> Sweet joy it always brings
> Everybody knows it, I'm wild about that thing
>
> Please don't hold it, baby, when I cry
> Gimme every bit of it, else I'll die
> I'm wild about that thing, Sha-da-jing-jing-jing
> All the time I'm cryin', I'm wild about that thing

Presenting the black woman in the blues as "assertive, sexy, sexually aware, [and] independent" (as noted above) the way that Smith did in this song and others was a hallmark of the blues era that categorically "redefined women's 'place'."⁶⁷ Though many of the songs, including the one explored here, were penned by men, this song and others held the integrity, passion, and authenticity of the singer which, according to Harrison, produced a "distinctly female interpretation."⁶⁸ These songs were sung by women and, because of the singer's positionality as a woman, catered particularly to women. Likewise, the songs were sung by gender and sexual nonconformists, and were lauded by audiences comprised of the same.

Rent Parties

Directly related to the blues was a primary setting in which the blues found its footing in blackqueer Harlem—rent parties. Though a source of income and entertainment, the gatherings offered much more through a suspension of sexual, gender, economic, social, and political constrictions.⁶⁹ Rent parties, along with buffet flats and speakeasies briefly elaborated below, aided in the popularization of the blues among working-class black people in Harlem who frequently found themselves in need of additional financial support. The gatherings developed as a necessity for persons struggling to maintain housing due to the increasing rents brought on by the greed of landlords during the migration of black people from the south, and the lower wages afforded them by racist employers.⁷⁰ One Bermudan immigrant, Bernice Gore, strategized, "With a sixty-dollar-a-month apartment on my hands, and no job, I soon learned, like everyone else, to rent my rooms out and throw these Saturday get-togethers."⁷¹ Through these parties, Harlemites "raised money [...] by charging guests a few cents for admission to their apartment and providing food, liquor, live music, and uninhibited dancing in a highly sexually charged, unrestrained environment."⁷² By providing a kind of economic empowerment to those of lesser socioeconomic means, the parties stood in opposition to the capitalist framework that prized independence over community as Harlemites turned to communal support for their wellbeing.

According to Wilson, the parties served as havens for "lesbians and gay men [who] relied on private parties as spaces safe from potential personal and professional scandal and from prosecution."⁷³ Though many of the invitations were extended broadly in the neighborhood and a variety of people could be present, the parties being held in private apartments meant gender and sexual nonconformists could exercise greater discretion about how and when they might be seen—often among people not unlike themselves—and enjoyed some degree of social safety. Rent parties offered connection and enjoyment, a reprieve from the prevalent hegemonic powers of racism and classism as black bodies swayed and touched, filled with laughter, food, and drink, and found distinct freedom among other black bodies.

Like rent parties, buffet flats were house parties "combining celebratory music with sexual activities of all sorts" while serving as "a major component of the black gay subculture."[74] Though buffet flats were blackqueer spaces that incorporated some of the same qualities of rent parties, they are not explored deeply in this chapter because they were more exclusive spaces known mostly through word-of-mouth and distinguished by their liberal access to sex workers, often a clientele rather than a general public.[75] Similarly, speakeasies, businesses that illegally sold liquor, also would have been spaces that provided the sexual liberation akin to rent parties, in addition to all manner of forbidden activities; however, because the primary interest of the space was anti-Prohibition and catered to such an audience as its main focus, it is not included here. In fact, historian Eric Garber argues, persons were expected to "hide their preferences" and "blend in" with heterosexuals in such settings.[76]

Held in the renters' apartments featuring illicit liquor and soon-to-be-well-known musicians, rent parties provided a setting through which sexual and gender nonconformity modeled sexual liberation. A more intimate level of engagement was available in these parties "infused" with "sexual energy" that were also critical to the development of a lesbian and gay subculture in Harlem (and beyond) through increased visibility and its crossing of racial and class boundaries. Wilson aptly identifies this period of increased visibility and identity formation as a "queer renaissance."[77] Lesbian activist and dancer during the 1920s, Mabel Hampton, describes the scene at a Harlem rent party, namely one for women, which she frequented:

The bulldykers would come and bring their women with them. And you wasn't supposed to jive with them, you know. They danced up a breeze. They did the Charleston, they did a little bit of everything. They were all colored women. Sometimes we ran into someone who had a white woman with them. But me, I'd venture out with any of them. I just had a ball.[78]

Hampton's statements illuminate the uninhibited sites that the rent parties provided, as well as the tensions that could exist along the lines of sexual expression and race. Rent parties, like the Hamilton Lodge Balls elaborated in the next section, troubled the color line through a practice of blackqueer subversion, specifically in terms of integration.[79]

Hampton's interviews also reveal the significance of a growing black community in Harlem that thrived through these parties, often away from an intrusive police presence.[80] However, the increase in blackqueer visibility in Harlem and much of New York City led to stricter policing and application of sodomy and decency laws,[81] greater hostility from moralists, and public discourse that disfavored sexual and gender nonconformists of all races. In one example, editor of *The New York Age* and the pastor of a Harlem church enlisted the help of the police commissioner in the task of preserving black respectability by tending to the growth of rent parties wherein "all manner of debauchery was engaged."[82] Wilson argues it was not the public nature of homosexuality that troubled the masses; it was that gay and lesbian presence was not ghettoized, but enmeshed throughout New York City that made it "frightful."[83] While the lack of containment of sexual and gender nonconformity certainly added to the fright, it is also important to note the visceral homophobic response evoked merely by their existence and visibility itself, especially among black institutional moralists with substantial platforms and distinctly respectable racial and moral aims.

The rent parties diminished as blackqueer sanctuaries as they grew in popularity and became an outlet for those who were not in financial dire straits, but who instead sought profits.[84] They also faltered in tandem with the blackqueer subculture that "quickly declined following the stock market crash of 1929, and the repeal of Prohibition, soon becoming only a shadow of its earlier self."[85] Still, for the contributions to black life in 1920s Harlem, rent parties were celebrated by Langston Hughes as "the one authentic black social event that was unspoiled by white tourism."[86]

Hamilton Lodge Ball

The Hamilton Lodge Ball was held annually at various venues in the heart of Harlem, hosted by the Oddfellows Society.[87] Though there were other smaller balls held in the neighborhood and others held across the country, the most well-known, which drew crowds in the thousands, was the Hamilton Lodge Ball. Beginning in 1869 as the "Masquerade and Civic Ball," it developed into a drag competition in 1923 and became referred to as "The Fairies Ball," "The Dance of the Fairies," or the "Faggots Ball."[88] For years, this event brought together an amalgam of people across socioeconomic status, sexual orientation, and (as was less frequent across the United States and in New York City) across race.[89] The balls could draw upward of 1,500 spectators each, notably increasing in popularity throughout the 1920s and early 1930s. One reporter noted in 1932 that lesbian women and gay men from nearly twenty-five states arrived to witness the annual ball, citing it as an "institution" rather than a hidden aberration,[90] and fantastically, nearly 6,000 attendees were recorded at the Ball the following year.[91] Local attendees, like white visitors from the bohemian Greenwich Village, often participated in the Balls in large numbers, joining the number of participants "in their gorgeous evening gowns, wigs and powdered faces."[92]

In a 1926 article from *The New York Age*, under the headline "Hamilton Lodge Ball: An Unusual Spectacle," the writer reported,

> "Although Hamilton Lodge is a colored organization, there were many white people present and they danced with and among the colored people. Many people who attend dances generally declare that the masquerade and civic ball was the most unusual spectacle they ever witnessed."

It is unclear whether it was the racial mixing that seems to be the most unusual aspect of the evening or solely the men who "mask[ed] as women for [the] affair."[275] A 1927 report of the same event went into deeper description of the contestants as they elaborated the racial scene:

From the garb of a biblical virgin, by way of the historic costumes of the early centuries, down to the very sparse attire only seen on the burlesque stage of today, accentuated with the feminine gesture and lingue, to say nothing of the contortions of the hip, formed the make-up of these male masqueraders. Color prejudice was thrown to the winds, as the Nordic contestants mixed freely with their darkskinned [sic] brethren.[93]

Again, race relations are presented in utopic fashion in this seemingly alien space of the ballroom.

Despite its popularity, the reception of the Hamilton Lodge Balls and its participants by black Harlemites was varied. Like the rent parties and blues environments, the Balls highlighted a class conflict among black people that hinged upon socially acceptable behavior, repeating the respectability politics prevalent among those concerned with racial uplift through behavior modification. At once a spectacle for some and a cause for aversion for others, Wilson notes the way participants, namely the "fairies," were received among middle-class black people as "'low class' in morality and social standing."[94] This "'low class' in morality" could have been a matter of gender performance or presumed sexual deviance, or in an era of establishing a black Harlem, possibly a critique of racial miscegenation. In any event, the Hamilton Lodge Ball was a site of controversy—one about which the local black press loved to talk.

That the annual article in *The New York Age* reporting on the Ball more readily shared the details of the evenings throughout the 1920s seems no small feat. The Ball often received agreeable coverage in *The New York Age,* but by the early 1930s, this view seemed to change. One article, from a March 1933 issue, focused mostly on the police presence and arrests for disorderly conduct that took place and referred to attendees as "males and females and the variety of she-males and he-females."[95] In the same issue of the newspaper, a sharp-witted gossip column entitled "Carrying the Torch" spoke of the event like never before as "an abomination" and the participants as "sex perverted." Attendees were also called "fagot [sic] supporters," "suckers," and "morons." The writer, called The Flying Cavalier, went on to speak of attendance at the event as a feeding on "one's baser appetites" and accused a local Baptist deacon of a "prominent church" of being "she-ish" at the event and zinged, "Will he burn in hellfire or will he burn?"[96]

Likewise, the annual article in 1938 focused on arrests of those "offering to commit lewd acts" at the Ball, and even went as far as to include not only names (which was also in the former article about arrests), but also addresses and races.[97] This was troubling, particularly considering most of the black people named were from Harlem, like the readers of the paper, and were, therefore, vulnerable to harm. Also, it marked a shift from reports in the 1920s that focused on those present from across the country, the winners, the racial harmony, the artistry of drag, and the grandeur of those gathered. As Wilson notes, the *Amsterdam News* shared like sentiments, referring to "the virus of the perverted," insinuating the ability for sexual and gender nonconformists to infect others with their deviant ways, while *Atlantic World* likewise invoked "perversion" language.[98]

The Hamilton Lodge Ball functioned as a space wherein black drag queens, as well as other gay, lesbian, and sexual or gender nonconformists could openly (albeit momentarily) celebrate their identities in their own neighborhood.[99] Through the performance of gender variance via drag—an expression that would not be welcome or celebrated in public life, but as a celebratory event, it provided opportunity for a celebratory reality—blackqueer participants, as performers and onlookers, established power that was counter to normative expressions generally celebrated in New York City publics. Though the Hamilton Lodge Ball was open to white participants and welcomed famous white and black elites, it offered a communality distinguished from the curious, but otherwise conformist communities. Blackqueer people formulated and participated in a concurrent counter-discourse that transcended the performative competition to create bonds of commonality across blackqueerness. Its power rested in its capacity to aid in the development of blackqueer culture governed by differing conceptions of goodness and communality, and, for a time, to subvert the values of a conformist society to allow possibility for and celebrate that which was publicly labeled abject.

This celebration of gender subversion met its untimely end by the beginning of the 1940s when "homosexuals" became more widely associated in the national psyche with "sex crimes," and the social understanding of their identity shifted "from silly oddities and sexual degenerates to dangerous psychopaths."[100] Yet, the counterpublic endured underground alongside various balls across the United States. They continued in their legacy in major cities where black and brown participants consistently formulated communal space for their belonging, expression, entertainment, talent, and thriving.

Promptings toward Integration and Community-Centered Sexual Ethics

At the start of this chapter, I began with the question of "What does it *mean* to theorize ethics from among those deemed immoral by the traditionalism of Christian ethical framings and those largely absent from liberative ethical conceptualizations?" I have sought to convey the doing of ethics from a layered, descriptive approach, not only in theory, but through the practices of a community. The counterpublic of blackqueer Harlem exemplifies the meaning that is made when communities are deepened, expanded, and troubled by grounding their moral imagination beyond the given traditionalism. As I noted, the ungrounding of Christian personal piety, anti-body logics and practices, whiteness, and sexual and gender conformity allows for a prioritization of communal becoming that creates space for the sexual and gender complexity of its members.

Through the blues environments, rent parties, and the Hamilton Lodge Balls, blackqueer Harlem developed a greater sense of communal identity notwithstanding the Harlem public and wider public with which it was often in conflict. They created space for distinct, integrative forms of "uplift" that celebrated their flourishing as black sexual and gender nonconformists; innovated body-honoring and creative expressions; and attended to their socioeconomic wellbeing and need for connectivity, which enabled them to exhibit a flourishing communality. By delving into the archive for gender and sexual microhistories, we better understand blackqueer Harlem as an integrative site that uniquely allowed for the incorporation of the gender and sexual self into what it was to be a black Harlemite and human. Even when places of blackqueer thriving were perceived as counters to sociopolitical uplift strategies, blackqueer Harlemites continued to establish their place in the larger community and, in turn, created their own.

Harlem's sexual and gender nonconformists embraced their deviance from normativity to help shape their Harlem as a space with the capacity to hold gender and sexual difference, and in the process fostered an ethos beyond survival. Though, as Vogel notes, it is clear that "spaces of sexual dissidence" existed among renowned writers, entertainers, socialites, and intellectuals of the age,[101] the everyday people of Harlem fashioned (and sometimes shared with these renowned citizens of Harlem) liberative sanctuaries that enabled them to imagine and cultivate vibrancy and yield beauty in their togetherness. In a notable way, blackqueer Harlem cared for the spirit that longed for relationality and belonging, the body that sought authenticity and expression, the mind and heart that craved exploration, discovery, and a leaning into its own knowing, and the communities seeking liberative practices amid racial, economic, gender- and sexuality-based oppressions. In the following chapter, I continue to examine integrative communality as the foundation of an ethic rooted in blackqueerness by exploring ethical and theological reflection firmly grounded in the experiences of black LGBTQ+ people that has reshaped the contours of religious discourse and textures a living archive by critically grappling with questions of sexuality, gender, and the sacred.

Notes

1 Thelathia Nikki Young, *Black Queer Ethics, Family, and Philosophical Imagination* (New York: Palgrave Macmillan, 2006), 60.

2 Traci C. West, "Constructing Ethics: Reinhold Niebuhr and Harlem Women Activists," *Journal of the Society of Christian Ethics* 24, no. 1 (Spring/Summer 2004): 46.

3 Beverly Wildung Harrison, "Doing Christian Ethics," in *Justice in the Making: Feminist Social Ethics*, ed. Elizabeth Bounds, Pamela Brubaker, Jane E. Hicks, Marilyn J. Legge, Rebecca Todd Peters, and Traci C. West (Louisville: Westminster John Knox 2004), 36.

4 Though "gender," as such, was not yet an established term in reference to people (though a concept) in the 1920s, my use of "gender" instead of sex speaks to the power dynamics and performativity that accompany the embodiment of masculine,

feminine, and nonbinary expressions, and not necessarily biological traits.

5   As mentioned above, I recognize that understandings of gender, as it is currently understood by some scholars as performative and constructed, were unknown in blackqueer Harlem. The deconstruction of gender norms present in blackqueer Harlem cannot be ignored, and the deliberateness of their nonconformity must be noted. Because categories of gender, womanhood, manhood, femaleness, maleness, feminine, masculine, and trans (including nonbinary) are lived in contested and often illegible and/or inaccessible expressions when through a black body, the conversation of gender and sexual nonconformity in Harlem is one that would benefit from greater exploration. For our purposes, I refer to gender and sexual nonconformity as a practice, as acts of living into difference with intention.

6   Michael Warner, "Publics and Counterpublics (abbreviated version)," *Quarterly Journal of Speech* 88, no. 4 (November 2002): 423–4.

7   Warner, "Publics and Counterpublics," 424. Cathy J. Cohen, "Deviance as Resistance: A New Research Agenda for the Study of Black Politics," *Du Bois Review* 1, no. 1 (2004): 27–45.

8   Embedded in my understanding of Harlem as a counterpublic is the understanding of its position as subaltern. Feminist philosopher Nancy Fraser draws a distinction between "counterpublics" and "subaltern counterpublics," though both understandings apply to blackqueer Harlem. For Fraser, a distinctive marker of subaltern counterpublics lies in communal self-understanding. That is, the power of subaltern counterpublics is discovered in its meaning-making, including its ability to make, or define, itself. This making requires the proliferation of a counter-discourse that allows members "to formulate oppositional interpretations of their identities, interests, and needs." Additionally, for Fraser, the primary purpose of counterpublics is support and training: "They function as spaces of withdrawal and regroupment [...] they also function as bases and training grounds for agitational activities directed toward wider publics." See Nancy Fraser, "Rethinking the Public Sphere: A Contribution to the Critique of Actually Existing Democracy," *Social Text* 25, no. 26 (1990): 67–8. One example of such activities lies in the attitudes with which *The New York Age*, one of Harlem's foremost newspapers, covered the Hamilton Lodge Balls over the years, shifting from ridicule and disdain to celebration, particularly when a black person won the competition. Unfortunately, in the 1930s, the local newspapers returned to their ridicule and disdain of the Balls. In a March 4, 1933, excerpt from the "Carrying the Torch" gossip column of *The New*

York Age, the attendees of the Hamilton Lodge Ball were referred to as "sex perverts [...] with sex perverted minds." Later issues of the newspaper primarily reported on arrests and named those arrested for crimes like soliciting sex. This was quite a shift from coverage in the 1920s that celebrated the extravagance of the evening's events and the "keen [...] competition" among the participants as well as the large numbers present. I say more on this shift later in this chapter. See "Hamilton Lodge Ball: An Unusual Spectacle," in *The New York Age* (New York), March 6, 1926, and "Hamilton Lodge, No. 710 in Annual Masquerade and Civic Ball," in *The New York Age* (New York), March 5, 1927; The Flying Cavalier, "Carrying the Torch," in *The New York Age* (New York), March 4, 1933.

9   For more on a black feminist politics of refusal, see Axelle Karera, "Black Feminist Philosophy and the Politics of Refusal," in *The Oxford Handbook of Feminist Philosophy*, ed. Ásta and Kim Q. Hall (New York: Oxford University Press, 2021).

10 Shane Vogel, *The Scene of Harlem Cabaret: Race, Sexuality, Performance* (Chicago: University of Chicago Press, 2009), 18–19.

11 As a counterpublic, blackqueer Harlem's spaces stood in juxtaposition to the "private sphere" where sexuality was often relegated in Western society and in Christian understandings beholden to traditionalism. For an invitation to black gay men to make oneself and one's community "from scratch," toward life and living, see Joseph Beam, "Making Ourselves from Scratch," in *Brother to Brother: New Writings by Black Gay Men*, ed. Essex Hemphill, conceived by Joseph Beam (Boston: Alyson, 1991).

12 For more on queer failure and its creative potential, see Jack Halberstam, *The Queer Art of Failure* (Durham: Duke University Press, 2011).

13 Harlem was frequently referred to as a "Mecca" for black people. The phrase gained popularity in the 1920s, connoting a city to which people flocked in large droves with religious-like devotion (i.e., as a pious Muslim would to the holy city, Mecca, Saudi Arabia). Harlem Renaissance novelist Wallace Thurman referred to Harlem as "the Mecca of the New Negro" in his *Negro Life in New York's Harlem: A Lively Picture of a Popular and Interesting Section* (1927). Harlem Renaissance intellect and activist James Weldon Johnson also said of Harlem, "[It] is indeed the great Mecca for the sight-seer, the pleasure-seeker, the curious, the adventurous, the enterprising, the ambitious, and the talented of the whole Negro world." James Weldon Johnson, "Harlem: The Culture Capital," in *Double Take: A Revisionist Harlem Renaissance Anthology*

(New Brunswick: Rutgers University Press, 2001), 21. In "The New Frontage on American Life" (1925), Charles Spurgeon Johnson's essay, he refers to the neighborhood as "the Mecca of Negroes the country over." Charles Spurgeon Johnson, "The Negro Frontage on American Life," in *The New Negro*, ed. Alain Locke (New York: Touchstone, 1992), 15–16.

14 Jill Watts, *God, Harlem, USA: The Father Divine Story* (Berkeley: University of California Press, 1995), 43.

15 "Black New Yorkers" violent encounters with civilian and police violence during the race riot of 1900, as well as entrenched overcrowding and landlord exploitation in the Tenderloin and then San Juan Hill, engendered the migration to Harlem, according to historian Shannon King. The race riot took place in the Tenderloin district, beginning with an incident at West 41st St. and 8th Ave., when a black man attempting to protect his partner from a solicitation arrest by a plainclothes cop killed the cop, and a "white mob—comprised of civilians and police officers" responded days later by attacking "Black pedestrians from thirty-fourth street to forty-second street along Broadway, Seventh, and Eighth Avenues." Shannon King, *Whose Harlem Is This, Anyway?: Community Politics and Grassroots Activism during the New Negro Era* (New York: New York University Press, 2015), 2.

16 Jervis Anderson, *This Was Harlem: A Cultural Portrait, 1900–1950* (New York: Farrar, Straus, Giroux, 1981), 45. An upstate New York newspaper read, "'San Juan Hill' [...] was the scene Friday night [of] a fierce race riot which required the reserves of no less than 17 police precincts, numbering more than 250 men, to quell after many shots had been fired and several persons had been seriously injured." "Race Riot in New York," in *Springville Journal* (Springville, NY), July 20, 1905, 8.

17 Gilbert Osofsky, *Harlem: The Making of a Ghetto; Negro New York, 1890–1930* (New York: Harper & Row, 1971), 79.

18 James Weldon Johnson, *Black Manhattan* (New York: Da Capo, 1930), 147–8.

19 Anderson, *This Was Harlem*, 62.

20 Osofsky, *The Making of a Ghetto*, 105.

21 Julie A. Gallagher, *Black Women and Politics in New York City* (Urbana: University of Illinois Press, 2012), 15.

22 Judith Weisenfeld, *African American Women and Christian Activism: New York's Black YWCA, 1905–1945* (Cambridge: Harvard University Press, 1997), 122.

23 Mark D. Naison, *Communists in Harlem during the Depression* (Champaign: University of Illinois Press, 2004), xvii.
24 Gallagher, *Black Women and Politics*, 49.
25 James F. Wilson, *Bulldaggers, Pansies, and Chocolate Babies: Performance, Race, and Sexuality in the Harlem Renaissance* (Ann Arbor: University of Michigan Press, 2011), 8. For more on religion in the Harlem of the 1920s, alongside the lens of literature in the New Negro Renaissance, see Josef Sorett, "The Church and the Negro Spirit," in *Spirit in the Dark: A Religious History of Racial Aesthetics* (New York: Oxford University Press, 2016) 19–53.
26 George Chauncey, *Gay New York: Gender, Urban Culture, and the Making of the Gay Male World 1890–1940* (New York: Basic 1994), 254.
27 "Dr. A. C. Powell Scores Pulpit Evils," in *The New York Age* (New York, NY), November 16, 1929.
28 "Dr. Powell's Crusade against Abnormal Vice Is Approved: Pastors and Laity Endorse Dr. Powell's Denunciation of Degeneracy in the Pulpit: Chorus of Commendation Is Heard as Eminent Men Express Approval and Give Promises of Their Support," in *The New York Age* (New York, NY), November 23, 1929.
29 Wilson, *Bulldaggers, Pansies, and Chocolate Babies*, 37.
30 Wallace D. Best, *Langston's Salvation: American Religion and the Bard of Harlem* (New York: New York University Press, 2017), 60.
31 Best, *Langston's Salvation*, 60. While the greatest majority of religious black Harlemites were primarily Baptist and Methodist Christians, religion took on various forms in Harlem including people who affiliated with black Judaism (e.g., the Moorish Zionist Temple), Father Divine's Peace Missions, Bishop Grace's United House of Prayer for All People, as well as Harlem Community Church (with Unitarian connections). Some also belonged to other Christian denominations and some were nonreligious.
32 Best, *Langston's Salvation*, 61.
33 Best, *Langston's Salvation*, 60–1.
34 Robert Weisbrot, *Father Divine and the Struggle for Racial Equality* (Champaign: University of Illinois Press, 1983), 38.
35 Best, *Langston's Salvation*, 59.
36 Qtd. in Jon Michael Spencer, "The Black Church and the Harlem Renaissance," *African American Review* 30, no. 3 (Autumn 1996): 455.
37 Weisbrot, *Father Divine*, 195.

38 In his study of the economic and racial campaigns of Father Divine and the Harlem Peace Missions, Weisbrot argues, what could and has been written off as a cult of deceived followers was actually "the largest, most cohesive movement in the northern ghettos" and became a formidable force against racial and economic disparities—a much more sympathetic view of Divine than many scholars offer. Weisbrot further states, "Rather than bask, immobile, in the adulation of his followers, [Father Divine] redirected their devotion outward, in support of the reform causes he valued: integration, equal rights, and economic cooperation." Such a perspective contrasts sharply with earlier significant historians, such as Lewis, who dismissed Divine as a symbol of Harlem's Depression-era "religious hysteria." See David Levering Lewis, *When Harlem Was in Vogue* (New York: Oxford University Press, 1979), 44. For insight on the sexual practices forwarded by the Peace Mission, in the case of the Movement in Philadelphia, see Judith Weisenfeld, "Real True Buds: Celibacy and Same-Sex Desire across the Color Line in Father Divine's Peace Mission Movement," in *Devotions and Desires: Histories of Sexuality and Religion in the Twentieth-Century United States*, ed. Gillian Frank, Bethany Moreton, and Heather R. White (Chapel Hill: UNC Press, 2018), 90–112. Another faith leader with a significant reputation arose in 1929, developing in prominence beyond the period emphasized here, but is worth naming to reflect further the rise of charismatic black faith leaders invested in healing and the material wellness of parishioners, as well as black women's groundbreaking religious leadership. Elder Rosa A. Horn, a worship radio broadcast pioneer, founded the Mount Calvary Assembly of the Pentecostal Faith Church—a church writer James Baldwin joined in his youth—and the Gleaner's Aid Home which provided rest, food, and clothing, as well as shelter (particularly for women and children). See "Pentecostal Faith Church Closes Revival Campaign," *The New York Age* (September 17, 1932).

39 Roberta S. Gold, "The Black Jews of Harlem: Representation, Identity, and Race, 1920–1939," *American Quarterly* 55, no. 2 (June 2003): 184–5.

40 Lewis, *When Harlem Was in Vogue*, 222, 223. The acts of one leader, Elder Warren Robinson, were horrifying: sexual exploitation of women members and the accumulation of a personal fortune stolen from members. There is no evidence that the community of people deceived by him and that existed beyond his leadership were at all a horror to their neighbors, but rather, evidence exists that they were simply devout practitioners of faith.

41 Frederick C. Harris, "Rise of Respectability," *Dissent* 61, no. 1 (Winter 2014): 33.

42 The subversion was not only related to sexuality and gender. As many migrated to the north from the south, bringing with them their southern, often rural, culture, many struggled to acclimate to life in the big city. See Isabel Wilkerson, "The Kinder Mistress," in *The Warmth of Other Suns: The Epic Story of America's Great Migration* (New York: Vintage Books, 2010), 223–431.

43 Wilson, *Bulldaggers, Pansies, and Chocolate Babies*, 30.

44 Wilson, *Bulldaggers, Pansies, and Chocolate Babies*, 39. Wilson's quote incorporates the word "hid," to connote sexual and gender nonconformists' relationship to the "veils of respectability" and their capacity to be less conspicuous in "large urban centers." I raise a contention with the word "hid," as it connotes that acts toward privacy or discretion (often for physical safety and to maintain connection) are associated with shame without a clear indication of why such steps might be taken (within the context of the paragraph). The intentions of blackqueer Harlemites requires deeper nuance on this point, so I omitted the word "hid."

45 In this examination of archive and queernesses, I am inspired by Saidiya Hartman and, in particular, her critical fabulation on the life of a fifteen-year-old called Mattie leaving Virginia for New York, whose story, much like the communities of nameless individual blackqueer nonconformists, "exceeds the archive." Hartman says of Mattie, "She hoped 294 nautical miles was sufficient distance to create a new life. Mattie wanted something else. It was as simple and elusive, as vague and insistent as that. *Something else* was never listed as one of the reasons people left home, only the appalling and the verifiable [...] yet the inchoate, what you wanted but couldn't name, the resolute, stubborn desire for an elsewhere and an otherwise that had yet to emerge clearly, a notion of the possible whose outlines were fuzzy and amorphous, exerted a force no less powerful and tenacious," *something else* beyond that to which generations before her were confined. Saidiya Hartman, *Wayward Lives, Beautiful Experiments: Intimate Histories of Riotous Black Girls, Troublesome Women, and Queer Radicals* (New York: W. W. Norton, 2019), 46.

46 I am thinking here of Eddie Glaude's popular essay on James Baldwin and his 1968 introduction of Martin Luther King, Jr. at a fundraiser, which draws out the ethical complexity involved in how historical moments are remembered: "[Baldwin's] was an effort to jog the memory and, by extension, the morality of the audience,

by telling a different story about what happened to a movement on the brink of failure." It prompts the consideration of the ethical possibilities that await when the story is told another way, signaling Emilie M. Townes' use of "countermemory." Emilie M. Townes, *Womanist Ethics and the Cultural Production of Evil* (New York: Palgrave Macmillan, 2006), 6, 23.

47 Townes, *Womanist Ethics and the Cultural Production of Evil*, 8.
48 Kelly Brown Douglas, *Black Bodies and the Black Church: A Blues Slant* (New York: Palgrave Macmillan, 2014), 32.
49 Angela Y. Davis, *Blues Legacies and Black Feminism: Gertrude "Ma" Rainey, Bessie Smith, and Billie Holiday* (New York: Vintage, 1999), 141.
50 Davis, *Blues Legacies and Black Feminism*, 10.
51 Davis, *Blues Legacies and Black Feminism*, 4.
52 Alain Locke describes the blues as an expression of black people's "emotion, folk-wit and musical inventiveness." Alain Locke, *The Negro and His Music* (New York: J. B. Lyon, 1936), 28.
53 Douglas, *Black Bodies and the Black Church*, 20, 63.
54 Qtd Lawrence W. Levine, *Black Culture and Black Consciousness*, 237. Davis, *Blues Legacies and Black Feminism*, 8, 9. Davis critiques Levine's reference to "'spokesmen' of the blues," which negates the crucial role of women in integrating elements of the religious in the genre.
55 Davis, *Blues Legacies and Black Feminism*, 153–4.
56 Douglas, *Black Bodies and the Black Church*, 170.
57 Alwyn Williams, "Jazz and the New Negro: Harlem's Intellectuals Wrestle with the Art of the Age," *Australasian Journal of American Studies* 21, no. 1 (July 2002): 1.
58 Davis, *Blues Legacies and Black Feminism*, 123. Davis refers to the blues as an "indelicate stepchild" of many Harlem Renaissance luminaries, apart from Zora Neale Hurston and Langston Hughes. There is a periodization debate as it relates to the actual years of the Harlem Renaissance, with all agreeing the 1920s were significant years for such a cultural, intellectual, artistic, and sociopolitical "rebirth." For more on the debate, see Venetria K. Patton and Maureen Honey, *Double-Take: A Revisionist Harlem Renaissance Anthology* (New Brunswick: Rutgers University Press, 2001), xxv–xxvii.
59 Williams, "Jazz and the New Negro," 1.

60 Davis, *Blues Legacies and Black Feminism*, xi.
61 Davis, *Blues Legacies and Black Feminism*, 154.
62 Davis, *Blues Legacies and Black Feminism*, 154. Qtd. Elaine Feinstein, *Bessie Smith: Empress of the Blues* (New York: Penguin 1985), 30–1.
63 Barnet states, in an anecdote featuring Rainey and her sexual expression, "[apparently] Ma [Rainey], who was openly homosexual, had been jailed one night for partying with naked girls." Andrea Barnet, *All-Night Party: The Women of Bohemian Greenwich Village and Harlem, 1913–1930* (Chapel Hill: Algonquin Books of Chapel Hill, 2004), 174. She also notes Ethel Waters's "homoerotic leanings." Barnet, *All Night Party*, 207.
64 The performances of the classic blues women—especially Bessie Smith—were one of the few cultural spaces in which a tradition of public discourse on male violence was established in the 1920s. Davis, *Blues Legacies and Black Feminism*, page 5 of insert.
65 Daphne Duval Harrison, *Black Pearls: Blues Queens of the 1920s* (New Brunswick: Rutgers University Press, 1988), 111.
66 Such invitations to embodiment in black music popularized among the working class and those who hold less commitments to elite class stratifications continues to the present in such dance forms as twerking.
67 Davis, *Blues Legacies and Black Feminism*, 296.
68 Harrison, *Black Pearls*, 111.
69 Wilson, *Bulldaggers, Pansies, and Chocolate Babies*, 18.
70 Wilson, *Bulldaggers, Pansies, and Chocolate Babies*, 16. Rent parties over time changed in function. According to Wilson, "rent parties, in particular, included a preponderance of the working class in Harlem, and while these parties were originally staged from economic necessity for Harlem residents, they became quite marketable for entrepreneurial residents and shadowy underworld figures." Wilson, *Bulldaggers, Pansies, and Chocolate Babies*, 12.
71 Qtd. in Wilson, *Bulldaggers, Pansies, and Chocolate Babies*, 15.
72 Stephen Robertson, Shane White, Stephen Garton, and Graham White, "Disorderly Houses: Residences, Privacy, and the Surveillance of Sexuality in 1920s Harlem," *Journal of the History of Sexuality* 21, no. 3 (September 2012): 461. Rent parties, according to historian David Levering Lewis, would have been open to "formally dressed society folks from downtown, policemen, painters, carpenters, mechanics, truckmen in their workingmen's clothes, gamblers,

lesbians, and entertainers of all kinds." Lewis, *When Harlem Was in Vogue*, 107–8. In describing the extension of invitations to rent parties, a journalist for *The New York Age* wrote, "The more business-like souls, who like to do things with due formality, usually resort to the nearest printer to have a hundred or so circulars struck off, bidding the public in general to attend the party on such an evening. The more exclusive individuals give verbal or telephonic invitations to their acquaintances, whose rent parties they have recently attended and upon whom they may depend for a reciprocation of patronage." "A Rent Party Tragedy," *The New York Age* (New York, NY), December 11, 1926.

73 Wilson, *Bulldaggers, Pansies, and Chocolate Babies*, 9.
74 Davis, *Blues Legacies and Black Feminism*, 133.
75 Robertson, et al., "Disorderly Houses," 461.
76 Eric Garber, "A Spectacle in Color: The Lesbian and Gay Subculture of Jazz Age Harlem," in *Hidden from History: Reclaiming the Gay and Lesbian Past*, ed. Martin B. Duberman, Martha Vicinus, and George Chauncey (New York: Penguin, 1989), 323.
77 Wilson, *Bulldaggers, Pansies, and Chocolate Babies*, 20, 28–9.
78 Qtd. in Joan Nestle, "'I Lift My Eyes to the Hill': The Life of Mabel Hampton as Told by a White Woman," in *A Fragile Union: New and Selected Writings by Joan Nestle* (San Francisco: Cleiss, 1998), 36.
79 Similar racial integration took place in the primarily white Greenwich Village among the bohemian camp, though it is known that more white people tended to travel uptown than black people tended to travel downtown. See Andrea Barnet, *All-Night Party: The Women of Bohemian Greenwich Village and Harlem, 1913–1930* (Chapel Hill: Algonquin Books of Chapel Hill, 2004), 7–9.
80 Wilson, *Bulldaggers, Pansies, and Chocolate Babies* (December 11, 1926), 40. Rent parties also carried risk, like most public spaces that integrate liquor and humans. One instance involved "the combination of bad gin, jealous women [two women vying for the attention of another woman], a carving knife and a rent party" which ended in *The New York Age* claiming this mix of events and people to be "dangerous to the health of all concerned." This only added fuel to the fire where rent parties were already looked down upon socially and politically. "A Rent Party Tragedy," *The New York Age*.
81 Wilson, *Bulldaggers, Pansies, and Chocolate Babies*, 31.
82 Wilson, *Bulldaggers, Pansies, and Chocolate Babies*, 40.

83   Wilson, *Bulldaggers, Pansies, and Chocolate Babies*, 38.
84   Wilson, *Bulldaggers, Pansies, and Chocolate Babies*, 16. See footnote 70.
85   Garber, "A Spectacle in Color," 318.
86   Wilson, *Bulldaggers, Pansies, and Chocolate Babies*, 18.
87   Wilson, *Bulldaggers, Pansies, and Chocolate Babies*, 82. Locations included the Rockland Palace, previously known as Manhattan Casino (West 155th St. and 8th Ave.) and the Renaissance Casino (West 138th St. and 7th Ave.).
88   John L. Fell and Terkild Vinding, *Stride! Fats, Jimmy, Lion, Lamb, and All the Other Ticklers* (Lanham: Scarecrow, 1999), 64.
89   Wilson, *Bulldaggers, Pansies, and Chocolate Babies*, 86.
90   Floyd G. Snelson, "Strange 'Third' Sex Flooding Nation, Writer Reveals," in *Pittsburgh Courier* (Pittsburgh), March 19, 1932, 6.
91   Wilson, *Bulldaggers, Pansies, and Chocolate Babies*, 85.
92   "Hamilton Lodge Ball an Unusual Spectacle," in *The New York Age* (New York), March 6, 1926.
93   "Hamilton Lodge, No. 710 in Annual Masquerade and Civic Ball," in *The New York Age* (New York), March 5, 1927.
94   Wilson, *Bulldaggers, Pansies, and Chocolate Babies*, 99.
95   "Third Sex Hold Sway at Rockland When Hamilton Lodge Holds 65th Masquerade Ball and Dance; Police Arrest Two," in *The New York Age* (New York), March 4, 1933.
96   The Flying Cavelier, "Carrying the Torch," in *The New York Age* (New York), March 4, 1933.
97   Ebenezer Ray, "Fifteen Arrested by Police as 'Fairies' Turn 'Em On: Oops My Dear, Fairies Stomp at Rockland," in *The New York Age* (New York), March 5, 1938.
98   Wilson, *Bulldaggers, Pansies, and Chocolate Babies*, 89.
99   Wilson, *Bulldaggers, Pansies, and Chocolate Babies*, 42.
100 Chauncey, *Gay New York*, 359. It is worth noting that the exclusionary attitude found in Harlem mirrored a national wave of conservatism in the era of the Great Depression.
101 Vogel, *The Scene of Harlem Cabaret*, 19. The cultural and literary Harlem Renaissance featured artists who utilized their platforms to offer insights into black sexual nonconformist life. Harlem's "princess," A'Lelia Walker (daughter of Madam C. J. Walker), held parties with as much sexual and gender abandon as Harlem's rent parties, and other parts of Manhattan allowed for sexual and gender nonconformity, like Greenwich Village.

2

Blackqueering of Ethical and Theological Discourse

A blackqueer ethics foregrounds communality in discourse, in practice, in approaching sexual ethics. Its orientation is ethical praxis (reflection and action) developed through integrative communality grounded in a collectively derived sense of the good, open to the possibilities of right relating. In this chapter, I expound upon a community of discourse within the living archive upon which I build a blackqueer sexual ethics, the scholarship that is blackqueering the terrains of ethics and theology. I offer a retelling, or "spill the tea," on the past nearly three decades of ethical and theological reflection grounded in black LGBTQ+ experience, being, becoming, questioning, expanding, contracting, shifting, and potentiating within religious worlds toward the cultivation of an ethically and theologically diverse community of discourse.

In this chapter, I employ the verb "blackqueering" to refer to the intervention of black lesbian, gay, bisexual, transgender, and/ or queer-centered discourses and populations, not necessarily as assigning an identity or politic to individual scholar's work. I am, however, referring to a methodological subversion of the dominant ethical and theological discourse toward which their scholarship moves through foregrounding and taking seriously black LGBTQ+ life. The verb, blackqueering, speaks to an active, continual process of reorientation and reconstructing that further illuminates the living nature of a blackqueer archive. One could also think of it as a verb and an active adjective that describes this new take on ethics and theology. As a practice, blackqueering disrupts hegemonic and normativizing logics and creates openings to possibility. Blackqueering challenges the status quo by destabilizing it toward more expansive epistemologies or ways of knowing, deconstructing the made-abject, and inhabiting the not-before-known, the liminal, the immaterial.

The purpose in this chapter is to classify some of the pertinent concerns within the scholarship as it relates to ethics and theology, religion (most often, Christianity), sexuality, and black LGBTQ+ lives. To that end, I offer a thematic analysis that serves as a generative base for the values I center in Chapter 4, "Constructing a Blackqueer Sexual Ethics." The primary themes I locate within black LGBTQ+-focused ethical and theological discourse are inclusion, subjectivity and identity, resistance and difference, embodiment, and power. While there is overlap in the content and meaning of each theme and the list of themes is not exhaustive, I offer an in-depth exploration of each framing for the profound ways blackqueering shows up in ethics and theology. I analyze the multiplicity of approaches to these themes (and movements beyond them) and aim to allow each theme to stand as its own conversation. Therefore, some of the scholars' specific interventions and theorizing may be addressed under more than one theme.

In the previous chapter, I introduced gender and sexual nonconformists of 1920s Harlem as a historical site of blackqueer meaning-making community, an archival example of integrative and communal moral imagination at work. Like the previous chapter, here, I aim to illuminate an enlivened archive in conversation with itself, as I bring together scholars interested in black LGBTQ+ experience in one genealogy to demonstrate the dialogical practice of communal reflection foregrounded within a blackqueer ethics. The following themes and analysis will evidence the ways blackqueering shows up in ethics and theology and serves as a point of departure for a blackqueer ethics. In the chapter that follows, I will share the oral histories of contemporary blackqueer practitioners as an act of further presencing and futuring the blackqueer moral imagination that inspires the constructive communal-sexual ethics I propose in Chapter 4.

The scholarship and scholars that make up this chapter formulate radically interested ethical and theological perspectives rooted in the particularity of black LGBTQ+ life/lives and firmly foreground their subjectivity. Beginning in the early 1990s, black LGBTQ+-focused discourse contributes to the liberative ethics and theology traditions by asserting black LGBTQ+ mattering in academic and religious spaces, as well as in families and communities, in struggles for black freedom, and as part of stories of black religion. It demands that people with HIV/AIDS be honored as integral to black life and that their lives be cared for in a time when some black churches called (and some continue to call) the condition God's judgment upon "homosexuals." It challenges liberation theologies to note their exclusion and erasure of LGBTQ+ people in their conceptions of blackness, ethical sexuality, and community. The blackqueering of ethical and theological discourse yields a sustained critique of heterosexism, homophobia, anti-blackness, and religion-based disembodiment. It confronts ethics, theologies, and often religious spaces (namely, black churches), imploring them to acknowledge, even to celebrate, the blackqueer among them and proposes means of LGBTQ+ thriving beyond these spaces. This blackqueering dismisses modernist objectivity[1] to assert the value of black LGBTQ+ experience for the development of ethics and theology.

Nomenclature referring to non-normative sexualities and genders has changed in substantial as well as subtle ways since the early 1990s. There are periods of overlap where terms are returned to and re-employed. For instance, "homosexual" was utilized by some as appropriate and affirming but was later rejected when "homosexual" faded from use among LGBTQ+ communities and was viewed pejoratively in social discourse. Additionally, terms like "gay" or "queer" were sometimes used interchangeably and "bisexual," for some, now transcends the gender binary where it was once thought to reify it. The employing of terms, as is often the case, is neither consistent nor linear. I attempt to employ the terms homosexual, lesbian, gay, bisexual, transgender, LGBT, LGBTQ, LGBTQ+, and queer in alignment with the ways that the scholarship does at the time of writing and as needed for consistency.[2]

Inclusion

As black LGBTQ+-focused scholarship in ethics and theology articulates concerns of significance to their subjects, each engages in an assessment of the relationship of queer, lesbian, gay, and bisexual (and less often, transgender) people to black churches and black communities, as well as to black academia in black liberation theology and womanist ethics and theology. The scholarship here invites a consideration of inclusion as an affirmation, a challenge to hegemonic norms, and a practice of care toward all members of a community. I acknowledge the importance of transforming attitudes toward inclusion over time in tandem with movements in queer communities, academia, and the United States; therefore, this section is as chronological as possible—recognizing linearity in time, not necessarily in thought. For clarity, in some cases, I distinguish between each thinker's earlier and later work with attention to the shifts in their arguments.

Concurrently, in 1993, Ibrahim Abdurrahman Farajajé (known then as Elias Farajajé-Jones) and Renee L. Hill offer a bold critique of the heterosexist and homophobic underpinnings of exclusionary black liberation and womanist theologies, respectively, in the signal second edited volume of James H. Cone's and Gayraud S. Wilmore's *Black Theology: A Documentary History* (1993). They subsequently interrogate the foundational assertions of these theologies that claim to include the experiences of black people, yet neglect bisexual, queer, transgender, gay, and lesbian persons in their construction of blackness. In the same year, Horace L. Griffin approaches the question of inclusion by challenging pastoral theologians in their research and practices to frame their constructions of family to include lesbian and gay persons. In these ways, each scholar contributes a foundational assertion of the presence and value of lesbian, gay, bisexual, queer, and transgender people to (black) Christian academic discourse and community. As they question the silences and lacunae, they invite black theologies and communities to contend with the bodies and lives that it erases.

"An avowed gay-identified, bisexual Black theologian" and "Black queer man," Farajajé, in "Breaking the Silence: Towards an In-the-Life Theology" (1993), begins his essay with an epigraph from a signal volume on black gay men's experiences, *In the Life: A Black Gay Anthology*, edited by black writer and AIDS activist Joseph Beam.[3] The fictional narrative, keenly representative of lived experience during the peak of the AIDS crisis in which it was written, is aptly entitled "Cut off from Among Their People." Craig G. J. Harris in part tells the story of a preacher who, during a eulogy, declared AIDS as a just punishment for those who practice "abominations."[4] Utilizing black gay men's literature and his own experience as an AIDS activist, Farajajé expands the resources of theological reflection and the epistemological potential within black liberation theology in the vein of womanist ethicist Katie G. Cannon's assertion of black women's literary tradition as an integral source for doing ethics.

Farajajé proposes an integrative "African-centered, womanist, in-the-life theology of liberation" that connects the struggles of those in-the-life with the oppressed peoples of the world and is concerned with the wellness of entire black communities (a womanist claim), though he specifically centers black gay and bisexual men.[5] Presenting a distinct in-the-life theology that honors the dignity and presence of black bisexual, gay, lesbian, transgender, and queer people without apology, he seeks inclusion because of the systemic intracommunal determinations that keep those "in-the-life" as outsiders, often leading to their demise—"cut off from their people" (as referenced in the biblical book of Leviticus) in their living and in their dying.[6] Such an assertion of the embodied, valued presence of black bisexual, gay, lesbian, queer, transgender, and AIDS-impacted people provides an important intervention in respectable discourse, and reveals the limitations that arise when blackness is essentialized and black subjectivity is conceived too narrowly. Farajajé's theology pushes a deep consideration of those who are marginalized because of gender and sexual nonconformity and the importance of amplifying queer suffering, even if it may risk aligning queerness solely with illness, abjection, tragedy, and oppressions.

Renee L. Hill, a "self-identified lesbian,"[7] likewise seeks inclusion through the dismantling of heterosexism and homophobia, concerns that Hill argues had been treated as "nonissues" among womanist scholars.[8] Her pivotal contribution to womanist dialogue, "'Who Are We For Each Other?': Sexism, Sexuality, and Womanist Theology," begins with an analysis of Alice Walker's "womanist" definition, which notably includes women who love women, both romantically and non-romantically. It is curious for Hill that all other aspects of Walker's definition are engaged by Christian womanists with the sole exception of romantic love between women. Black women in relationship to other black women—celebrating one another, shaping communities—form the foundations of womanism, Hill argues,[9] and no aspect of these relationships between women should be subject to exclusion. As a matter of justice, Hill claims womanism must integrate lesbian voices, which would open the door more widely to addressing a variety of significant intracommunal gender and sexuality injustices impacting black women.[10]

Both Hill's and Farajajé's focus on the interconnections between religion and spirituality, sexuality (including but not limited to sexual orientation), and justice are distinctly revolutionary as a just engagement with sexuality remains a topic in need of greater exploration within black theological and ethical scholarship.[11] They contest entities that claim concern with black communities, but with exclusions. Together, they seek inclusion for gay, lesbian, queer, bisexual, transgender, and AIDS-impacted people in the theological, ecclesial, and social environments in which they have been shaped, even while sexuality (especially, of the non-normative kind) was held beyond the delimitations of acceptable theological topics.

Additionally, in 1993, Griffin, who writes from his positionality as a "middle-class, African American, gay Christian man," argues for the inclusion of African American gays and lesbians to validate their familial norms and construction of family.[12] Distinctively, Griffin offers the most extensive discussion advocating ecclesial and pastoral inclusion of black gay and lesbian people in pastoral theology. In his latter works of the early 2000s, Griffin's sustained desire for inclusion resides alongside a weightier call for affirmation. Shifting the framing of "inclusion," Griffin articulates a community of liberation that is not exclusively for gender and sexual nonconformists, but all who would actively resist the bonds of homophobia, heterosexism, racist standards of sexual purity, discriminatory biblical interpretation, and like oppressions.[13] To argue that the heterosexual, who had been bestowed with superior sexual morality simply by virtue of their normative sexual orientation, has room for liberative transformation in their sexual selves marks an audacious moral egalitarianism for black theology and communities.

Griffin pointedly argues that accepting, affirming, and celebrating people of all sexualities create space for "our sisters and brothers who, in their faithful commitment to their sexual gifts, allow us to appreciate the beauty of God's diverse creation."[14] For black theology in particular to take on this approach to gay and lesbian people would have been to "take seriously the reality of Black people—their life of suffering and humiliation" and would extend liberation to all oppressed, as Jesus sought to do.[15] Inclusion, argues Griffin, of all erotic selves is the way to "proclaim a *true* Black liberation theology, and in so doing, [...] honor God" (emphasis mine) through affirming the multiplicity of black identity.[16] Inclusion, then, means delving more particularly into the sufferings, as well as the joys, delights, and power of being black and in tune with one's erotic self.

While Griffin pushes pastoral caregivers to "uphold all covenanted loving relationships as normative,"[17] he centers covenanted relationships. Subsequently, this marginalizes sexual acts and relationships that exist primarily for temporary, playful, desire- and pleasure-oriented sexual connection. It sanitizes sexual nonconformity and proscribes limits in the name of normalizing gay and lesbian expression. Such approaches present a further burden to LGBTQ+ persons by morally heroizing them, as Roger A. Sneed names, and subjecting them to the violence of normativizing processes, in the manner Thelathia "Nikki" Young describes and I address later in this chapter. Griffin's and like approaches to inclusion strive toward a kind of respectability politics that celebrates/rewards gay and lesbian families through Christian heteronormative characteristics, and relies on characterizations of "homosexuality" as innate/ "homosexuals" as "born this way" in order for them to be worthy of inclusion. This sanitization reifies hetero- and homo-normativity and the hegemony of the dominant discourses that demonize black sexualities.[18]

Also, in the early 2000s, Victor Anderson addresses the inclusion of "the curious body of the black homosexual" by interrogating the paradigm of a public/private dichotomy that exists in the logics of black churches and leadership. According to this paradigm, as argued by social theorist Michael Eric Dyson and Christian social ethicist Robert M. Franklin, many black churches have elected to espouse "conservative/preservative" views as it relates to sexuality—"private matters of marriage, the family and sex"—and more "liberal/progressive" views in matters of other social justice concerns.[19] For Anderson, the exclusion is not paradoxical because he does not accept the idea that the Black Church and their clergy are necessarily as justice-driven as some leaders and theorists suggest. Ultimately, Anderson proposes a more critical lens in examining black churches' commitments to justice, rather than an assumption of solidity of position in the progressive camp.[20]

Additionally, Anderson constructs, in part, inclusionist arguments for gay and lesbian people by asserting black gay and lesbian presence as faithful Christians and members of the Black Church.[21] Many black gay and lesbian persons do not leave the churches in which they grew in faith because they have not allowed ecclesial homoantagonism to force their acquiescence. Anderson's argument invites a broadening of the term inclusion as it troubles the conception of who has the power to include and exclude, though in some cases, that power to say who literally can and cannot be present as their fullest selves lies with vehemently anti-LGBTQ+ parties. He forwards a "let live" ethos, based on a God-granted right to be a part of the church that is Christ's body and to participate in its ministry as one's full self. Yet, Anderson, speaking as "one Black gay believer," does not go much farther than "let live"—not demanding advocacy for gay and lesbian sexual freedom by the Black Church, but simply and realistically asking "that it not hate us when we advocate for ourselves [sic] sexual liberty."[22] The distinction lies in quelling one's repressive scrutiny of the "homosexual" versus cultivating an openness to the expansive diversity existent within the body of Christ.

For some theorists engaged in blackqueering discourse, inclusion in settings that do not fully affirm black queer people in presence and ministry is tantamount to self-betrayal. Arguing counter to Griffin and Anderson, Sneed is one of the few black religious scholars (apart from Farajajé and Dorinda G. Henry) to name presence in homophobic settings as acquiescence and, ultimately, approval of the discrimination.[23] While this could be perceived as victim blaming, Sneed reframes sexual difference apart from the status of victimhood[24] and asserts black queer dignity. This dignity should not be sacrificed for the sake of inclusion. He poignantly states:

> Black queer experience is real and in need of serious attention. The desire for attention echoes a desire for belonging. The desire for belonging may be read as desire for reconciliation with the larger Black community. However, this reconciliation cannot happen if Black queer experience is merely tolerated and addressed only in the service of fighting white supremacy, for Black queer life is far more than an endless, heroic struggle against the forces of white racism.[25]

The parallel concerns of hyperfocus on liberation from white racism's effects and erasure of sexualities, namely marginalized ones, are significant themes for Sneed.[26] This invites greater mindfulness of the various aspects of human and communal existence beyond any one identity marker.

Writing in the mid-2010s, Pamela R. Lightsey, "African American queer lesbian womanist scholar," argues that inclusion is necessary for the sake of the soul of the Black Church even as she affirms the Church's "Blackness—that spiritual DNA commitment to the liberation of all oppressed."[27] While I caution against locating such a spiritual DNA within the Black Church because its presence is questionable, as Anderson notes above, I concur that the souls—the aliveness, the interconnecting energy, the sense of self—of the Black Church and black churches are compromised by exclusion and those logics that inform utilizing power to exclude. Likewise, Lightsey affirms the integrity of the Black Church is endangered by collusion with white "right-wing fundamentalist [evangelicalism]" that pointedly excludes queer people.[28]

For Lightsey, inclusivity is also a matter of research method as she gives considerable attention to queer lived experience, including and beyond those categories that reflect her positionality, an important practice for any theology or ethic that claims to be liberative, by grounding her queer womanist theological interventions in the work of gender expansive and transgender persons like Monica Roberts, Georgia Black, and Pauli Murray.[29] Accordingly, Lightsey argues queer womanist theology is a theology of wholeness and bodily freedom, which affirms the expansive inclusion of entire selves in community, church, and academy and liberation from racism, sexism, homophobia, transphobia, poverty, war, and the rigid powers that uphold the status quo.[30] Yet, the particular task of queer womanist scholarship is the inclusion of LGBTQ lives in the communal conception of black lives.[31]

For many of these scholars, the pursuit of inclusion lies in interrogating the ideological underpinnings of exclusion. For example, in analyzing womanists' disassociation with lesbians, Hill cites womanists' refusal to contend with being aligned with what was perceived as a feminism that rejects men, and their aversion to the risk of being labeled lesbian and being accused of "airing the dirty laundry" of black communities by naming sexism.[32] Farajajé decries communal stigmatization through "AparthAIDS" (discrimination on the basis of an AIDS diagnosis), AIDSphobia, and the correlation of AIDS with queer communities—many in the 1980s and early 1990s naming AIDS the "gay man's disease"[33]—in addition to the subsequent erasure of harmed and impacted communities. Griffin finds the widespread argument of "homosexuality" as a sexual orientation not practiced in Africa until it was proposed by white

Europeans to be racist because it assumes that Africans do not engage sexuality in the way that the rest of humanity does. He claims some African American Christians duplicitously invoke Africa when it is convenient, much like their use of the Bible.[34] This then also points to the use of the Bible as a disingenuous means of preventing the inclusion of lesbian and gay persons. For Lightsey, "bhomophobia"[35] is a basis of exclusion because it hinges upon a desire to be accepted "by oppressors" (presumably right-wing Christianity entrenched in the whiteness that has diminished black sexuality for centuries) and to receive the benefits of heterosexual supremacy. By analyzing the benefits accrued to black communities through its sacrificing its most vulnerable members, the call for inclusion both seeks to hold black and womanist theologies and communities accountable and to assert LGBTQ+ dignity by telling hard truths toward the goals of collective reckoning, integrity, and liberation.

Finally, blackqueering interventions say little about God beyond God as being on the side of the oppressed and as an expansive Creator—one who creatively fashions persons of varying orientations and expressions and, therefore, welcomes them. Particularly when referring to Griffin's scholarship, Sneed notes that there is little to be said about who God is and why God is supportive of gay and lesbian folks; this argument could extend to nearly all the ethicists and theologians in this chapter, who typically depend on the Christian liberationist vision of God. If it is a construction of God and of "God's word" that prevents the inclusion of LGBTQ+ persons in the discourse and some black religious spaces and communities, then Sneed addresses the root cause of the problem with a nontheistic solution: a humanist ethic of openness. While there are responses like providing support for pastoral care providers faced with "clobber texts" or the affirmation of a God who includes LGBTQ+ persons without contradiction, there is also the option of removing the assumed barrier altogether.

Subjectivity and Identity

Blackqueering ethics and theology contends with limited and limiting framings of blackness and queer sexual orientations through their framing of subjectivity and identity. Their scholarship explicitly or implicitly says something of who and how queer people are, grounded in the particularity of being simultaneously and non-dichotomously black and LGBTQ+. As Jennifer S. Leath argues, without the willingness and space to proclaim particularity, those who are not subjects remain subjugated.[36] Identity politics, alterity, self-naming, claiming the term "queer" and queerness all signify the particularity of black LGBTQ+ existence.

Like many black feminists, womanists, and queer theorists of color argue, identities exist at various intersections. Inattentiveness to this reality by institutions, communities, and even interpersonally often forces people with marginalized identities to attempt the impossible task of "picking" an identity with which to align. When Farajajé states, "While we do not place our sexuality before our Blackness, we do live out our sexualities within the context of our Blackness,"[37] he speaks to an inseparable weaving of subjectivities and identities. "No one of our self-identities is subordinate or should be made subordinate to the other," Lightsey claims; that is, they are always simultaneously so.[38] For some Christian ethicists and theologians who are both black women and concerned with life at this intersection, the desire for integrated subjectivities in academic study led to the founding of womanist discourse. For some black scholars of a sexually marginalized community and/or who are concerned with life at this intersection, the interventions explored here present a new black LGBTQ+ hermeneutic and subject-hood.

By and large, black LGBTQ+ Christians' experience has been and is one of alterity. For black men "in-the-life," Farajajé contends, "in our experience of alterity, of otherness, we are doubly or triply the ultimate Other, the Different One"—as black men, as queer men, as black queer men.[39] Likewise, Sneed identifies themes of alterity in fictional tellings of black gay experience by black gay men: alienation, longing for belonging and home, reconciliation, and revision. Methodologically, for illumination of black gay men's experiences, Sneed finds in fictional literature a "thicker" examination of black queer life than theological scholarship offers.[40] Though alterity can be a rejection that leads to dehumanization and even death, it can also be a source of liberation and resistance. In the othered space, one and their community are afforded the fluidity, expansion, and freedom eluded them by whiteness, compulsory heterosexuality, and patriarchal dominance.

Conversely, black LGBTQ+-focused discourse conceives of its subjects not as a despised other, but as a uniquely good representation of God's diversity and desire for humanity. For example, Griffin frames gay and lesbian people and their love as representations of God's presence and love.[41] Griffin presents a God who disrupts the notion that what is normative is what is good. I agree with Sneed that Griffin offers a palatable version of marginalized sexual orientations by consistently referring to "homosexuality" in terms of love-relationships. Sneed argues further, "Griffin has to present black homosexuals as an aggrieved party suffering great injustice at the hands of heterosexual oppressors. In other words, Griffin has to follow the same model presented by Cone and others in the formulation of Black liberation theology."[42] This model often creates static categories of "oppressed" and "oppressor" that mask the messiness of reality with uncritical labels or essentializations (even strategic ones).

Thwarting the dichotomy, Sneed (like some black gay, bisexual, lesbian, and queer-centered scholars before him) perceives marginalized sexualities "not [as a] problem that [needs] to be fixed,"[43] but as simply human. Young continues along these lines by asserting black queer moral agency against the prevailing narrative of black queer victimhood in the face of institutional, communal, and interpersonal oppressions.[44] What Sneed and Young's scholarship represents is the power of black queer people naming themselves for themselves (to paraphrase Audre Lorde). In Sneed's method, black queer cultural productions accomplish such an aim. Similarly, Young forwards black queer narrative. The telling of these narratives by black queer people serve as a form of resistance to erasure and an act of reintegration of the self: "Lives that are lost through the narrative can be restored through a counter narrative."[45] Early on, by self-telling through stories and self-naming in response to AIDS and its stigma for those "in-the-life," Farajajé similarly claims life's vibrancy rather than disinheritance.[46]

Griffin adds that through telling their own stories, black gay Christians, who are also full representations of the *imago Dei*, reflect Christian faith and witness—a counter-argument to "homosexuality" as incompatible with morally good forms of Christian sexuality.[47] In identifying the value of black gay Christian narratives, drawing from pastoral theologian Larry Kent Graham,

Griffin states that sharing these stories will "demonstrate that all human beings are capable of reflecting the *imago Dei*—when their concrete and everyday lives and relationships are truthful, loving, creative, just and diverse and consequently assist in transforming the understanding of many black heterosexuals so that they will come to recognize that black gays and their loving sexual relationships are also moral."[48] According to Griffin's explanation, sharing these narratives seems to serve more to counter a heterosexist *imago Dei* and to persuade heterosexuals than to create space for black LGBTQ+ people to know and affirm one another's worth. Though decades of (primarily) gay and lesbian nonfiction narratives exist, Griffin insists that those harmed act as a catalyst for the spiritual growth of the primary enactors of the harm, a considerable part of the onus carried by the party to whom the harm is directed.

Stories within black LGBTQ+-focused scholarship in ethics and theology have generally focused on cisgender men's narratives and concerns that most impact them. This aligns with a larger fixation on male homoeroticism. Concerns specific to women largely have not been much examined beyond the scholarship centering women named in this chapter.[49] In a later essay, Hill affirms the need for narratives—those that reveal "the breadth and depth of human sexuality"—as resources for (black) theological reflection and responsiveness to the complexity of human experience.[50] For Hill, the narratives are less about proving and more a resource for shifting collective orientations to sexuality toward greater expansiveness. Moreover, Roland Stringfellow affirms the need for faithful black queer people to "come out and offer their distinctive voice."[51] While Stringfellow concedes that this bold manner of coming out may yield rejection, greater attentiveness must be given within the discourse to the ways that in many parts of the United States and world, coming out or sharing one's story may mean more than rejection, which is a signficant loss in itself. It may mean retaliation, unsafe living conditions, or death. This risk of exposure to death is especially prevalent for transgender people who face physical violence at higher levels than other members of the LGBTQ+ community.[52]

Though I uphold the generative potential of narrative, I note that while coming out to others can be liberative, affirm black LGBTQ+ moral agency, and strengthen one's capacity to engage risk with resilience, coming out can also lead to dangers and ought not be compulsory or a tool for LGBTQ+ persons to police one another's politics and decisions. Greater attentiveness to existing LGBTQ+, and especially transgender, narratives could provide a better understanding of the challenging realities that sometimes result from appeals for black LGBTQ+ people to come out to others and share intimate aspects of their lives with a public.

Assertions of black LGBTQ+ subjectivity and identity through the act of self-naming are further developed by the use of the term "queer." The fluidity of queerness, beyond serving as an umbrella term, also deconstructs rigid categorizations related to sexuality and gender to create more space for self-determination and expansive communality. While black LGBTQ+ discourse utilizes "queer," it is not without some interrogation of the limits (or lack thereof) of the term to offer insight into identity and subjectivity. Farajajé's use aims to be a reclamation and a form of resistance to "white male-dominated heterosexual culture."[53] On the other hand, Lightsey critiques the term for its whiteness, but utilizes it to refer to "gay men, lesbian women, bi-sexual [sic], transsexual, and intersexed [sic] persons in ways that do not limit—as does 'gay'—our lives to the intimacy of lovemaking nor the attractions we may or may not have."[54] The term adds layers of multiplicity, in-betweenness, and opacity to what it is to be a full person, including, but not limited to, sexuality. Such a move responds to a concern Farajajé names that "in the minds of most people, our lives do not exist apart from sexual acts."[55] The use of "queer" can decenter sexual acts, or more accurately hypersexualization, and instead proclaim ways of relating: subversively, curiously, and toward justice.[349]

Uniquely, Leath incorporates "quare," as coined by performance theorist E. Patrick Johnson, which reflects a relational imperative in self-naming and "[embodies] the newness and now-ness of a discourse of Afro-diasporic queer LGBT SGL (same-gender loving) simultaneity."[56] Utilizing Alice Walker's definitional framework employed for "womanism," Johnson states, "quare is to queer as 'reading' is to 'throwing shade'," like "womanism is to feminism as purple is to lavender." According to the renowned film in black and brown gay, trans, and queer culture, *Paris Is Burning* (1990), as stated by Dorian Corey, "Reading comes first," that is, before "throwing shade." Johnson's definition seeks to assert the deeper, primary meaning that "quare" offers for describing black life. From Johnson's essay, Leath draws the following definition:

Quare (Kwâr), n. 1. Meaning *queer*; also, opp. of *straight*; odd or slightly off kilter; from the African American vernacular for queer; sometimes homophobic in usage, but always denotes excess incapable of being contained within conventional categories of being; curiously equivalent to the Anglo-Irish (and sometimes 'Black' Irish) variant of queer, as in Brendan Behan's famous play, The Quare Fellow.

—adj. 2. a lesbian, gay, bisexual, or transgendered [*sic*] person of color who loves other men or women, sexually or nonsexually, and appreciates black culture and community.

—n. 3. one who thinks and feels and acts (and, sometimes, 'acts up'); committed to struggle against all forms of oppression—racial, sexual, gender, class, religious, etc.

—n. 4. one for whom sexual and gender identities always already intersect with racial subjectivity.

5. quare is to queer as "reading" is to "throwing shade."[57]

By invoking *quare*, Leath asserts a black queerness that avoids the whiteness of queerness and troubles the assumed heterosexism of blackness. Quaring is an act of justice with an orientation that grows out of the experiences of black lesbian, gay, bisexual, transgender, and queer folks and seeks justice for all black people. Like the communities of black sexual and gender nonconformists in 1920s Harlem, "quare" serves as an example of the potentiality for individual and shared subjectivity to act toward means of justice-making.

The tension of complex subjectivities—for instance, as persons who are black and LGBTQ+ and often beyond normative gender—and the desire to claim them represents a significant point of departure as blackqueering contends with queer theory's deconstruction of identity and the postmodernist critique that claims the unintelligibility of group identity.[58] While Lightsey decries the damages of identity politics and essentialism, she, with Young, is careful to retain the cultural particularity that makes up the experiences of being black queer and black women, as well as the real consequences that persons encounter in their black queer bodies.[59] Leath agrees, "'Queer' [...] does not supplant racial discourse, [though] we might strategically and occasionally conceive of it as *another* Black—or (alternatively) a Blackness. Similarly, Black might be conceived of as *another* queer—or a queerness."[60]

Young's black queer ethic challenges the hegemonic labeling within identity-making rather than identity. She asserts, "Troubling the concept of stable identities is more a matter of troubling the technologies of normalization and processes of categorization than it is a matter of dismantling the identities themselves."[61] Young further refuses a monolithic black queerness which, according to Johnson and Roderick Ferguson, reifies "the racist and homophobic thrust of ethnic and sexual genealogies."[62] There are "norms, behaviors, values, and virtues" Young ascribes to black queerness, though this is not essentialism or heroizing through a hierarchical moral dichotomy that uncritically pedestalizes black queerness, but a move toward greater multifarity.[63] For Young, black queer people have something distinct and valuable to contribute to moral discourse through their subjectivity, agency, and imagination.[64]

Blackqueering ethics and theology distinctly describe black LGBTQ+ life to create space for complex subjectivity. It does not theorize a homogeneous, utopic expression of what it is to be black and LGBTQ+; rather, it theorizes black LGBTQ+ becoming, resistance, and mattering from a lens that, to varying degrees, refuses heteropatriarchal logics. These scholarly interventions illuminate the creative tension within subjectivity as black and LGBTQ+ in engagement with religion—the power of unapologetic existence, the "shame and self-hatred," and the liberative means of embracing selves that are diminished in church/religious spaces and society.[65] Some of the scholarship theorized black LGBTQ+ subjectivity beyond Christianity and normative communality. Black LGBTQ+-focused discourse imagines an understanding of being in community that, in some cases, aims to integrate blackness and (marginalized) sexuality, and in others, acknowledges the inseparability of the two.

Resistance and Difference

Resistance in this discourse primarily asserts black LGBTQ+ value, goodness, creativity, imagination, and means toward thriving. "Black queers' efforts to resist," Young affirms, "is a critical first step in the longer, creative process of generating a notion of the good." Resistance is then transformed into resilience, which can lead to thriving.[66] Resistance is present in the scholarship that follows by not shying away from but affirming the fecundity and critically engaging the difference that LGBTQ+ experience, cultural productions, activism, and relationality represent. Some of the scholarship here resists destructive understandings about sexuality and LGBTQ+ identity that have dominated Christian and Western thought, while other inquiries are located beyond countering oppressions brought about by difference. I explore resistance and difference through their approaches to troubling authority, (re)constructing family, embodying pleasure, employing experience-based research methods, and embracing difference.

Blackqueering ethics and theology addresses authority in the Bible, in black communities and society, and within academic discourse. Authority equates to validity and, subsequently, shapes moral and theological norms. Griffin challenges "clobber texts" and the weaponization of the Bible by invoking the argument that scriptures supposedly addressing "homosexuality" must be rethought, just as those related to enslavement were. Further, he disrupts the pervasive narrative of gay presence in the church by going beyond the stereotype of the "gay choir director" (presumably as the only acceptable and useful queer presence in the church) to include concrete examples of black gay and lesbian ministers who founded churches where queer people could see themselves in leadership positions, without forsaking a culturally connected worship experience.

This communal self-sufficiency is also reflected in Irene Monroe's essay, "When and Where I Enter, Then the Whole Race Enters with Me: Que(e)rying Exodus" (2004), in which resistance takes the form of self-love through "Black bodyrights," a reclamation of the body from demonization "by white culture."[67] Communal self-love resists valuelessness and practices black LGBTQ+ mattering. Young calls self-love among black queer congregants a "radical, revolutionary, creative, and resistant act." She goes on to say, in loving self and one another;

> [Black queer people] resist three things: first, that black lives are unlivable and unworthy of protection, care, justice, and love; second, that material realities of oppression are inevitable

outcomes of black subjectivity. And third, that black queer subjectivity is devoid of moral and ethical reasoning and practice.[68]

Similarly, in her essay, "Inner Dictum: A Womanist Reflection from the Queer Realm" (2011), Lightsey asserts queer value by divorcing it from the need for heterosexuals' support. In contrast to Griffin and others who attempt to convince heterosexuals of "homosexual" worth, Lightsey and others who subvert "societal expectation and constructions of what presents as 'normal'" pronounce queerness as good without qualification.[69]

Within pastoral theology, Griffin first interrogates the conception of family and the roles of black gays and lesbians therein. In "Giving New Birth: Lesbians, Gays, and 'The Family': A Pastoral Care Perspective" (1993), Griffin delineates the experiences that gay and lesbian families encounter socially and within pastoral settings, including socially rewarded, heterosexist, rigid conceptions of "the family," while offering care alternatives that attend to the individual and to social injustice. Young comprehensively takes up the question of family from a black queer ethical position. She utilizes narrative to explore family that black queer people embody over and against society's familial norms and examines openings to black queer relationality through everyday black queer folks. To this end, the notion of family as contingent upon the marriage of a (Christian) heterosexual, presumably cisgender man and cisgender woman, is disrupted to include a diversity of sexualities and relational modes. Young argues that, in fact "the American family *is* a queer family."[70] It is black queer families' disruption and irruption of normalizing technologies by recognizing, naming, evaluating, and re-orienting themselves in relationship to these technologies that enable profound moral imagination to help formulate distinct, liberative constructions of family.[71]

Womanist ethicist Emilie M. Townes, in her lecture "The Dancing Mind: Queer Black Bodies and Activism in Academy and Church" (2011), offers an entry into black queer Christian moral thought within womanism that is unapologetic in its embrace of the body, pleasure, sensuality, sex, and sexuality and which acts as a counter to the oppressive proscriptive norms and systemic injustices that pervade black Christian contexts.[72] The black queer body itself (as well as the black woman's body as a beyond-normative body) is conceptualized as a site of resistance that pursues pleasure against the command of repression, that asserts its sensuality and corporeality in the face of duality, and that embraces the sex and sexuality that white, heteronormative society has deemed hypersexual. The practice of embodiment in difference, for Townes, is resistance.

Black LGBTQ+-focused discourse also uses method as a means of resistance through queering, or in the case of Leath, quaring. In Lightsey's theological use, queering allows for a re-examination of gender norms by destabilizing the categories and taking these reflective insights together with the traditional resources for theological and ethical reflection, with a liberative God at the foundation.[73] According to Lightsey, queering and womanist theology can work complementarily and in solidarity toward more just ways of relating as gendered selves.[74] Similarly, though she does not use the term queer, Hill's "Human Sexuality—The Rest of the Story" (2010) challenges religious discourses of sexuality to take more spacious and fluid approaches to theology, community, and identity categories.[75] Communality rests in embracing ambiguity, an approach also employed by Sneed, wherein black queer people abandon "neat resolutions" to embrace the creative potential of liminality for their collective well-being.[76]

Further, as a mode of resistance, the use of narrative enables blackqueering scholarship to provide a counternarrative to the "thin" view presented by black theologians and cultural critics that revolve around victimhood as a result of homophobia and HIV/AIDS, and the notion of black LGBTQ+ people as "immoral and unnatural" held in some black ecclesial spaces and communities.[77] Lightsey's *Our Lives Matter* (2015) builds upon the epistemological value of black transgender and cisgender women's and black queer and trans people's narratives and, subsequently, centers the experiences of the black women that are often overlooked within womanist theologies.[78] Similarly, for Sneed, black gay men's fictional narratives provide a foregrounding of black queer experience as resistance to alienation.[79] These writings offer voice and visibility that signals the multiplicity and complexity of black gay men (and subsequently people of all genders), beyond homophobia and HIV/AIDS, reflecting the words offered by black gay writer and activist Joseph Beam that Sneed espouses, "visibility is survival."[80]

Leath takes resistance a step further by deepening the conversation of visibility and black LGBTQ+ liberation. Inspired by womanist ethicist Katie G. Cannon, she locates the hyper(in)vis/audible among black queers, whereby both bodies and voices are simultaneously overly focused upon, yet eclipsed in their abjection.[81] Further, Leath agrees with Evelynn M. Hammonds, who argues, "Visibility in and of itself does not erase a history of silence nor does it challenge the structure of power and domination, symbolic and material, that determines what can and cannot be seen. The goal should be to develop a 'politics of articulation'."[82] Articulation, including expanding the resources for knowledge production in (Christian) ethics discourse, is an imperative of quaring justice to create space for the hyper(in)vis/audible. To quare justice is to assert black queer subjectivity as a means of disrupting epistemology and ontology toward the end of challenging all oppressions, intersectionally and beyond superficiality.[83]

Lastly, the label "deviant" has served as both epithet and moniker for black queer people claiming their difference as an act of power. Black queer discourse that recovers deviance neither does so for the sake of being contrary nor haphazard. Influenced by Cathy J. Cohen, Leath forwards a strategic deviance that claims "dignity in shame," so that the "sociopolitical integrity of people and communities" may be gained and maintained.[84] Leaning into the potentiality of deviance enables black queer subjects to enact alternatives often limited by normativity. Within the framework of deviance, Sneed's humanist ethic of openness articulates resistance through multiplicity for the sake of black queer integrity. Located outside of theo-centric discourse, this humanist approach asserts black queer subjectivity and worth by asserting human responsiveness/responsibility as a criterion toward the good.

Embodiment

To theorize embodiment from the space of blackqueering, asserting the presence and reality of experience within a body that is black and LGBTQ+, is to reorient the theoretical gaze from a focus on a problematized object to a multiplicitous subject. Victor Anderson argues, "There is no body (literally) more contested in black churches than the curious body of the black homosexual."[85] Black LGBTQ+

bodies, for many in black and non-black Christian settings, hold no legitimacy or value.[86] And for this reason, the black LGBTQ+ body is a vulnerable body. The black LGBTQ+ body is simultaneously a black body, so it is a doubly (or triply) stigmatized, abject body. The black LGBTQ+ body is also representative of beyond normative expression, a symbol of potentiality. The black LGBTQ+ body is a holy body.[87]

Some ethicists and theologians here build upon the work of womanists and black cultural critics who have written about black sexuality and its maligning in the historical and contemporary United States context. The black body is read not only within the racist narrative that has shaped much of the public imagination about black sexuality, but also the internalized shame experienced by black people regarding their own bodies. Townes decries the black body as stereotyped and as that of which some black people themselves are made to be "terrified."[88] Griffin concurs:

> The internalization of dark skin as ugly and in need of lightening; coarse hair texture as bad and in need of straightening; writhing Black bodies as nasty and in need of saving; sexual attitudes as dirty and in need of purifying; Black sexual longings as uncontrollable evil and in need of taming; and sex talk as inappropriate and in need of silencing, have made it difficult for Black people to love their bodies and contributed to an understanding of their own sexual expression as nasty.[89]

Within the context of internalized and external anti-black racism, discourse of the body (in black liberationist/liberative theorizing, as well as in the public imagination in the United States) often problematizes the sexual body. Much of black LGBTQ+-focused scholarship seeks to counter this messaging and to focus on the good of the body.

Theorizing the black body in the era of Black Lives Matter, Leath argues that black ("Afro-Diasporic") bodies only seem to matter when they are abjectified.[90] In "(Out of) Places, Please! Demystifying Opposition to Procreative Choice in Afro-Diasporic Communities in the United States" (2014), she argues that the "questionable mattering" of black bodies "signifies a perennial marginality and thus a perennial abjection." Leath considers the place of meaning-making (of *making* something matter) to be queer and, therefore, instructive in the understanding of the black queer body as one among the many black bodies that do not matter. Where black bodies matter, they are still always already marked from their beginnings by meanings that counter their value and forces that vie for their nonexistence.[91]

Within black queer expressive culture, Sneed locates illuminations of the complexity of black queer life that occupies liminal space and attempts to make sense of that space by imagining new, creative, dynamic meanings toward a "humanist conception of the self"; that is, a human-centered approach to countering that which seeks to limit the flourishing of black queer bodies and lives.[92] To name this queer space of not belonging here or there as liminal, as opposed to disempowered, recognizes the subject's power and possibility in ways the discipline has not. The outcome is not a new hegemonic discourse like the one refused, but it is contentedly ambiguous—neither queerness nor blackness is resolved.[93] Sneed finds "the black queer body, in the final analysis, is not a problem, not a marginalized figure that will always point back to the heteronormative body at the center of discourse. Nor is the black queer the heroic yet still marginal body that will deliver us from our wayward ways."[94] The flourishing of the black queer body lay not in decentering the heterosexual body so that the queer can be centered but occupying the liminal space unmanaged by the hegemonic discourse that created liminal bodies in the first place. This offers a powerful disruption to the aims of legibility—not to be centered, but to make oneself according to one's own desires rather than as directed by normativizing discourses.

Hill's critique of the absence of a lesbian experience in womanism affirms sexuality and sexual expression as a viable womanist imperative, namely as a check to womanist discourse that seeks to be committed to the well-being of whole people, including their bodies. Where there is a concern for "physical health, wholeness, and wellbeing," there are bodies that cannot be ignored.[95] As Hill explains, the embodied experience of GLBTQ people goes beyond that of exclusion and rejection from churches, but also includes the social injustices that limit survival and thriving, like various forms of violence and discrimination related to housing, healthcare, and employment.[96] To be attentive to these embodied realities can yield ways of relating interpersonally and activism that is concerned with healthy sexuality, as well as all aspects of communal and social existence.[97]

For Lightsey, a primary starting point in discourses of the body is to claim the body as good, particularly for black women and black queer people.[98] Her queer womanist theology argues that LGBTQ bodies are essential for aiding in the task of building a better world, a world wherein the presence of LGBTQ bodies makes a difference.[99] Through her framing of "woman love," Lightsey becomes a primary celebrant—openly and without innuendo or veiled language—of what one black woman's body can do for another in an embodied and sexual way.[100] Contemporary theological and ethical discourses often conceive of meanings of queerness apart from sex or shy away from explicit representations of sex acts, particularly when referencing bodies that have been hypersexualized, which makes Lightsey's invocation of black women's bodies engaged in sexual pleasure all the more poignant.

Despite blackqueering, the ethical and theological discourse has frequently neglected attentiveness to the ways that black queer bodies express gender, beyond normatively cisgender women and men. With the exceptions of Pamela Ayo Yetunde, who considers the health and community care of transgender people, and Lightsey, who incorporates trans experiences by referencing activist, writer, and Episcopal priest Pauli Murray, actress and activist Laverne Cox, writer and activist Janet Mock and others, the discourse largely misses the opportunity to explore how being, for example, transgender, a femme, nonbinary/enby, masculine of center[101]— particularities perceived and often expressed through/with the body—could carry real implications for some of the issues explored as black queer realities, such as serving in ministry, embodied liberation, resistance to violence, and simply queering gender. The politics of these varied queer positionalities of the black queer body creates an opening within a blackqueer ethics to, again, think of the self more holistically and to consider the implications of current body-talk for transgender and gender nonconforming bodies.

Power

According to Hill, "in our [US] culture sex and power go together." Cultural barometers of power and status determine insiders and outsiders, worthiness, leadership, norms, and the capacity to practice self-determination.[102] Blackqueering discourse analyzes power dynamics demonstrated in the practices of black churches and communities, and in the conceptual assumptions in womanism, black theology, and broader academic disciplines. They contend with the hegemonic power to construct family and community in exclusive terms, to direct dialogical parameters, to restrict embodied realities of black LGBTQ+ people, to maintain existing power imbalances, and to collude with whiteness's aims.

Systemic and ideological expressions of power are at work in constructing both "the black family," "the black community," and their conservative/preservationist approaches wherein people beyond the normative are framed as threats.[103] Essentially, though social understandings of family are ever subject to change, there is power to gain by clinging to a narrative of an inherently moral heteronormativity and by inciting fear via a "current moral breakdown" with "homosexuals" at the helm.[104] One example exploring this power dynamic is located in Victor Anderson's essay, "The Black Church and the Curious Body of the Black Homosexual" (2004), which in part analyzes Christian ethicist Cheryl J. Sanders's understanding of family and "homosexuality." According to Sanders, it is because gay and lesbian people are nongenerative—both physically (in terms of procreation) and morally—that they are invalid in and unwelcome to remain as they are in ecclesial spaces; they are a threat to the wellness of the black family.[105] Such a rigid family construction is disrupted as scholars like Griffin and Young draw from biblical tradition and black LGBTQ+ life to rewrite or reinterpret constructions of family rooted in inclusivity and imagination. As mentioned above, Griffin prompts theology to be attentive to the concerns of (black) gay and lesbian persons in their practices of care, while Young affirms the expansiveness of family from black queer moral imagination and practices of black queer thriving.

Blackqueering discourse offers a critique of the ways that black liberation theologies and the leadership of the Black Church/black churches have exerted their power to direct dialogue at the intersections of black religion and LGBTQ+ lives. For instance, when Yetunde notes the limitations of a womanist methodology that does not integrate black lesbian literature and marks the distinction of Walkerian womanism, one that is attentive to Alice Walker's definition of womanism in taking seriously women who love women, she brings attention to and asserts the power, even from a marginalized position, to shape how a discourse is developing.[106] Additionally, by offering a "Black Buddhist Womanist lesbian hermeneutic," she critiques the power of a Christian-centric approach, and its often heteropatriarchal commitments frequently employed in black ethics and theologies.

Farajajé critiques black religious communities' utilization of power to silence and their ability to direct a discourse of sexuality to exclude and diminish gay, bisexual, and queer people. Arguing against the silencing of cries against homophobia/biphobia and calling out the silences of the Black Church regarding sexuality, Farajajé names the exclusion and dehumanization plainly: "In the eyes of the Black Church, queers have a 'lifestyle' and not a life"[107]—that is, they are not whole beings and they are disconnected from black life. Whereas silencing has taken the form of the excuse, "Black folk have bigger issues than that!,"[108] blackqueering discourse seeks to problematize the commitment to overlook LGBTQ+ presence that some in black communities, churches, and academia hold, not necessarily for lack of knowledge or access to knowledge of existing concerns, but by choice.[109] The early reluctance of theologians and ethicists, whose research centers countering race and cisgender women's marginalization, reflects a hesitancy and gap in generative dialogue about black sexuality. To confront sexism alongside heterosexism is a means of reclaiming just power for black people of all genders and sexual orientations. Such a critique does not disregard the significant contributions to counter homophobia, hetero/sexism, and anti-body logics in ethics and theology from black feminist Traci C. West or womanists such as Kelly Brown Douglas, M. Shawn Copeland, and Cannon but pushes for an expansion of established bounds of womanhood and what is needful for the thriving of all black people.[110]

Blackqueering critique confronts the power that labels "homosexuality" as solely a problem, with a refusal to learn about and learn from the stories of black LGBTQ+ people. Griffin identifies this problem at its core as an unwillingness to see gay and lesbian people as "equal members in the body of Christ," which keeps black LGBTQ+ folks in a perpetually subordinate position, and leads some scholars to render apologetic responses in the face of demonization and erasure.[111] In subordinating black LGBTQ+ communities, some black heterosexist and homophobic people seek to grasp the illusion of moral dignity systematically denied by anti-black and gender-specific racism, but at too high a cost—the fracturing of communities, the harm to LGBTQ+ and heterosexual people's relationships to their sexuality, and the indissoluble loss of pandering to whiteness. As Griffin makes clear:

> negative understanding of homosexuality causes Black people to internalize another negative understanding about themselves, about their sexual longings, their lovemaking and their capacity to appreciate sexual intimacy and orgasm. Thus, heterosexual supremacy, like white supremacy, male supremacy and so forth, further imposes bondage upon Black people, a spiritual estrangement that prevents them from loving their black bodies.[112]

Griffin illumines the ways that oppression begets oppression and points toward the need for an alternative means of engagement between heterosexual and gay and lesbian black people. This often takes the form of aiding black heterosexual people to see gay and lesbian people as fully human by hearing their stories and eventually struggling in support of shared, equitable power.

As shown above, Sneed views such methods to gain heterosexual sympathies with reproach. He observes sensationalism, namely by non-LGBTQ+ persons, when engaging gay experience by focusing solely on HIV/AIDS, homophobia, men who are "on the down low"/ who practice sexual dishonesty or discretion, and other stories of "the tragic homosexual."[113] Sneed argues, "It seemed that the only way to gain an audience among black heterosexuals was to present gay experience and existence through the lens of victimization."[114] In order to counter the oppressive power of a constructed discourse wherein gay men are not allowed to speak for themselves,[115] Sneed utilizes black gay (and later black lesbian and queer) cultural productions to present a more complex representation of black queer subjects through the power of a people to tell their own stories.

To maintain heteropatriarchal structures, inflexible binaries in sexuality and gender are frequently employed. Hill believes this may have been why bisexuals and transgender people who trouble the categories of sexuality and gender incur such vehement phobia.[116] According to Young, systematic oppressions frequently function as stabilizing forces that limit the capacity for human relationships. Black queer ethics disrupts that power by prizing such values as interdependence, potentiality, and becoming.[117] Each of these values counters the binaries that buttress hegemonic power and normalize discrimination. However, similar binaries are also employed among those seeking justice to solicit commitment in combatting a singular oppression. While black communities and black liberationist scholars have gathered considerable thrust in combating racism, Monroe argues this power came by treating racism as "the only and ultimate oppression" black people face in the United States, to the neglect of the manifold ways black people are impacted by various intersecting oppressions. Sexism and homophobia will remain unaddressed, she maintains, until the calculus incorporates various oppressions.[118]

The problem of whiteness's power in shaping black sexual mores is taken up through blackqueering ethics and theology, as well as black liberative traditions. As Griffin states, "historical circumstances that demonized Black sexuality are largely responsible for African Americans' current prudishness or public silence about sexuality."[119] While both Griffin and Farajajé identify silences regarding sexuality in black ecclesial spaces and communities, it is more accurate to say the spaces are not silent, but instead are not producing generative dialogue as they criticize "homosexuals," abortion, gender "disorder," adultery, and fornication. Yet, social and ecclesial demonization of black sexuality produces a wariness among black people regarding publicly engaging conversations about sexuality in helpful ways.

Monroe sharply critiques the accommodationist stance that she argues the Black Church has taken to maintain power and relevance in society—"megachurches, prosperity gospel, and the selling out of its social gospel message of justice in return for government money for faith-based initiatives."[120] To this end, like Lightsey, she interrogates the collusion of African American ministers with the "religious right" to subjugate (African American) LGBTQ communities.[121] Implicit and explicit collusion with the aims of anti-black racism forfeits the power black people possess to shape their own understandings of sexuality that celebrate and uplift the black body and its pleasures—without shame and with the fecundity of agency.

The Urgency of a Blackqueer Ethics

In this chapter, I highlighted how blackqueering and its community of scholars reshaped black ethical and theological discourse, evidenced over the last nearly three decades. The invitation to examine blackqueering through the scholarship in this chapter thematically records the decades-long conversations concerning black LGBTQ+ life in ethics and theology and illuminates potential openings toward a blackqueer ethics expounded in greater detail in Chapter 4. Blackqueering discourse affirms the moral generativity of those who are marginalized sexually (with room to grow for those of marginalized gender identities). It orients talk about sexuality toward right relationship to power, to the body, to identities and subjecthood, to justice, to one another. It seeks to integrate the fullness of what it is to be human through honoring the spirits and bodies of black LGBTQ+ persons, and of what it is to be in community—struggling against oppressions, as well as reformulating communal goodness for the well-being of the collective. I turn now to the everydayness of blackqueerness as a source for moral imagination through blackqueer transreligious practitioners who enliven the archive through their lived religious experience and moral imagination about gender, sexuality, the sacred, community, the body, and their whole selves.

Notes

1   Roger A. Sneed, *Representations of Homosexuality: Black Liberation Theology and Cultural Criticism* (New York: Palgrave Macmillan, 2010), 8.

2   My use of LGBTQ+, in referring to an expansive and growing community, instead of LGBTQIA+ is intentional. The scholarship in this chapter does not specifically and pointedly address intersex or asexual persons and their experiences (it also rarely reaches transgender persons and their experiences). I am reminded of the words of one of my former students, an intersex activist, to our Queer Theologies and Ethics class whom I attempt to quote: "If you're not *really* talking about intersex [and asexual] people, why use the [LGBTQIA+] acronym?" However, because there seems to be

an aim among these scholars of thinking of and with a community of people who are not normative in their sexual expression and in some cases are gender nonconforming, using LGBTQ+ seems in integrity and even aspirational.

3   Elias Farajajé-Jones, "Breaking the Silence: Towards an In-the-Life Theology," in *Black Theology: A Documentary History (Volume Two: 1980–1992)*, ed. James H. Cone and Gayraud S. Wilmore (Maryknoll, NY: Orbis Books, 1993), 139. It is worth noting that Farajajé identifies himself in this manner in the notes on the first page of his essay. His was one of two openly LGBTQ+ voices at the time of publication. Given what the archive now reveals of the life of Pauli Murray, they may be identified as another LGBTQ+ voice in volume one of Cone's and Wilmore's series. See Pauli Murray, "Black Theology and Feminist Theology," in *Black Theology: A Documentary History (Volume One: 1966–1979)*, ed. James H. Cone and Gayraud S. Wilmore (Maryknoll: Orbis 1993), 304–22.

4   Farajajé-Jones, "Breaking the Silence," 139.

5   Farajajé-Jones, "Breaking the Silence," 141. "In-the-life," according to Farajajé, has traditionally been utilized in African American communities to indicate a variety of sexualities. He utilizes it because of its inclusivity and "because of the rich spiritual connotations of the word 'life', especially for a people continually confronted with suffering and death." Farajajé-Jones, "Breaking the Silence," 140.

6   The many people who died during the beginnings of the AIDS crisis in the United States serve as an example of how "outsiders" meet untimely fates without transformative intervention from those in power, the "insiders." It also testifies to how creating communal "outsiders" allows such atrocities to unfold, largely unabated.

7   Renee L. Hill, "'Who Are We for Each Other?': Sexism, Sexuality, and Womanist Theology," in *Black Theology: A Documentary History (Volume Two: 1980–1992)*, ed. James H. Cone and Gayraud S. Wilmore (Maryknoll: Orbis 1993), 345. It is worth noting that Hill names herself in this manner in the notes on the first page of her essay featured in this signal volume.

8   Hill, "Who Are We for Each Other?" 346.

9   Hill, "Who Are We for Each Other?" 346.

10 Hill, "Who Are We for Each Other?" 349–50. According to Hill, "Christian womanists, like their male counterparts, focus for the most part on the impact of racism on the black community." Hill, "Who Are We for Each Other?," 346. In the same year, womanist

theologian Delores Williams raises a value akin to Hill's in stating, "Among womanists and feminist theologians, heterosexual women and lesbian women can come together for serious dialogue to discover if there are ways heterosexual female culture oppresses lesbian women on the basis of homophobic responses to the question of what is 'acceptably female'." Delores S. Williams, *Sisters in the Wilderness: The Challenges of Womanist God-Talk* (Maryknoll: Orbis 1993), 183.

11 Foundational womanist theologian Delores S. Williams's integration of womanhood and sexual identity in her scholarship prompted black feminist Christian ethicist Traci C. West's own reflective hopes and critiques for womanism in its failure to interrogate heteropatriarchy critically. See Traci C. West, "Visions of Womanhood: Beyond Idolizing Heteropatriarchy," *Union Seminary Quarterly Review* 58, nos. 3 and 4 (2004): 132. Notably, a recent contribution to womanist discourse that focuses on sexuality, including lesbian identity, is the womanist sexual ethics proposed by Monique Moultrie. See Monique Moultrie, *Passionate and Pious: Religious Media and Black Women's Sexuality* (Durham: Duke University Press, 2017).

12 Horace L. Griffin, "Giving New Birth: Lesbians, Gays, and 'The Family': A Pastoral Care Perspective," *Journal of Pastoral Theology* 3, no. 84 (1993): 88. Taken together with Farajajé and Hill's self-identification, the developments in gay and lesbian studies, queer theory, and activism in the United States it is likely that Griffin is also participating in a politics of disclosure befitting of the time. I name his positionality (and that of Farajajé and Hill above) given this context and because the scholar does so, and will do the same for other scholars who overtly self-identify.

13 Horace L. Griffin, "Toward a True Black Liberation Theology: Affirming Homoeroticism, Black Gay Christians, and Their Love Relationships," in *Loving the Body: Black Religious Studies and the Erotic*, ed. Anthony Pinn and Dwight Hopkins (New York: Palgrave Macmillan, 2004), 139, 145–6.

14 Griffin, "Toward a True Black Liberation Theology," 150.

15 Griffin, "Toward a True Black Liberation Theology," 143.

16 Griffin, "Toward a True Black Liberation Theology," 151.

17 Griffin, "Toward a True Black Liberation Theology," 142; Horace L. Griffin, *Their Own Receive Them Not: African American Lesbians and Gays in Black Churches* (Cleveland: Pilgrim 2006), 218.

18 Roger A. Sneed, *Representations of Homosexuality: Black Liberation Theology and Cultural Criticism* (New York: Palgrave Macmillan,

2010), 94. Griffin's aim may have been to dispel harmful myths about black lesbian and gay people by promoting respectability and sacrificing queer/nonconformist sexualities. He addresses the pejorative assertions being argued in the same era by major white Christian evangelical figures like Jerry Falwell and Pat Robertson (Griffin, "Giving New Birth," 91). He also may have written with the din of incessant black antigay critics in mind like gospel singers Debbie and Angie Winans, or Martin Luther King, Jr.'s niece, Alveda King, as well as others, clergy and lay, spreading panic about homosexuals luring children to be gay and other purported gay pathologies (Sneed, *Representations of Homosexuality*, 89). This offers some context to his apologetic stance that seeks to pave the way for gay and lesbian inclusion by countering every excuse for exclusion. Griffin is not alone in his apologetic approach. Lightsey identifies "other apologists of the time" that she juxtaposes with Douglas and her significant critique of homophobia and the Black Church's negligence regarding HIV/AIDS, while noting Douglas doesn't say enough to disentangle the stereotype of HIV/AIDS with gay identity or to celebrate the gift of queer sexuality and its expression. Pamela R. Lightsey, *Our Lives Matter: A Womanist Queer Theology* (Eugene, OR: Wipf and Stock, 2015), 6. Sneed calls Griffin's stance "near apologetic." Sneed, *Representations of Homosexuality*, 94. Given the context of Griffin's arguments, including unapologetic contributions like Hill's and Farajajé's, I find value in removing the preposition.

19 Victor Anderson, "The Black Church and the Curious Body of the Black Homosexual," in *Loving the Body: Black Religious Studies and the Erotic*, ed. Anthony Pinn and Dwight Hopkins (New York: Palgrave Macmillan, 2004), 297.

20 Anderson, "The Black Church and the Curious Body," 304–5. Sneed likewise rejects the notion that such a dichotomy necessarily exists and that black churches have been consistent bastions of justice. See Roger A. Sneed, introduction to *Representations of Homosexuality: Black Liberation Theology and Cultural Criticism* (New York: Palgrave Macmillan, 2010).

21 Anderson, "The Black Church and the Curious Body," 310.

22 Anderson, "The Black Church and the Curious Body," 311.

23 Roger A. Sneed, "Like Fire Shut Up in Our Bones: Religion and Spirituality in Black Gay Men's Literature," *Black Theology* 6, no. 2 (2008): 245; Farajajé-Jones, "Breaking the Silence," 146; Dorinda G. Henry, "'I, Too, Sing Songs of Freedom': A Theo-Sociological Praxis toward an Emancipatory Ethic for the Black Church and Its

Trans—Same-and-Both-Gender-Loving Members," in *The Black Church Studies Reader*, ed. Alton B. Pollard III and Carol B. Duncan (New York: Palgrave Macmillan, 2016), 288. Henry identifies as an "African American woman and lesbian."

24 Sneed, *Representations of Homosexuality*, 14.

25 Sneed, "Like Fire Shut Up in Our Bones," 247.

26 The racialized focus in black liberation theology excludes sexuality because the framing of the primary agenda as countering white supremacy does not include a gender or sexuality analysis, though later waves of black theologians, womanists, and black cultural critics of the 1990s disrupt this narrative. Sneed makes the argument that "this implied linkage of homosexuality with womanist ethics feminizes and marginalizes black gay men." It is challenging to understand Sneed's critique of inclusion within womanism as a loss without noting the sexism in the statement. Though Sneed is careful to name womanists as admirable in addressing homophobia pointedly and as "a grievous sin," he decries gay and lesbian inclusion as a "subset" in womanist discourse and that when their sexuality is mentioned, it is often as "a problem to be solved" (e.g., homophobia, HIV/AIDS stigma), not as a means of celebrating difference, diversity, or queer life. He also rightfully critiques how womanism has not allowed black gay men's experience to speak for itself methodologically. Sneed, *Representations of Homosexuality*, 13, 53.

27 Lightsey, *Our Lives Matter*, xix; Pamela R. Lightsey, "Inner Dictum: A Womanist Reflection from the Queer Realm," *Black Theology* 10, no. 3 (November 2011): 345, 340.

28 Lightsey, "Inner Dictum," 345.

29 Lightsey, *Our Lives Matter*, 71–2. Lightsey describes Pauli Murray as living in an "intersexed [sic]" body in the 2011 article, and as transgender in *Our Lives Matter* (2015). According to Murray's archive at Harvard's Schlesinger Library, the former is inaccurate. In "Inner Dictum," Lightsey quotes historian Rosalind Rosenberg's biography of Murray, stating, "Ashamed to be thought a lesbian, [Murray] reasoned that her attraction to 'very feminine and heterosexual women' was an indication that she was biologically male." Lightsey, "Inner Dictum," 340. Given the extensive gender questing pursued by Murray, I and other scholars and organizations recognize Murray as a person of trans experience. I affirm the need for differing pronoun choices and understandings of Murray beyond "she"; this distinction is crucial for recording more rigorous and robust trans experiences in histories. See Naomi Simmons-Thorne,

"Pauli Murray and the Pronominal Problem: A De-essentialist Trans Historiography," *The Activist History Review*, May 30, 2019.
30 Lightsey, *Our Lives Matter*, 99.
31 Lightsey, *Our Lives Matter*, 99.
32 Hill, "Who Are We for Each Other," 346.
33 "Young People and the History of the Ryan White HIV/AIDS Program," Health Resources and Services Administration: Ryan White and Global HIV/AIDS Programs, accessed April 14, 2019, https://hab.hrsa.gov/livinghistory/issues/youth_1.htm.
34 Griffin, "Toward a True Black Liberation Theology," 140–1.
35 "Bhomophobia" is a distinctly African American form of homophobia that identifies queer people as race traitors, diminishes white queer people, creates a hegemonic relationship between black heterosexual and black LGBTQ people, and protects a one-sided relationship with the "family-values lobbyist" with whom the bhomophobic person can connect on matters of marriage (though they cannot expect support for concerns impacting black communities). Lightsey, "Inner Dictum," 344.
36 Jennifer Leath, "(Out of) Places, Please! Demystifying Opposition to Procreative Choice in Afro-Diasporic Communities in the United States," *Journal of Feminist Studies in Religion* 30, no. 1 (Spring 2014): 160.
37 Farajajé, "Breaking the Silence," 153.
38 Lightsey, *Our Lives Matter*, 16.
39 Farajajé, "Breaking the Silence," 141.
40 Sneed, "Like Fire Shut Up in Our Bones," 247.
41 Griffin, "Toward a True Black Liberation Theology," 150.
42 Sneed, *Representations of Homosexuality*, 94.
43 Sneed, "Like Fire Shut Up in Our Bones," 247.
44 Thelathia "Nikki" Young, *Black Queer Ethics, Family, and Philosophical Imagination* (New York: Palgrave MacMillan, 2016), 33.
45 Thelathia "Nikki" Young and Shannon J. Miller, "Asé and Amen, Sister!: Black Feminist Scholars Engage in Interdisciplinary, Dialogical, Transformative Ethical Praxis," *Journal of Religious Ethics* 43, no. 2 (2015): 300, 311–12. Young takes up the argument of feminist ethicist and philosopher Hilde Lindemann Nelson in making this assertion alongside her own paradigm of listening and telling as ethical imperatives.

46 Though Sneed later takes issue with Farajajé's use of "in-the-life" because it historically includes a variety of people that Farajajé does not mention (e.g., pimps, sex workers), Farajajé was adamant about asserting "life" in connection with all oppressed peoples because these populations so frequently need to resist "suffering and death." Farajajé-Jones, "Breaking the Silence," 140. According to Sneed, "The term in-the-life had traditionally been used to refer to unsavory elements within Black life [...] If Farajajé-Jones wants to take in-the-life seriously, he has to contend with the negative associations that this term entails." Sneed, *Representations of Homosexuality*, 60. Sneed's critique of Farajajé must include Farajajé's conception of those in-the-life as "inextricably bound" in the struggle for liberation with all the oppressed peoples of the world, perhaps including pimps, sex workers, hustlers, and drug dealers—persons oppressed by socioeconomic injustices. These rejected populations exist in a distinct alterity because they, too, struggle against oppressions and a kind of disinheritance that black LGBTQ+ people needn't create distance from, further disinheriting them, even if there is critique to be made of harm or the ethics of the behavior of anyone in-the-life. Farajajé-Jones, "Breaking the Silence," 140-1.

47 Griffin, "Toward a True Black Liberation Theology," 149.

48 Griffin, "Toward a True Black Liberation Theology," 149.

49 Griffin includes lesbians distinctively in Horace L. Griffin, "Revisioning Christian Ethical Discourse on Homosexuality: A Challenge for Pastoral Care in the 21st Century," *Journal of Pastoral Care and Counseling* 53, no. 2 (June 1999): 215, 218. In Roger A. Sneed, "Dark Matter: Liminality and Black Queer Bodies," in *Ain't I a Womanist Too?: Third Wave Womanist Religious Thought*, ed. Monica A. Coleman (Minneapolis: Fortress Press, 2013), Sneed draws from black woman writer Octavia Butler and black lesbian singer Meshell Ndegeocello's cultural productions.

50 Renee L. Hill, "Human Sexuality: The Rest of the Story," in *Walk Together Children: Black and Womanist Theologies, Church and Theological Education*, ed. Dwight N. Hopkins and Linda E. Thomas (Eugene: Cascade 2010), 186.

51 Roland Stringfellow, "Soul Work: Developing a Black LGBT Liberation Theology," in *Queer Religion: Volume I*, ed. Donald L. Boisvert and Jay Emerson Johnson (Santa Barbara: Praeger, 2012), 124.

52 See "Fact Sheet on LGBT Youth," Religious Institute, accessed May 8, 2019, http://religiousinstitute.org/resources/fact-sheet-lgbt-youth/.

53 Farajajé-Jones, "Breaking the Silence," 140.

54 Lightsey, *Our Lives Matter*, 34.
55 Farajajé-Jones, "Breaking the Silence," 141.
56 Jennifer S. Leath, "Is Queer the New Black?" *Harvard Divinity Bulletin* 43, nos. 3 and 4 (Summer/Autumn 2015), https://bulletin.hds.harvard.edu/articles/summerautumn2015/queer-new-black.
57 E. Patrick Johnson, "'Quare' Studies, or (Almost) Everything I Know about Queer Studies I Learned from My Grandmother," *Text and Performance Quarterly* 21, no. 1 (January 2001): 2.
58 Lightsey, *Our Lives Matter*, 21.
59 Lightsey, *Our Lives Matter*, 32, 24.
60 Leath, "Is Queer the New Black?"
61 Young, *Black Queer Ethics*, 80.
62 Young, *Black Queer Ethics*, 59.
63 Young, *Black Queer Ethics*, 50, n. 12.
64 Young, *Black Queer Ethics*, 2, 7.
65 Griffin, *Their Own Receive Them Not*, 3.
66 Young, *Black Queer Ethics*, 195.
67 Irene Monroe, "When and Where I Enter, then the Whole Race Enters with Me: Que(e)rying Exodus," in *Loving the Body: Black Religious Studies and the Erotic*, ed. Anthony Pinn and Dwight Hopkins (New York: Palgrave Macmillan, 2004), 123.
68 Young, *Black Queer Ethics*, 107.
69 Lightsey, "Inner Dictum," 342. Lightsey chooses to frame same-gender attraction through the lens of "loving relationship," an approach that Sneed critiques in Griffin because it presents a respectable form of sexuality without acceptance that all relationships that queer (or heterosexual) people engage are not aiming to culminate in romantic love. Even if the connotation were that all Christians should practice loving relationship, the emphasis on "loving" relationships carries with it the weight of sanitization that some scholars employ because of the stereotypes that deem LGBTQ+, and in a particular way black LGBTQ+, relationships "dirty."
70 Young, *Black Queer Ethics*, 5. To this end, Young offers, "America comprises households led by same-sex partners, interracial families, interreligious families, immigrant and transnational families, single-parent households, multigenerational households, co-parenting units due to separation or divorce, and more."
71 Young, *Black Queer Ethics*, 5, 57, 85–6. The constructed term, "family," carries with it real benefits in society from which

unmarried people or people without children are often precluded (e.g., sharing a joint health insurance plan with a partner, the ability to be "next of kin" for a friend in medical emergencies). I question the moral value imputed to (namely, narrowly defined) "family" and its usefulness as a social value, as it serves as a means of upholding inequitable access to resources in our current institutional structures, though a deeper exploration of this topic goes beyond the scope of this project.

72 Emilie M. Townes, "The Dancing Mind: Queer Black Bodies and Activism in Academy and Church" (Gilberto Castañeda Lecture, Chicago Theological Seminary, Chicago, IL, April 28, 2011).

73 Lightsey, *Our Lives Matter*, 27, 49.

74 Lightsey, "Inner Dictum," 339.

75 Hill, "Human Sexuality," 192.

76 Sneed, "Dark Matter," 147.

77 Sneed, "Like Fire Shut Up in Our Bones," 242, 255–6.

78 Lightsey, *Our Lives Matter*, xx.

79 Sneed, "Like Fire Shut Up in Our Bones," 257–8.

80 Sneed, "Like Fire Shut Up in Our Bones," 246, 260.

81 Leath, "Is Queer the New Black?" Leath articulates, "Katie G. Cannon notes the ways that Afro-Diasporic or black women's bodies are particularly visible as abject objects to be targeted for oppression and incomprehensibly invisible as subjects deserving dignity and respect. In my work, I hope to respond to the 'hyper(in)visibility' and the 'hyper(in)audibility' of these same women." Katie G. Cannon, "Sexing Black Women: Liberation from the Prisonhouse of Anatomical Authority," in *Loving the Body: Black Religious Studies and the Erotic*, ed. Dwight N. Hopkins and Anthony B. Pinn (New York: Palgrave Macmillan, 2007).

82 Leath, "Is Queer the New Black?"

83 Leath, "Is Queer the New Black?"

84 Leath, "Is Queer the New Black?" See also Michael Warner, *The Trouble with Normal: Sex, Politics, and the Ethics of Queer Life* (Cambridge: Harvard University Press, 1999), 36.

85 Anderson, "The Black Church and the Curious Body," 297.

86 Anderson, "The Black Church and the Curious Body," 311.

87 Townes, "The Dancing Mind."

88 Townes, "The Dancing Mind."

89 Griffin, "Toward a True Black Liberation Theology," 133.
90 Leath, "(Out of) Places," 157.
91 Leath, "(Out of) Places," 157.
92 Sneed, "Dark Matter," 142, 145, 147.
93 Sneed, "Dark Matter," 147.
94 Sneed, "Dark Matter," 147.
95 Hill, "Who Are We for Each Other," 347.
96 Hill, "Human Sexuality," 185.
97 Hill, "Human Sexuality," 185.
98 Lightsey, *Our Lives Matter*, 85.
99 Lightsey, *Our Lives Matter*, 84.
100 Lightsey, "Inner Dictum," 341, 348–9.
101 While some of these terms can be perceived as offensive, many black queer people have reclaimed these terms to express their unique way of expressing gender while being gay, lesbian, bisexual, transgender, and/or queer. Monroe has dismissed terms like "butch" and "femme" or even "lesbian," "gay," or "queer" as belonging to white queer vernacular. Still, this dismissal seems unfounded considering black folks and people of color (presumably in cosmopolitan areas, especially) have utilized these terms for much of the twentieth and into the twenty-first century. Irene Monroe, "Between a Rock and a Hard Place," in *Out of the Shadows, Into the Light: Christianity and Homosexuality*, ed. Miguel A. De La Torre (Danvers, MA: Chalice Press, 2009), 40.
102 Hill, "Human Sexuality," 185.
103 Anderson, "The Black Church and the Curious Body," 309.
104 Griffin, "Giving New Birth," 88–90. This narrative also centers the white, mythological family in social and political definitions of in the United States a standard that is distinctly unreachable by black people of any sexual orientation.
105 Anderson, "The Black Church and the Curious Body," 309. See Cheryl J. Sanders, "Sexual Orientation and Human Rights Discourse in the African American Churches," in *Sexual Orientation and Human Rights in African American Discourse*, ed. Saul Olyan and Martha C. Nussbaum (New York: Oxford University Press, 1998), 178–84. For more of Sanders's insights about lesbian and other "homosexualities," as well as her critique of womanism's potential connections with lesbianism, see Cheryl J. Sanders, "Roundtable Discussion: Christian Ethics and Theology in Womanist

Perspective," *Journal of Feminist Studies in Religion* 5, no. 2 (Fall 1989): 83–91.

106 Pamela Ayo Yetunde, "Black Lesbians to the Rescue! A Brief Correction with Implications for Womanist Christian Theology and Womanist Buddhology," *Religions* 8, no. 9 (2017): 175.

107 Farajajé-Jones, "Breaking the Silence," 146.

108 Lightsey, "Inner Dictum," 342.

109 As noted above, Hill identifies the fear of association with lesbians and accusation of being a lesbian as potential reasons why womanists may choose to exclude lesbians in their analyses of black women's lives.

110 See the critique in Kelly Brown Douglas, "Homophobia and Heterosexism in the Black Church and Community," in *Sexuality and the Black Church: A Womanist Perspective* (Maryknoll, NY: Orbis, 1999). See also M. Shawn Copeland, *Enfleshing Freedom: Body, Race and Being* (Minneapolis: Fortress 2009), and Cannon, "Sexing Black Women."

111 Griffin, "Revisioning Christian Ethical Discourse on Homosexuality," 217. Sneed, "Like Fire Shut Up in Our Bones," 260.

112 Griffin, "Toward a True Black Liberation Theology," 135.

113 Sneed, "Like Fire Shut Up in Our Bones," 241, 244–5. Sneed includes in his critique Douglas, a foremost voice on sexuality among womanist scholars and in the black liberationist tradition, who chooses to write about men "on the down low," and the unfortunate framing of black gay men as "uniformly promiscuous and carriers of plague." He goes on to say, "[Douglas] accepts [the media presentation of men 'on the down low'] uncritically as a complete representation of the lives of black men who have sex with other men and keep that a secret." This practice has also been common among popular black women figures like Oprah Winfrey and Terry McMillan, and black men such as Tyler Perry.

114 Sneed, *Representations of Homosexuality*, 9.

115 Sneed, *Representations of Homosexuality*, 14.

116 Hill, "Human Sexuality," 186.

117 Young, *Black Queer Ethics*, 185–6.

118 Monroe, "When and Where I Enter," 130.

119 Griffin, "Toward a True Black Liberation Theology," 134.

120 Monroe, "Between a Rock and a Hard Place," 58.

121 Monroe, "Between a Rock and a Hard Place," 49–51.

3

Spirit in the Dark Body: Blackqueer Expressions of the Im/material

To engage with experiences of blackqueerness signaling moral imagination is to encounter mystery. It is to lean into intentional and strategic obscurations. It is to perceive clearly and otherwise.[1] It is to listen to the indiscernible and through the unintelligible for the story between the words. It is to suspend expectation and open to possibility in the everydayness of blackqueer folks living into their frequently hard-fought moral imagination. It is in the quotidian that values are shaped, ways of being are practiced, and ethics are made. The words, stories, scholarship, and images contribute to a record that affirms, to borrow from womanist ethicist Emilie M. Townes, blackqueer "is-ness."[2] With a blackqueer ethics' methodological grounding in theory and practice, it is necessary now to turn to stories of blackqueerness intersecting with religion and/or spirituality in the quotidian, as practiced in the lives of contemporary, everyday people.

Employing oral histories, that is, subjective narratives that expound on and provide insight about experiences and/or events, contributes to the building of a living blackqueer archive in conversation with the content of the previous chapters. These narratives offer *something else* toward blackqueer life engaging with, shaping, deconstructing, and reconstructing religion in academic discourse and lived religion.[3] It is important to remember that though these stories are of blackqueerness, they are not centered solely in questions of sexuality or gender. They are concerned with the whole person informed by this politic. Because, as I have stated, a sexual ethics is always a communal ethics, I aim to present these subjects as full people, including but not limited to their sexuality and gender.

Story is essential to any construction of liberative ethics because it enables expansiveness in individual and collective moral imagination; questioning, embracing, and interrogating one's own stories; and materializing the real lives being spoken to or about in academic discourse. Thelathia "Nikki" Young argues for the importance of narrative as "a tool for getting to the substance of black queer lives, allowing people to speak for themselves from lives that they have not only written and directed, but also ones which they have enacted and evaluated."[4] Utilizing narrative in ethics is presencing lived moral imagination and agency in questing toward more just ways of doing ethics. As with any sacred story, the stories within this chapter serve as invitations to tarry, to earnestly stay with each subject's words as a liberative praxis of witnessing, connecting, and welcoming the unexpected.

As a blackqueer ethicist committed to blackqueer liberative ways of life, I have in mind the value blackqueer stories hold for the speaker and blackqueer people who will read these stories, as well as for the disciplines of black religion and religious ethics. The oral histories in this chapter contain the subjects' own interpretations, creativity, epistemologies, rituals, self-reflection, theological understandings, and moral positions that suggest what it is to be one's own and belong—complex, alive, part of faith and just communities, transformed and transforming. Blackqueerness in histories and in ethics or theology subject to blackqueering tell a part of the story; oral histories, shared through a lens of blackqueerness, tell another part. While these stories are offerings toward how *some* persons live into their religious and ethical selves, they are not included here to offer a comprehensive or definitive framing of blackqueer spirit, religion, or ethics. The fluidity, multiplicity, and heterogeneity of the lives shared in these stories can expand and/or challenge existing bounds within religious ethics, religious studies, and black religion, as well as how sexuality and gender with race can inform engagement with religion and spirituality. In their diversity, the oral histories significantly shape the ethos that informs the "a" in this study's "a blackqueer ethics."

These histories refer to spirituality and religion, at times interchangeably, oppositionally, and complementarily. They inspire the transreligious approach taken in this book. From a "black queer mystic warrior poet" to a Christian pastor and energy healer, the subjects reflect a spectrum of engagement with religion that is *trans*, inclusive *across* various traditions, faiths, and practices and *beyond* the confines of religion, even if they are still an active part of or informed by a religion after their departure from it. The transreligious approach counters Christian traditionalism that has shaped both academic and lived expressions of black religion. This is not to say that blackqueerness is the singular space that yields a kind of transreligious practice of religion and/or spirituality that permits (even celebrates) a flow between and among various traditions, expressions, ethical and theological understandings, rituals, meditative practices, and forms of veneration and devotion, but it is worth noting the liberty these subjects feel to engage the various spiritual, religious, healing, and justice-seeking paths that call to them.

This chapter contributes to a growing collection of diverse black and queer religious and spiritual oral histories and collections of narratives.[5] Examples like Akasha Gloria Hull's *Soul Talk: The New Spirituality of African American Women* (2001) excerpts of Darnell Moore's memoir, *No Ashes in the Fire: Coming of Age Black and Free in America* (2018) and oral histories like E. Patrick Johnson's *Sweet Tea: Black Gay Men of the South* (2008) and *Black. Queer. Southern. Women.: An Oral History* (2018) are invaluable in their record of the stories of their subjects. Like Johnson names in *Black. Queer. Southern. Women.*, I have elected to create space for these oral histories as "a quotidian form of self-fashioning and theorizing," not attempting to create knowledge from them as a blackqueer ethics in action.[6] They speak for themselves as meaningful depictions of blackqueer life. While the stories inform my thinking on the constructive ethics in the next chapter, they are presented here as oral histories that offer their own explanation and insight on the religious and the spiritual in the lives of the practitioners. Countering extractive practices around the stories of persons pushed to the margins, the value of the stories lies not in their ability to forward or fit into a theoretical framing—though we do gain from engaging their moral imagination—but more so in the hereness and nowness of blackqueer folx doing religion and spirituality in their own words. Akin to the subjects in Chapter 1, wherein I analyze gender and sexual nonconformist communities in 1920s black Harlem and find in their counterpublics ways of being and doing that demonstrate moral imagination, in addition to the blackqueering discourse of the ethicists and theologians in Chapter 2, these subjects' engagement with religion and spirituality is an enlivened, generative source of and for moral knowledge toward a blackqueer ethics.

Though many narratives and studies of black LGBTQ+ people and religion explore religious trauma, my intent was to gain a comprehensive picture of the subjects' journeys and its varying twists and turns, primarily through the lens of their agency, by posing open-ended inquiries and not framing them to probe potential traumatic experiences, though the subject could be broached by the storyteller. While some of the oral histories may reference moments of challenge with (namely) Christian traditionalism, they more broadly reflect an alive relationship to religion/spirituality centered in its usefulness and transmutability toward fostering a good life. I employed the terms "spirituality" and "religion" in my prompts to include a wide range of practices and so that those who I knew to have a disconnect with religion might feel open to decenter institutions, faith leaders, doctrine, etc., if they so chose. I was also aware through interactions with the subjects that many had more resonance with the word "spirituality" than "religion."

The subjects are persons I have been fortunate to meet through years of friendship or as family, as kin of kin, or simply as part of informal networks of blackqueer community (physical and virtual). In this respect, my method is autoethnographic. They are everyday people, their everydayness lying in their regular spiritual and religious practices toward integration and liberation. The storytellers have origins primarily in the United States: Ohio, New York, Washington, DC, Florida, Virginia, Pennsylvania, New Jersey, and Delaware, and, at the time of the interviews, resided in metropolitan areas of the Midwest, Northeast, and South of the United States. Two of the subjects also share deep ties with the Caribbean alongside the United States. One shortcoming of this small collection is a lack of representation from the West and North. More than half of the subjects have a degree from a seminary or school of theology and are leaders of various kinds in their communities. This factor could account for some of the extensive thought that has already taken place, prior to our recording, regarding thinking identity and positionality with religion and/or spirituality. At the time of interviewing, each subject associated with the terms "black" and "queer," though in our most recent check-in, one (Michael) explicitly identified as "gay." Many of the subjects are nonbinary or genderqueer, contributing to my aim of disrupting queer narratives that solely center lesbian cisgender women or gay cisgender men. Participants were encouraged to share only what they felt like sharing and were permitted the time to speak as they chose.

Like most histories, these oral histories have said much more than can be recorded or described here. Some interviews were as short as twenty minutes and some exceeded an hour. Though the oral has been made written word, the process of storytelling served as its own kind of exercise in blackqueer subjectivity, agency, performativity, and world-making. It is also a lesson in opacities within queerness—some things cannot and will not be revealed for and perceived by a reading public. All is not intelligible. And, this is okay. As is often the case in spaces of blackqueerness, the subjects and I were glad to *kiki* and to digress, to delve into the mundane and the depths. Further reflecting a living archive and the liberative practice of persons/communities in communal dialogue, the subjects' words are integrated with one another, grouped by like subject matter for ease of readability. The oral histories have been edited for clarity and with great effort toward retaining the integrity of the subjects' speech; reflecting the most robust presentation of the histories as possible given space constraints; and aligning with their representation of their reality at the intersections of race, sexuality, gender, and religion.

Upon recording, listening to, transcribing, reading, and rereading the oral histories, certain themes arose across each of the subject's narratives that provide guidance for this chapter. I have named the themes as Origins in Religious and Spiritual Becoming, A Practice in Connecting, Cultivating Access, Queering Belief, Journeying Toward and Away/Redefining, Blackness and Queerness, and Benedictions. These are not the words that the subjects have chosen; rather, they are my attempt to name the cohesion I see. There is overlap among the themes, and the storytellers' words may not fit squarely under one topic. The themes should be understood as providing insight rather than framing. Further, they are not intended to mark sameness or to present a monolith of blackqueer experience; the histories certainly contradict these notions. Essentially, the headers serve as an invitation to the reader to read for these shared ideas across the oral histories and to read beyond them where needed.

A Word about Visuals in the Archive

Picturing the black, queer, and sacred, both literally and imaginatively, is an act with futuring at its root. As the archive is a record of something past, the visual representations of the subjects, like the oral histories, also serve as a means of presencing blackqueerness intertwined with religion and spirituality, further asserting the matter(ing) of the featured subjects. Some of the photos in this chapter are from my photo-sonic exhibition, *Spirit in the Dark Body: Black Queer Expressions of the Im/material.* "Dark body" speaks not only to race, but to darkness as a symbol for intentionally inhabiting mystery. This mystery is reflected in terms of sexuality, spirituality, and other unknowable parts of deviant (in the Cohenian sense) selves. Where blackqueer spirituality has at times been considered insignificant or even non-existent—that is, immaterial—I aim to reclaim immateriality (also known as spirit) through blackqueer materiality, the dark bodies that house the immaterial. The photo-sonic exhibition, whose amended name also entitles this chapter, is thought together with Aretha Franklin's "Spirit in the Dark" (1970) and E. Patrick Johnson's "Feeling the Spirit in the Dark: Expanding Notions of the Sacred in the African-American Gay Community," and further inspired by Josef Sorett's *Spirit in the Dark: A Religious History of Racial Aesthetics* (2016). The exhibition premiered at the L Street Fine Arts Gallery in San Diego, California, at the 2019 annual meeting of the American Academy of Religion, sponsored by the African Diaspora Religions Unit. Some images and interviews from the photographic and sound series have been removed for the sake of space and to honor the nonconsenting participant-subjects, and additional participant-subjects have been integrated.

In a 1964 oral history recording with famed black photographer Gordon Parks for the Archives of American Art at the Smithsonian Institution, Parks asserts the importance of "keep[ing] the record straight pictorially," in an effort to reflect through photographs the various and specific elements of a time for future generations.[7] Taking Parks's words as a pun within the context of a blackqueer living archive, it is the "straight"-ness—homogeneity, "normalcy," sanitization, and heteronormativity—of existent records of black religion and spiritualities that I hope to trouble through the photos and accompanying stories of blackqueer practitioners. Further, in the spirit of Parks, I aim to do so in the service of countering erasure and contributing to a more multifaceted picture of black religion and spiritualities in the United States toward more liberative religious ethics.

In our increasingly social media visuals-driven culture, one can take for granted or minimize the value of an image, particularly those that do not reflect normativized ideals of beauty. There are temptations to project meaning or to approach an image with the aim of receiving something—a positive feeling, resonance, fodder for critique. While a receptive posture may not be inherently harmful, such a posture is as that of a consumer because there is not a reciprocal exchange between art and viewer. Elsewhere, I have posited aesthetic intimacy as an ethical approach to engaging art as it enables a viewer to approach art as an intimate, one willing to be in vulnerability with the art—the subject and the process of art-making—to yield an indeterminable encounter. In this way, both the viewed and the viewer are shaped in the moment of mutuality.[8] Because caution and care are to be exercised in viewing blackqueer bodies, blackqueer lives engaging the sacred (and isn't all sacred?), these photos serve as an invitation to quieting and noticing, a counterintuitive practice of listening, a liberative move toward releasing preconceived ideas of (black) (queer) religion and spirituality and allowing the photos to *be,* rather than *do* for the archive or even for those with whom the photos resonate.[9] While I acknowledge there is a function being served by the photos being included here, I invite the posture of aesthetic intimacy as an experiment in attunement to all that is present.

FIGURE 3.1 *"black queer feminist planet" (New Orleans, 2019).*

For Alexis, her enmeshed blackness and queerness constitute an aesthetic of difference, which underlies a "daily practice of being alive and living in relation to other living realities." This is spirituality as she knows it.

Beauty lies at the center of Alexis's conception of spirituality: the beauty of gratitude, of the aromatic, of making art, of arranging flowers, of Nina Simone's voice, of an altar—like the one in her home dedicated to Erzulie Freda ("a goddess of women" and of love and beauty, "particular to women who identify as lesbians").

In finding that we are all made of cosmic material, she asks, "If a planet is simply an independent body orbiting in time and space, then what's to say that humans are not planets as well?"

Alexis is a writer, poet, and activist originally from Harlem.

FIGURE 3.2 *"strength and blessing/blessed strength" (Philadelphia, 2022).*

Koach possesses a spirituality that is deeply and necessarily integrated with his embodiment. This connection has also aided in his self-understanding as a trans person.

From a lineage of African Methodist Episcopal Church ministers, Koach practices his spirituality and religion through ancestral connection; as a spiritual leader in movements for social change; through sensorial means; and as "a black trans Jewish person who is learning how to live with deep grief and high key anxiety and love—love of self and love with [his] partner."

He says, "As a queer person, as a trans person, I just understand that it's okay. That it's nothing that I need to fight. I ain't got to argue with nobody. I do what *da Lawd* let me do and if *da Lawd* allows me to do all of these different things, then I want to do them, because that's actually the freedom of spirituality and the plurality of humanity and divinity."

Koach is a spiritual leader and co-founder of the Tzedek Lab.

FIGURE 3.3 *"black queer mystic warrior poet" (New Orleans, 2019).*

storäe advises, "You stay true to your queerness and your blackness and your spirituality, and it will stay true to you." A far stretch from the conservative Presbyterian household in which they were raised, storäe came to a deeper understanding of spirituality through "exploring different sensations in [their] body, which [they] came to know as spirit, as Universe speaking," and "recalling the parts of [themself] that experienced Spirit as a child."

Integral to storäe's constantly transforming spirituality has been "listening to Mother Earth and listening to black women," as well as their intuition and curiosity, embodiment ("[their] fashions" as the energy that connects them with others), and art (namely, as it "lives in [their] writing").

storäe is an interdisciplinary scholar-artist, writer, and performer.

FIGURE 3.4 *"i am a listener, an observer" (New York City, 2019).*

Olivia frequently uses "the tools of astrology, tarot, and Afro-Indigenous spirituality" toward "constant self-reflection, listening to [their self] and the world around [them]." They say of spirituality that it is inherent to humanity and involves "positioning yourself with the least amount of harm to yourself and others."

Olivia believes that blackness and queerness (even more so) share the qualities of the Divine—they are timeless, always "on the way," and embody love. Perhaps, this correlation exists because, according to Olivia, black and queer people by virtue of their existence in the West are "pushed to become more spiritual." They name the importance of having been prompted most frequently by black queer persons to live more deeply into their spirituality.

Olivia is a storyteller and healer.

FIGURE 3.5 *"being so that i can be in the quest of becoming"* (New Jersey, 2022).

Nala says of herself, "I am a goddess. I am a daughter. I am a friend and a sister." She is a "woman of trans experience and defining."

Being raised around a variety of religious and spiritual expressions in Bushwick, Brooklyn, "helped [her] because it was a fusion of all different spiritualities and the way that folk communicated to the God of their understanding."

She locates both her becoming identities and expressions of spirituality within the realms of fluidity and earthiness, naming water, evolution ("[I am] a person of many transitions like seasons"), herbs, Earth ("[I am] one with Earth, sometimes dis-attached from Earth"), and soil (particularly that of South Africa about which she says "I didn't know I was looking for home. I didn't know home was looking for me.") as elements and support for living into her self-understandings.

Nala is an activist, influencer, and healer and is founder of Reuniting of African Descendants (ROAD).

FIGURE 3.6 *"black queer believer" (Atlanta, 2019).*

Natasha's exploration of a more expansive spirituality comes from a sense of "feeling bamboozled" after discovering the truths of the religion of her childhood. Her journey now encompasses "existing as a whole self [and] determining what works for [her] and what doesn't," and leaning into "[her] truth and lived experiences" which, for her, holds as much import as the sacred texts of religions.

Natasha defines spirituality as "the process of connecting to God, self, and others," and as the ways that persons do so in community. Employing various modalities to connect spiritually, Natasha is part of an African-centered Christian ministry, communes with ancestors, honors the orisas, meditates, carries stones, and shares her practice as a Reiki (energy healing) Master.

Natasha is a pastor and healer.

FIGURE 3.7 *"black ethical liberation humanist" (New York City, 2018).*

Jé thinks of art, inspired by the root of the word in Sanskrit, as "truth." Their art is their spirituality. It makes them feel free and rapt as they live out their truth as a performance practitioner, as they live "more authentically, unapologetically, and securely." Spirituality as artistry is rooted in process, which enables them to "grow, develop, change, evolve, go through metamorphosis and in turn, be inspired to create again."

Jé's blackness and queerness are "a force of nature to be reckoned with," their disruptiveness "a projection of what spiritual life and spiritual living can do for others."

Jé is a performance practitioner and Humanist clergy leader.

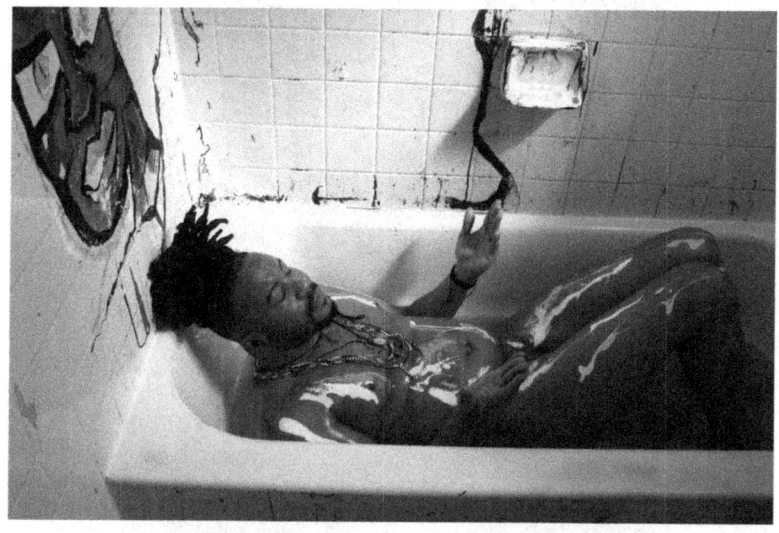

FIGURE 3.8 *"i am a gatekeeper [...] i am multiplicities"* *(New York City, 2019)*.

Charly connects spiritually through their art. It is his ritual.

Raised in part in the Dominican Republic, Charly was mothered and nurtured by women there in various African diasporic spiritual traditions and forms of ritual. Today, they carry that same multiplicity in his understanding of his "multidimensional," "multi-faith," "multi-spirit" spirituality.

Charly says of spirituality that it is "the core of every soul in connection to the multiplicities in the universe" and includes "the dimensions that you travel in … the multilayers of experiences … quantum leaping … memories that bring you back to stages … it's all intertwined."

Charly is a multitalented artist.

FIGURE 3.9 *"african american gay man who still carries the energy forces, or the souls, of my people" (New York City, 2019).*

"As above, so below," Michael frequently states regarding his metaphysical conception of spirituality. He understands human existence as an opportunity to learn a lesson not previously gained in former levels of evolution.

Pursuing, a "great life *now*" through his higher vibrations, Michael says of his relationship to Divine Energy, "I believe in self […] I get my approval from myself." Further, he affirms, "You are the God-Force. You are the Energy Force. You are everything."

Michael was one of the first people to have a legal gay marriage in New York.

Origins in Religious and Spiritual Becoming

Charly: I think that the cultural diffusion of being not just an African descendant, but also being in the United States where everyone is blended [...] it's a whole different experience than being back in the Dominican Republic or in other islands where the community of that culture is still very intact and fluid. When you're coming across biases of people who don't understand your spirituality and don't understand your queerness and don't ... all of those things become obstacles in your path of your own liberation, as well as the liberation of the people that you're supposed to shed light to as you're walking through.

[...] I was born here [in New York City], but as a child, we were raised both places. My mother would send me and my sister (sometimes, me and my sister and my brother) to stay there for months or until school started. Then it would just be summer vacations or Christmas. [...] In the Dominican Republic, as a child they recognized these things in me. I was mothered by the women in the community and saw certain things with the spiritual system. So, they mothered me, they nurtured me. They taught me things. I saw them in trance. They saw me in trance. I was able to distinguish what was going on and who was there or who was speaking or what it looks like when it's something that you don't want (laughs). You know, those kinds of things, they taught me.

The reason I don't specify [the names of the religious/spiritual traditions] is because it's convoluted. You have the Catholicism [...] You have the Twenty-One Divisions. You have the Vodoun. You have the Hoodoo. You have Ifá ... all mixed in there. But because people are not anchored in certain ways of separat[ing the traditions], ways of gathering, it becomes a chaotic whirlwind.

Natasha: As far as starting out in a faith tradition, I was a part of a Pentecostal church. I was heavily involved with the music departments [and] youth departments. I started discerning a call to do more, to be more involved as a child. As a teenager, I gave my initial sermon—at like fifteen [years old]—and then followed down that path, which ultimately led me to seminary right out of undergrad.

It was in seminary that I was exposed to different ways of believing, different ways of thinking and theologizing and interpreting in ways that I had not been exposed to. Being exposed to so much in a short period of time, it just really got me thinking and reflecting and trying to figure out what was true and what wasn't. And at some point, I settled on, "My truth and my lived experiences are just as valuable, if not more, as these sacred texts that are passed down in the name of religion and spirituality."

So, it was that process and just being able to be mentored by and to sit with other scholars who have already done that work for themselves and the truths that they settled upon. And then, just accepting that there's a freedom to do and to be and to believe in the way that works for you. (I think, particularly in the Christian tradition, there's this box of what Christianity is and what it has to look like. Being able to exist out of that box was freeing, especially since because of my sexual orientation or identity—however we want to call it—it wasn't appropriate for that box.) ... Just being able to exist out of [the box] as my whole self and to determine what works for me and what doesn't and being okay with that.

Koach: I grew up in a household where the African Methodist Episcopal (AME) Church was a major part of my life. I come from a long line of AME preachers, including my grandfather, his grandfather, my aunt. I had an uncle who passed away, who was also an AME minister. It's all in the family and on my mother's side. I couldn't get away from wanting to be with other people in my spiritual practice, and the music of black spirituality—which lives not only inside of the Black Church, but also outside in other black spiritual traditions—has always and will, I think, be with me.

That being said, I needed something else. I needed something that felt resonant with me. The moments in time when I came home to Judaism ... the music, the words, the Hebrew, the Aramaic felt familiar. Wrapping myself in the wings of *Shakhinah*, as it were, with a *tallit* when I pray, to literally strap Torah onto my body. All of these things resonate with me. They're embodied. I needed them. Much like when I go to a black Jewish *shul* and they shout and I'm like, "Yes, I need that, too!" I need that release that we know as black folks we gotta have, or else it stays bottled up in us and can be destructive in some ways. I needed all of that. And so, I found home in Judaism.

I explored so many other different things. I explored Islam. I explored Hinduism and Buddhism. And ultimately, I explored African Traditional Religion (ATR). I'm very, very interested in the connections between Judaism and ATR, mainly because Judaism comes from ... it was literally started on the continent ... and so, I see connections that are resonant in my body. Like, I just know. Then, I read something, and I'm like, "Oh, right, yeah, yeah. I already knew that. I already knew that there's this connection between Ifá and Jewish practice that remains so clear."

Michael: I'm not Christian in the sense of Catholic or Baptist or Protestant or anything like that, although my family was Baptist. And of course, as a child you grow up in church ... at least I did for a little while, until Dad said, "You don't have to go," and we all stopped going. Great relief (laughs). We didn't have to go. But over time, I think I evolved into the realm of metaphysics. [...] I was always, quote, spiritual (as we all are) and more connected, growing up with plants and gardening and [...] fishing, and all the little things that are part of me. But I think what *really* happened to me is becoming grounded in myself.

I'm also the middle child in my family and that's significant. I had two older siblings and two younger siblings, so I was a real middle child and left alone, pretty much, because my mom had to take care of two above and two below. If there was any time left over, there was time for Michael. If there wasn't, then Michael had to take care of himself. I think early on in my life, in my development, I just started getting this sense of identity for myself, sense of security for myself, a sense of fight for myself. Like, I came to New York not knowing a soul (except a dance partner) for a little while, but I wasn't afraid because I was so grounded in who I was ... and I was twenty years old.

I didn't know about metaphysics at that time. I studied that later in time to try to ... I guess, I sort of found it because we found each other. And conversations with people, books at the "buy-in," and all these different things that you read and learn over time ... It fit the way I was feeling, what I was thinking. So, it wasn't a long journey. In between going to funerals and that kind of thing, you revisit the church. But as far as going there for spiritual awakening or anything like that, I didn't have time and I didn't believe because it was still something outside of me. And I was so grounded in what was in me.

Even today, its what's in me [...] my Energy Force that gives me the strength to wake up and do things I do every day. I'm not praying for God to give me the strength to wake up every day and to *do*. Maybe I should (chuckles). Maybe I wouldn't have so much stress. But I don't. I'm grounded in myself.

Olivia: Growing up in Dayton, Ohio, I grew up in a black Baptist church. Not for long. For a long time, we just didn't go to church, which was a relief. I think at that point, it was [somewhat because of our region], but it was mostly just family [being] like, "*This* is what we do, and *that's* what we do. And, if you're going to be in *this* family, *this* is what you're going to do."

Growing up the Midwest ... I mean, it's the Midwest: religion ... conservative. I really didn't think about religion growing up. It was just a task. A chore. When we didn't go, I really didn't ever think about it. But it just became a norm ... Like, everyone you meet, you just assume they're Christian. I started having animosity toward Christianity, Christians. I was just like, "I'm sick of it. I don't want to hear Jesus's name again. I don't want to hear *Holy Bible* ... any of it. Just get it away from me."

It wasn't until I went to Spain my junior year of high school and I lived there for nine months ... I lived in this very small town in Castile La Mancha, which is in the middle of Spain. Of course, they're super Catholic. I would go to Catholic Mass occasionally. It was during Holy Week when I started to ... I don't know what felt different about it, but it just felt different. I was able to just relax and appreciate it because they weren't ... maybe because they weren't telling me I had to [go to Mass], knowing that I'm not Catholic. Also, because it was very cultural, a deep cultural experience. Spain is old. And so, it just became ... I don't want to say more beautiful, but more of a celebration, a cultural celebration. It brought community together. Whereas, in Dayton, it was an obligation. And so, I was able to release some of that animosity.

But even when I had the thought, "I want to be a priestess," my second thought was "I'm in the Midwest. I'm going to have to wait." And that was my thing: I'm just going to have to wait until a priestess pops up in front of me and it's not going to happen in the Midwest. Nobody I know does that. I don't even see it. There's not even a space where you can see it underground. You just don't ever see it. I didn't even know what it looked like. My whole thing when I was little was, "I'm just waiting until I can leave and see more." And so ... yeah ... spirituality in the Midwest was ... It wasn't a great experience. It wasn't at all.

Nala: [An] "aha moment" for me was the self-determination, the self-actualization, feeling the feminine energy and the shift within my body, and the yearning to have that energy be reflected outward so that folks were communicating with me how I saw myself. That happened at seventeen [years old], right up to eighteen, and then nineteen. But as a child, I always felt that way.

[...] Somebody asked me, "When you see yourself die, how do you see yourself?" And it was right there instantly. God provided me with these images. God always communicates with images. [...] I don't dream as often, but as I'm sitting [next] to you, it's like I can see ... like how you can see auras or colors. I can see auras. And it's almost like I can see images in real time with my eyes open. Unfolding. And it was in that moment when that person asked, I saw myself old, so I knew I was going to have a long life. And when I say old [that] would mean that I had experienced life. I had long salt and pepper, wavy hair that had a silver tone to it. I saw myself in the casket. Right before that, God had shown me an image of kids. I was on a porch, rocking back and forth, and my partner was behind me at the screen door looking above me. And there were children, about three or five children running around. There was a fence. It was green and I saw nothing else but a mountain or something in front of us. I was like, "Wow, it's so vivid and so clear." And it was in that moment back in [2010 or 2011] that made me [know] "I need to start my journey to myself."

[...] There was a time that I could distinctly remember at my first address known to self, where I can vividly remember imagery. I was living at 118 Covert Street between Evergreen and Central, right across the street from a park, right? So detailed. I was in the kitchen, and I was looking out the window where I could see my grandmother's garden. She had tomatoes and all this stuff. As I was looking, I just heard a voice. I could hear the voice communicating to me, but it was something for my mom. [...] "Mom, do you know God is trying to really get your attention right now?" And it was like, "Mom, you don't hear God calling you? You don't hear God talking?" I didn't understand what was so powerful at that moment for my mother, but it did something. I could feel something because there was a sense of release that happened in that moment for her, where I could hear her in a bathroom crying or releasing. I didn't understand. The "aha moment" was that there was something bigger than me that can communicate to me even when I'm not expecting it. However, the consciousness of me from a young age got worried and nervous. I would watch my mother, as it seemed like she was talking to herself or someone. And it made me feel afraid because I'm like, "If my mom's not talking to me, who is she talking to?" There was a part of me that actually resented it. I shared that because there was a moment when I wanted my mother to be present, and I found that she was not. So, I had prayed. I said, "God, I don't want to dream like my mom. Makes her too tired. Makes her unavailable. So don't make me as tired as that. Don't make me have to dream." Not understanding that God gives us gifts in many different ways.

Alexis: I was born and raised in Harlem, in New York City. On my mother's side, I'm from the Caribbean. We're from Haiti and The Bahamas and Barbados and Cuba (KOO-bah). That's how my grandfather would say "Cuba." He would never say Cuba (KYOO-buh); he'd say Cuba (KOO-bah). And on my father's side, we're from North Carolina, a little town called Ahoskie, North Carolina. When I grew up, I understood myself as black. As I've gotten older and more mature and thought about it, I understand myself as Afro-Caribbean.

That was the heyday (chuckles)! When Harlem was a ghetto, that was the heyday! I don't know what it is right now. But when it was the ghetto, when only *we* lived there ... that was the heyday. Whooo, baby! [...] Harlem definitely paired my racialized identity to a spiritual one. There's no way you could live in Harlem or be raised in Harlem, particularly in those years, and not know that the fact of being alive is sown to, wedded to your blackness. There's just no way to get around it. There's no thinking that there's "this" and then there's "spirituality," you know what I'm saying? It's a wedded reality.

I grew up until I was a teenager in the Baptist church. I was deeply embedded in it, because of my grandmother who taught Sunday school. She was also in charge of the children's programs every holiday. Because I was adored by her, it was my job to recite.

My grandmother taught me to read the Bible as poetry. It doesn't get more black and more spiritual than that! When you come out of the Black Church tradition, you also come out as a poet whose sense of herself is situated in the black poetic, in the black spiritual, in the black Baptists.

Now, today, I don't feel the need to be in a Baptist church, but I have gone to them. No sooner than I'm there, all of those things come back. They resurface. The songs, the ... I can still remember the way my grandmother walked down the aisle. My grandmother was a member of the Usher Board and certain Sundays, she'd wear all white everything. I can still remember. My grandmother was about that high (gestures a short stature and laughs). I'm not much taller than she was. But, when she walked, she was like six feet tall. You could see my grandmother coming from six blocks away and know that was her. Harlem definitely put those things together for me as [a black person] and raised Baptist. That is the basis for thinking about any kind of queerness and any kind of spirituality.

storäe: I feel like I've been on a journey with spirituality. I grew up in a Christian household—extremely conservative, Presbyterian household. My grandmother was a Presbyterian minister for probably over twenty years up until her eighties. And even then, she still practiced as a Spiritual Counselor for others. For a very long time in my life, I thought that spirituality was denoted simply by what religious affiliation you had.

It wasn't until college that I started to reclaim spirituality for myself. In undergrad, I realized that I felt a sense of Spirit that I hadn't felt before when I was just restricted to religious actions: going to church, taking communion, doing the prayers. I remember being five and being obsessed with memorizing all the books in the Bible—backwards and forwards, literally—and having people clap for me.

As a young adult, I began to explore what these different sensations in my body meant, which I came to know as Spirit ... as Universe speaking. And, also, recalling the parts of me that had experienced Spirit as a younger person, where I would have dreams of my ancestors and they would talk to me and tell me things and show me things. And I thought it was just a normal thing that everybody had happen to them. But when I started talking to other people, they were like, "That's really unique."

A Practice in Connecting

Jé: If I was to play with the teaching that says, "There is no sorrow heaven cannot heal," I'd change it up and say that "There is no sorrow knowledge cannot heal." [...] Spirituality has been a great framing of knowledge, and those knowledges and those wisdoms being very rooted in the ideas found in *Nsaka Sunsum* that resonates with me as a voice of conscience, a voice of experience. [... I know] these elements to be like voices of ancestors. One is, for me, this voice of reason. Then, there's now the voice of imagination because both of them need to exist. When we do our work and when we lean into that wisdom, that knowledge, it serves us collectively. So, if I go to a psychologist or a therapist, I'm gonna unpack voices of ancestors that help me outline and clarify what my trauma is or possibly generational curses or what so have you, or aspects of my character that I have yet to unlock. I value that. I find that the voice of consciousness ... it's this deep, resonating factor in which I need to know myself. That's what spirituality has become for me, the multilayered voices.

I think "voices" is the best way to distinctly define spirituality because it deals with frequency. And as one who loves the power of homiletics, I like to see the voice take on a formation, or, if you will, if I use a choral word, "decorum." That decorum offers the voice a distinct refinement in articulation. And that Spirit is constantly about refining and articulating and speaking or singing or vocalizing itself so that one is edified, one is transformed, one is moved, one is touched. That's what spirit and spirituality have done for me through those voices within an expanded context of the *Nsaka Sunsum*.

Natasha: Spirituality is the process of connecting to God, self, and others. The way we connect with a higher power, how we connect to ourselves, how we collectively [connect], and how we relate to one another in community.

Alexis: I think of my spirituality as a daily practice of being alive and living in relation to other living realities: other human beings, other animals, plants. Although I grew up, until I was a teenager, in the Baptist Church, I moved away from the Baptist Church when I had a sense that the church that I was going to (which was my grandmother's church) was not embracing me as a queer person or as a young woman who liked other women—which is how I understood it at that time.

For me, the practices of spirituality don't have to do with religion. They have to do with an intellectual understanding ... an evolving intellectual understanding of life, what it means to be alive, and to be grateful for life. Every morning when I wake up, the first thing I say is, "Thank you," because I'm thankful for that breath. I could wake up and not be woke up! You know what I'm saying? I could wake up and, "Oh shit, I'm dead!", which would not be in my plans when I wake up. I'm thankful that I have [woken up], and that's usually my first thought. If I don't remember it, I'm like, "Oh, what?! It's noon, and you still haven't said your gratitude?!" For me, that constitutes a sense of the spiritual, of living in relation and also gratitude, in terms of understanding this thing that we call life, which is basically breath.

When I was younger, [books and other spiritual tools and technologies] were critical to shaping me. I think now, thirty, forty, or fifty years later, I don't so much require those tools to get to that place [of spiritual recognition, of inhabiting spirituality]. What I require is a life of beauty to get there now. [My spouse and I] live in a way that constitutes what we understand to be the beautiful and to be blackness centered in beauty. So, that could be anything from my gratitude in the morning, [to] playing Nina Simone, to burning the incense, to rearranging the flowers, to making an altar somewhere.

Koach: My understanding of spirituality is deeply embedded in my body. I don't understand spirituality without trying to understand my body. My spirit and my body are connected; without one or the other I couldn't exist. I spend a lot of time trying to make the connection real for myself. Oftentimes, I feel like there're moments where I feel like, "Oh, I'm in a spiritual place," but I can't locate myself in my body. And then I'm like, "Oh, maybe this is not the way I want to do this." But there're other times where I'm in my body and I can't locate my spirit. I feel like whenever there's a disconnect, that's when I feel the least confident in myself and my understanding of the world. And when I feel those two being connected, then that's my most, um, safe ... I don't like the ... I don't use the word safety often, but I feel safe, you know, when that connection is there.

This is where I rely on sometimes the external and/or the internal messages that I get. Sometimes it's real clear; somebody will say, "Hey, Koach, you don't seem like things are well for you." Or "It doesn't seem like you're your regular self." That's a reminder. I'm just trying to be aware of the messages I get from other people, but also there's an internal awareness that sometimes can come. It may be like the whisper of my grandma or God/*Shekhinah*/*HaShem*, whatever the name will be for Them at the moment, but They are calling toward me and like, "Hey, hello ... Uh, you all right?" which also feels nice, you know?

storäe: [Spirituality is] really just intuitive. [...] It's more of a felt thing where I understand what energies benefit me and what energies don't. Spirit, I find, is typically the energies that feed me, that sustain me.

Nala: I think of the quest. I always think the word "journey" and "quest" ... its being able to walk through and with air and all the elements the God of our understanding provides. What I have learned in my walk is that spirituality could come from air. It can come from wind. It could come from soil and Earth. It can come from sun. It can come from the remnants of life and all that life has. What I find refreshing for me when I look at what spirituality is for me and my queerness, it's fine tuning how God communicates to me and what may be needed for me. What's next or what I'm trying to manifest. It's that whisper at 3:00 a.m., that is disrespectfully waking you up and you really want to go to sleep (No shade!). It is a stranger bumping into you aggressively that invokes emotions in you, and then you get to look at why are you upset about this. What are you missing? Why does it have you in a reaction? It's all of those conscious moments that have you to really just think. It has *me* to think, I should say.

And so, spirituality has been trying. It is really trying. And when I say trying, I mean it can be challenging when you think one way and then everything around you allows you to shift and then you have to decipher if it's God, if it's circumstances, if it's life, or it's just a thing that is a thing. But also understanding that there is no coincidence. Spirituality can be quite complex for me and confusing because sometimes [I'm like,] "Give it to me plain, God. Give it to me plain. Don't give me all these metaphors and ... just give it to me straight." I also think about spirituality as the product of breath for me. Oftentimes I'm like, "Give me a miracle!" I have found that sometimes a miracle is just a breath of life (takes deep breath). It is where I go back to my center.

[...] What I've learned is that when I'm emotional or irrational, sometimes I can't go to Spirit by myself. Sometimes I need to go to a *babalao* or an *iya* to get a *Diloggún* reading, or divination, to know what is the next step for me to go. The interfaith of myself is I am willing to hear God and ancestors in many different languages that are outside what I know.

Olivia: I am a listener and observer, and I frequently use the tools of astrology, tarot, and Afro-Indigenous spirituality to do that. I would frame spirituality as constant self-reflection, listening to yourself, and to the world around you. But then I also, in another way, think spirituality is just inherently what we're all doing. It's just the inherent being human in this world. In a way, I can make anything spiritual. Yeah, every coincidence, every noncoincidence, everything that happens in my life, I can connect to a meaning, a spiritual meaning. I think spirituality is just something that we all do. Some do [it] better than others. I think one way to actively do it is to just listen to yourself and the world around you. [...] Constantly positioning yourself in this world with the least amount of harm to yourself and others.

Michael: "As above, so below." I hear that as my mantra in my life. That there's good and there's bad. And everybody's trying to reach the Light, but what is "the Light"? In metaphysics, we deal with vibrations. As you elevate your vibrations, you attract certain types of energy to you. You can also repel different energies away from you. That's how I live my life. I strongly believe that we are an Energy Force. We are here to learn the lessons we hadn't learned before. And I think as an Energy (or a spirit or whatever you want to call it), we come back time and time again until we learn the lesson, whatever that lesson is. We/I may not even know the lesson. I may have been on Earth a million times already, reincarnated as a different person each time because somewhere along the way I did not learn a lesson. So now I'm relearning a lesson so I can go to the next level of my evolution, wherever that's going to take me. I firmly believe that and in so believing it, we temper. [...] You've seen those copper pots where they have those indentations all over them? That's tempering ... where your concentration is so focused that you spend your life tempering, as if to find the lesson, to find the beat that gives you the rhythm that you feel you need to go through. And that's what I believe.

Through that, with meditation, and trying to get a proper diet (whatever that means), that's where my spirituality has really evolved into. And there is a God in that sense because He is (relative as to what you mean by God, but) an Energy Force that we interpret [as], "As above, so below," which means there's good, there's evil. There's bad, there's good. Not everything is good, and not everything is evil. And with this religion, if you want to call it that, or this practice, I do believe that there is evil. [...] When you become more spiritually bound in your vibrations, you do see the evil side of people, and the good side of people. That's where I have found myself to be. [...] You can walk into a room and you can attract negative energy if your vibration is so low or you can elevate your vibration to such a level that you only attract higher energies. In so doing, you are invisible. You see everyone else, but they don't see you. That's what I'm working on in my life, to be totally invisible, but be present. Because my vibrations are so high, I'm physically there, but you don't see me. But I see you. That's the Third Dimension.

Charly: I am a gatekeeper. I'm a water gatekeeper. I also work with fire shrines. I am very queer because I am multiplicities. I am many different things. I'm many different existences as Charly and I'm aware of that .... So, I'm multiplicities. [...] [Spirituality] is the core of every soul in connection to the multiplicities in the universe: the dimensions that you travel in... the multilayers of experiences ... quantum leaping ... memories that bring you back to stages ... it's all intertwined. [My multiplicity] is Spirit.

Cultivating Access

Koach: Judaism is my main religious practice and spiritual practice. And it involves using what Reb Zalman [Rabbi Zalman Schachter-Shalomi] (of blessed memory) would say, "prayer-phernalia." Like I have a *tallit*, which is a prayer shawl, and I have *tefillin* which I'm hoping to wrap again. That's one of the things in which I know that kind of external and the internal working together and [showing me I am] feeling disconnected. The last time I wrapped *tefillin* was the day before my dad died. I haven't been able to do that spiritual practice for an entire year because my body and soul connection has been disconnected because of this grief, this deep grief that I'm in. But I've leaned toward other things, like toward my music. I drum. I play the banjo a little bit. I'm learning how to play instruments that connect me to the continent of Africa. I pull tarot [cards]. I make amulets. I make prayer beads. Like very almost tactile ... here again, I'm using my body to interact with spiritual activity.

[...] I have always felt like I was both hypervisible and really strangely invisible to most people. People notice me because I'm different. I'm black. I'm trans. I'm Jewish. But then they also ignore the hell out of me. They don't listen to me. Oftentimes, people just bump into me as if I don't exist. It's just really interesting. I feel like growing up in the Midwest, it's also felt that way.

I was there during the Ferguson Movement and was out in the street as an energy worker with my drum, and again I was hypervisible. I had a drum. People knew who I was because of that. And I was also invisible, particularly as a trans person, as a Jewish person, as a spiritual person with other people on the street. For them, spirituality was not a connecting force, particularly in the Movement. And then as I kept being out there, folks started to actually, I think, kind of consider that there was a connection to be made, particularly through their bodies because we used our bodies so much. Our bodies were essentially our instruments against the power structure.

To understand the spiritual nature of that stance of "I will be in my power with my body," I think actually really helped, particularly for queer and trans folks who have been told—we were almost excommunicated from the movement because of our identity as queer people—"Don't be bringing that queer stuff up in here," and blah, blah, blah. And, "This ain't about queer people. This is about black men being shot by police." We had to meet at my house to decide whether or not we were going to keep going. We understood that we were called for a different purpose. It wasn't for us to be on the news. It wasn't for us to be in front of nobody, but that we actually had a spiritual agenda that involved us understanding who we were as people, who we were as a collective, and to know our power, to understand our power. I think that through that experience I really grew, I think, as a spiritualist, as a spiritual leader.

I leaned into ancestor veneration and learned how to call on them for help. I was never taught how to play this drum. I was taught how to play a trombone, which I still have. But the only way I can explain is that with God and the ancestors, they move my hands and I make beats on that drum. And there were times—and people would say this, and I would be like (dismissively) "Mmhmm. Mmhmm."—people would say, "I can hear the drum talk [when you play]. The drum was telling me things." And that's not anything that I can control. But I also know that we have used the drum. Our people understand the rhythm and the music and the cadence of a drum, and they know when it talks to them. And sometimes they said, "I felt that the drum was actually doing that work of pulling us together. And sometimes that drum was there to scatter us about so we could do what we need to do. And sometimes it was a warrior spirit drum." Like, literally, there were times where I would see (I call them young folks. They were younger than me, but I'm also not old) ... I would see these young folks coming toward us and literally, without even knowing it, the cadence and the movement of the drum changed, and their movements changed. It became less chaotic, and they started dancing. There was just something kind of magical about what happened out on the street. And I know that it was not just, "Oh, somebody brought a drum, and they started playing it." I understand that there was ancestral and spiritual connection that I think actually helped us be in our power and in our bodies.

Natasha: I still attend church weekly. I attend an Afrocentric Christian ministry, so I feel like it gives me ... I don't want to say the best of both worlds, but I get to tap into both parts of those sides to myself ... the part that identifies with African spirituality and connecting to my ancestors and the orisa, being able to honor the orisa. I'm not initiated to Ifá or Orisa or anything like that, but I do recognize the role of the ancestors in a very real and present and meaningful way [...] Existential experiences led me to that. I was a little apprehensive about it upon being introduced to it, but you know, when they come and talk to you, you start to listen.

[...] Connecting with the spirits. I still attend church. Meditation. For me, meditation is not about silencing my mind, but about following where my mind goes and seeing why and what the significance of that thought or the train of thought is. I'm also a licensed Reiki Master. I don't do it as often as I would prefer to. But, doing healing circuits or something like that. Or chants and mantras that kind of get the body in check. I'm also an avid stone carrier. I typically carry one or two stones every day.

For me, [engaging with ancestors] started out with having dreams. It was one dream in particular where I just saw a lot of faces and they were all talking. I was scared out of my mind. Like, "*What* is happening? What's going on?!" But in the dream, I saw a familiar face. One of my former professors [was] like, "Tasha, it's okay." After that, I kind of sat with it for a little while, trying to figure out what was going on, what I was experiencing. I went to one of the elders in my community and I said, "Hey, I'm hearing things. I need somebody to help me figure this out." So that's what I did. I sat with an elder who mentored me for, I think, twelve weeks and helped me to figure out how to use my gifts and how to manage and negotiate what that looked like.

I definitely do connect with my own ancestors, first and foremost, in my own familial lineage. At times, because I am open to it, other people's ancestors will try to communicate messages. That has been a new experience in the last couple of years of like, "Oh, hey! Do you know your great grandmother on your father's side?" (chuckles) Like ... how do you segue into *that*?

Alexis: This is an altar that we are just working on now. It's for Erzulie. Sokari, who is my spouse, decided that ... well, we had it outside, but it was really hot. And, the candles all melted, like, "Oh my God, this is not gon' work." We brought the elements inside and then built this structure so that we can begin to grow the altar inside. This is actually just starting.

The construction of altars and altar spaces, the making of art, gratitude, living life in beauty ... those are daily expressions for us. When we say, "Oh, we need to get some flowers," it's because we want flowers. But also because flowers are a part of our lives. Flowers grow and they constitute the Earth's spirituality, so we bring them in so that we can share that.

Erzulie is Haitian, but also Dahomey. Goddess of women. She's also goddess of love and beauty. She likes to smell really well, so we have a lot of oils everywhere around. She's particular to women who identify as lesbians and also businesswomen. There're several kinds of Erzulie. There's Erzulie Freda, which is the one that we follow, whom I just described to you. There's Erzulie Dantó, who is sort of the opposite. And there's Erzulie with the Red Eyes. And Erzulie with the Red Eyes ... it's like, you don't want to ... Yeah. Yeah. You just don't want ... because it's just bad news. You know what I'm saying?

storäe: My spirituality lives in my dreams and my dream world. As an artist, my spirituality lives in my ritual of writing. Often when I write, I don't know where it's coming from. I don't know if it's coming from me or if [the words are] literally being spoken or whispered to me as I type or write. My spirituality kind of encompasses whatever I'm drawn to. I am a very curious person and I like to explore. I always try everything once. My spirituality guides me in those directions where I meet people or go to places or find items and things. I don't know what [the things] mean at the time, but then later on, it manifests itself and shows me what it is.

[...] I think that Spirit can speak through others. I don't think that Spirit always has to manifest itself in just the whispers of my ancestors. I think that sometimes it's when I speak to an elder or a child and they say something profound or something that resonates with me in a very unique way. I understand that Spirit is all those things. It's moving. It's energy that flows from one thing to another. I spoke about my art, but I even think my fashion is a collection of Spirit and what Spirit wants to manifest to me. I have ancestors that were seamstresses and into fashion. I believe that they speak through me, and a lot of the ways I like to be in the world or present myself in the world are through them, too.

Now, I have on a choker, a cast of a finger, a necklace of Isis [Ancient Egyptian goddess of fertility], and a crystal quartz. Most of my jewelry, I tried to get from actual artists who handmake them. This [choker] is by Zana Bayne. She handmakes most of her items. The finger cast is a small Italian jeweler, and [the crystal quartz necklace] was made by a man in Ecuador, in Quito. He braided around it and created an encasement that has lasted [a long time].

But it's right here (pointing near navel). I had him put it at my core because it reflects out all negative energy and harvests my own. Isis was something that I found by a man named Dr. Foots who's from here in New Orleans. [...] I always have three because three is my number of power. I try to wear three necklaces every day. That's my uniform.

[...] When I first started my spiritual practice, it was all about crystals and I had crystals everywhere in the house. Oh, lizard (sees lizard on ground)! Hi, lizard friend. Okay. I'll walk around you. I found some crystals that absorbed my energies in certain ways and grounded me and made me feel whole. And, then I found ritual and spiritual practice in communities when I was in Durham. Going down to the [Eno] River ... I was obsessed with going down to the river. I was collecting water when I went to Zambia to Victoria Falls and collecting sand and doing rituals around that. It's something that always changes. It's never the same ritual. And I think that's because I'm just always open to understanding something new about myself and something new about my spirituality.

Currently, my spiritual practice comes from my art. I see my art as my ritual and my spiritual practice. It's a ritual that is grounding, but nerve-wracking at the same time, because when it comes to my art, I want to make sure I'm able to communicate my own thoughts, my own spiritual thoughts through my artwork in a way that people can access and connect to. In that way, it is not just for me. It's for community.

I feel like ritual, for me ... it's just transformative. It's just always shifting, changing. My spiritual practice is to be open to whatever the Universe provides that day, that moment ... To be open to hear the words of others and not just feel like I have to have everything together myself.

Michael: If you sit at an oceanside or lakeside where there are waves and you meditate on the waves, they will reveal to you, as it flows in and out, your past, your future, and your present. But can you see it? Because the story comes right in front of you with the waves. It reveals to you your present, your past, and your future. But do you recognize it? Do you want to see it? And if you do you see it, can you change it? Do you want to change it? Are you even granted the opportunity to change it?

Meditation is not grounding me in the present because I am in the present, but it elevates me out of [the present] because, for me and I think most people who really meditate, it takes you to a realm of a different kind of reality. That's why when people say when they meditate, they see things, they hear things, or they come back a changed person. That means they can't be in the present because something happens with the Energy Force—I don't want to say the Soul. Some people might say the Soul, because it's more relevant [...] as opposed to just an Energy Force that actually transcends you.

Olivia: I first really looked at my birth chart this past March. It was funny because I looked at my birth chart at the exact moment that a really big transit was happening that would change me completely. For many reasons I could explain astrologically, I've always been the person that just, like, *does me*. I just do me. And I don't think about it. Then, this past year, the Universe was just like, "Okay, pause and slow down. *Why* do you do that?" It wasn't [me] doing something different, but it was just reflecting and listening and observing myself and [asking], "Why *do* I do these things?" Which, again, [the chart] helps you. It's very easy to coast off of doing you, but sometimes there're things that you do that come from a place of trauma or hurt or pain. When I looked at my birth chart and I really studied it for the first time, I was able to see ... I was able to put words to why I do certain things. And I was able to understand the potential of what I *can* do because I see the birth chart as potential energy. It's not like you can look at an astrology chart and know exactly what your life's going to look like, but there's a potential to it. There's a way you can shape and move things. And so, it was just really big for me. It happens in small ways where I'll meet someone and they'll say, "Oh, you do this" or "You do that." And I'll say, "Hmm, I *do* do that." Before, I never thought about what I do. Looking at my own birth chart, I'm the one that's sitting there looking and recognizing the potential that I have for harming others, the potential that I have for success ... for all of these things. That was kind of like observing myself in a way.

Tarot is a way that I help listen to myself. [...] Tarot for me is just checking in with my intuition and listening to myself. A lot of people want tarot to tell them their future or make a decision for them or something. [...] If I want to know something that will happen in the future, a tarot deck is not going to tell me. But in a good reading, the images, the numbers, the words, the art on the card will spark some subconscious part of you that knows what you need to do. I've seen that happen where sometimes I can literally sit there, shuffle my cards, ask a question and be like, "I already know," and then don't even need to do a tarot reading. But occasionally, it is just a tool I use to listen to myself and get a little help when I feel lost.

[...] I don't necessarily think I would say I believe in a God, but I believe in bigger forces influencing us. I put a lot of like weight on Indigenous, ancient practices. And astrology is like one of the oldest things we've ever been doing as humans. [...] Also, it's something where no matter how much I practice it, I will never know it. It's something I can always practice and learn more about.

Charly: [My practice of spirituality] is fragmented. It's multidimensional, multi-faiths, multi-spirits ... "horse of many spirits." It's bloodlines coming to and from, but picking up on other people's spirits coming through, as well.

For me, art is my ritual. But those rituals also come from very spiritual existences. And they kind of show themselves and reveal themselves through work, through art, through trance, through interconnection with people, through sex, through kisses, through sensuality. All of those things come into play with the creation of ritual.

I work in all mediums. Primarily, I was a dancer. Okay, so that was my first love. Coming up, I was a dancer and that's what I thought I was going to be famous for. I thought I was going to be known for dance. In my high school years, I had a very tumultuous kind of experience being queer and being in society with a lot of issues around coming out, homophobia, not being tolerated in school or, you know, those kinds of things that ... not broke me away from dancing but broke me away from everything else that was set as a structure. I actually left school and that swayed my drive with dance. It just kind of started to bleed out into other things. Visual art in general, body art in general became my poetry and my journal.

I do [my art] with myself. That's how I started. I was my first muse. I was taking nude photos, like in my late teens, and I didn't want to just take nude photos. I thought that was kind of boring. So, I just started to paint on myself. I started to adorn myself and my spirit guides started to transform through me. [...] It's just awkward [to explain] because it's an awkward process for me. It takes you out of your comfort zone. It makes you feel like, "Oh, I'm doing something foolish," or "I'm behaving in a way that's not going to be looked at as normal or appropriate." A lot of the spasms and a lot of the things that happen when Spirit is coming through, I feel are awkward, you know? It makes me self-conscious.

Nala: I am an empath, very sensitive. I feel like I often am tapped in. It's almost like if I go in a room and my head starts pounding and my third eye is really heavy, I know that there's a lot of energy moving. I have to decipher if I'm being called to do work or I'm being called to protect my third eye. The instrument, the tool, my body is the vessel. The tool that I have been using is [asking], "What is my body communicating?" It's when the heartbeat stops or pulsates [...] what does that mean? It is in my shortness of my breath. I'm like, "Oh, I'm not breathing. Its stagnation. How do I move this through?" So, for me, the first core thing is the body. And then the sensation that comes with that: sight, hearing, taste, feel, [smell], like all those things, right? And then it's prayer. What I have learned now through the teachings of many others is that prayers are not just prayers. They're words, and words are spells. The intentionality of how I choose to communicate my words has really shifted because before I would just say shit (and I say that with the most respect). Now I'm like, "Oh, let me be careful what I say and how I say it," because I understand words are spells.

[...] I blend and I make my own (Jamaican accent) "calabash." I make my own mixture of spirituality from what is called to me. It's literally around what I hear, the hearing. If God say (Nala speaks in an accent, in and out of both Jamaican Patois and Brooklyn), "'ey, I need you to go make ya'self a spiritual bath. Y'know, this week, it's somethin' dutty in the air, somethin' nasty going on, y'know? Somethin' real vexed goin' on. Go take a shower!" And so, I'm like, "God, what herbs should I do?" So I might go to some lemons. I might go to some sea salt. I may go to some bay leaves to really cleanse myself. Or if I'm really feeling like I need to cut some cords or something, I'll go to coffee. Or Spirit communicates to me. Like when I know my ancestors [are communicating], I'll just get a sniff of coffee. I'm like, "Ooh, one of my ancestors need coffee." Or they're telling me to pay attention. Or they're saying, "Hey, you haven't spent time at your altar. You need to come to the altar and be with us." Maybe it's just a weep and cry ... that is also a tool. Sometimes when I know that I have stopped myself from crying, spending a whole day just weeping—that's also been a tool for me that has worked.

Dance. Dance and music! Yeah. Oh, my goodness! There's something about the rhythm of drums and the sensation when the body is able to connect with energy that's flowing ... the molecules that's in the air ... to make movements and to interpret whatever is need[ing] to be expressed. There's something that feels good for me. I find that when I'm doing West African dance, or I find that when I'm voguing or when I'm doing a good ol' wine or headtop or whatever the case may be (I can't headtop now. That was a whole 'nother life!). But those are tools because I told you when we started, my body is the first vessel; that is the tool. When I have been on my journey of being a vessel, I have irresponsibly become a container for a lot of things. Right now, what I'm learning is (although I'm a vessel) to become a channel, right? Vessel does not mean I have to hold everything ... as an empathic person, to hold it. [I can] just be a channel, so that I can redirect it to where it needs to go. Connecting all those things with dance and movement, [it's] that dance allows me to move that out ... the things that have been holding. Whether it's through kizomba (the intimacy of two people dancing and swaying their hips together), bachata, merengue, all those things allow me to release. The movement. I think there's a thing where people hold so much trauma in their hips. I find liberation when I see women and people twerking, I'm like, "Yes! Get it, sis!" "Get it, cuz!" "Get it, sib!" "Get it, auntie!" Like, really *get it*, because there's something spiritually that happens with the hips [...] you're breaking something up. For me, that is also a tool of releasing.

Queering Belief

Jé: In 2008, after my diagnosis with HIV, I remember being very angry with God. Not enough that I didn't believe in God, but just angry. I remembered people saying to me, "Trust God." "Trust God." "Trust God." "Trust God." And I said, "I can't trust You. I'm not gon' trust You. That's not what I need. I don't even need You to love me because You clearly can't do that either." And that was tough. I remember having that conversation sitting in my car, my little red Saturn Vue, and I had my two dogs with me. I said, "I can't trust You. And I don't need You to love me. What I need is simply for You to like me." It was the moment where I actually realized I was asking God not to affirm me, but just respect me. Respect me. Because I don't know this other God that everybody is talking about. And I didn't want to know that Person. I didn't want to know a God like that. I wanted to know a God that actually was just like, "You really don't do anything I want you to do, but hey, I like you!"

As someone who does engage humanism and atheist communities, I love to think of the moments that I bring God into question; I like to say that I am a friend of God's. I'm probably the closest friend. Because when I don't see results with my friend, I could place them into question. I could call her out. I could say to them, "Mmm, now you said this, but you did another, and that don't make no sense." Everybody wants to be in God's favor. I'm just trying to be a friend that can call You out, and You still gon' love me because I called You out. But we don't want that relationship. I like to think of my relationship, even in my nontheistic approaches, to be the closest thing to what God is probably doing with me as a friend: testing me and refining me to ensure that I'm fashioned for the life and the time that I live in. You ain't gon' call me into purpose, and I don't [likewise] call You into purpose.

Nala: My father passed away. I've learned ... I hate to say it this way ... I learned unconditional love in reverse. The absence of him ... not being in my life made me learn what I did not want to become. It also made me expand my capacity to cultivate a lot of new traditions ... of what that meant with my feminine body to be a relationship to men and masculine energy in all the ways that it shows up. And understanding that men or beings can hold multiple energies. It was in the absence of him that I learned to be who I am and release resentment for him not being there. Really choosing understanding. He could not give what he could not give. The impact hurts, completely.

When he passed in 2019, I knew a year later, in 2020, I wanted to do something to release. And I called some Ifá practitioners, and we went to the water. We did a ceremony around so many people in

July. I saw my dad come down, while my eyes were closed. It wasn't the conversation we had. He was just so like nothing was wrong. He was just laughing. He was like, "(sucks teeth) You know how I am." Like, true Leo shit. Just laughing in this vision. He was like, "Yeah, you all right. You're going to be fine. You okay." Just real Leo. Like real just, "You good" and laughing. "I'm always around. Even though I'm not there, I'm always around. And I am protecting in the ways that I can now." I feel like I've gained in my relationship with spirituality and the unseen, to know that there are angels and entities who are covering me when I cannot see the next step, the next road. The moment was accepting how ancestors are present. Always talking, always giving messages.

My father will come in my partner's dreams. Remember, I prayed to not dream. God didn't say He was going to put me in a relationship with people who don't dream. You understand what I mean? It's been weird and very interesting because in 2020 to now, I've gone through three relationships. And the number three is very important for me. I don't know why. Things happen to me in threes. I noticed that when I'm not listening, he would go into someone else's dream, Like, "Hey, can you tell her 806 is her number? That's the number. So, when she sees that, know that I'm here trying to give her a message." His number is 806. I didn't know that. Things like that, I know it's … it's so complex to share, but I know it's me! It's mine! It belongs to me.

Alexis: I now know that we're all made of stardust, and I found that out when I was doing research for my last book, *Yabo*. The notion that we're all made of cosmic material was quite striking to me. If a planet is simply an independent body orbiting in time and space, then what's to say that humans are not planets, as well? Some planets […] can support life, such as Earth. For all we know, or, up until what we know now, there are other planets that cannot. I am a planet that can support living. Do you know what I mean? And I can support life. My body can support life and I'm thankful for that. Let me just knock on wood (knocks on table). I'm thankful.

When I was in my fifties, maybe even when I was in my sixties, I was kind of trying to look at what it means to be a human being and how that is kind of tethered to Earth in some ways. But now that I'm in my seventies, I think that being a human being is not tethering to Earth. I think Earth-ness is only one orbit that we're in. It's only one.

What if we all understood that we were stars and planets? What if we all kind of *got* that? How would we then treat each other? How would we then respect each other? How would we then give each other the room to revolve and rotate, all at once. Would we have a different relationship to each other if we understood life is more cosmic than we do? We tend to want to ground life. Like, "You live here (points on table). You live only here. You live in this square." But actually, you live on the whole table because you're living in that square. You know what I'm saying?

Michael: You know "The Wiz" song, "Believe in Yourself"? You can have the ruby slippers, [but] I can't make you hit those slippers together to take you back to a world you want to be [in]. No matter how much I believe in you, how much do you believe in yourself that you can take yourself back to Kansas if that's where you want to go? And therein lies the Michael that you're now looking at: I can click my heels and take me back to where I want to go. I'm not asking God or some other religion that people are familiar with to say, "Get me back to where I want to be. Help me ... show me how to get there." I say, "I know how to get there within myself. Now, let me take that journey, however long it may take." No matter what happens along the way, I think I can find my path through my tempering, through my exercise "as above so below" and everything in between.

So, God is at the top—whatever the God is—of the Energy Force, the Life Force. But all of us are searching for the same thing. The interesting thing about a pyramid is we know [we all] can't fit at the top. We know as we climb up, some people have to climb down or be knocked down. What is the purpose of that? And purpose is the Light [...] The Energy is within you. You are the God. You are the Light. You are It! It's not someone saying, "I'm imposing It upon you." You are *It*. Now, recognize your Energy Force. Recognize your ability to be [...] whatever it is you want to be. It's not outside of you. It's inside of you.

And I think because it's been inside of me ... Where you look at material things and successful things, if you judge life in that way, I've done pretty good. But I always say I'm lucky. And people say, "You're blessed." And I always go back to them I say, "How am I blessed? I'm just lucky." I say, "Because when you say I'm blessed, that means the other person who doesn't do this is not blessed?" Think about it. I'm not blessed more than you are. We're the same. I just have a different Energy Force than you do. That's why I say I'm lucky. Because if I'm blessed, that means I got this because I'm blessed. Alright, so people don't have this, they ain't blessed? Can't be. Not what I believe. But that's what religion tells us right? Where does the "I'm blessed" come from?

Koach: I've really tried my best to explore all of who I am. That's also led me to really understand myself as a trans person and as somebody who doesn't need to pick a gender unless I'm *made* to pick a gender, and to understand the spirituality of the fluidity of gender and its connection to spirit. [...] I think one of the things that it helps me [to do is] not try to choose a side, as it were. I have an understanding of the multiplicity of humanity and divinity. It doesn't need to be one thing. God can be "It" or "They" or "He" or "She" and all of the above. I've actually gotten into calling God, "It." It's really helped me in my process, not needing a pronoun for God. I feel like it gives me permission ... especially in many religious and spiritual settings, things are so gendered. It's like, "The girls and the women do *this*. The boys and the men do *this*." Is that true? Does it have to be that way? Is that what God desired of us? Or are we able to figure out what part of the spectrum of spiritual technolog[ies] we are resonant with? And then we do that. Also, that might change from moment to moment or from season to season, and we get a chance to explore. In Jewish tradition, the women usually light the candles. The men say the blessings over the meal or blah, blah, blah. But the women can't do ... ? (Exasperated pause) We get to do whatever we want.

[...] I was talking to one of my teachers, Rabbi Toba Spitzer, who just wrote a really fantastic book about metaphors for God, and particularly in Jewish tradition. I was like, "Let's talk about pronouns." We talked about God is rock and God is fire and God is water, which all really resonated with me, and all are in the *Tanakh*. If God is a rock, then God is "It," right? Because a rock isn't gendered. [...] And she says she long ago started calling God "It" or referring to God as "It." [...] I was just with her a couple of weeks ago, but I could message her like, did you get that from *The Color Purple*?

Natasha: As far as Christianity goes, by and large, same-sex relationships are frowned upon. You know ... abomination, going to hell, all that stuff. I don't take on those aspects of the tradition. But there are components of it that I find are helpful for me ... fruitful. I don't want to say pick and choose, but it's really [that] you got to find what fits. You've got to try things on. It might not be the right cut. It might not be the right size. But I like the fabric. Trial and error.

Jé: What the Spirit does with you is very different than how It moves me. How maybe the Spirit whispers in your ... look, the Holy Ghost is polyamorous. It can whisper in your ear and say something very different because It knows what's going to trigger me and knows what's going to trigger you, all right? And if It's going to turn you on, let It turn you on in the way that the Holy Spirit needs to move you, not me. The Holy Spirit is polyamorous.

Journeying Toward and Away/Redefining

Nala: I grew up in a Caribbean family [where] church and God were very important, and from what I understood was Christian. I went to an Episcopal church. I grew up in the Episcopal Church for most of my life, right up until about, I feel like, middle school. And then because of my relationship with matriarchs in my life (my mother wasn't the one to force me to go to church) ... it was my grandmother who would say, "Come on, we're going to church." For me, I just think about church being the fellowship.

I'm choosing to be a Minister in Training in a nondenominational church under Rivers of Living Water, which is under TFAM (The Fellowship of Affirming Ministries) Global [with] Bishop Yvette Flunder. I've chosen that path. What feels comfortable, safe, and the language that allows me to understand how God shows up is saying "interfaith," or choosing the word "spirituality" and using all those forms of spirituality. Because for me, what I have learned is that religion is like a love language. I think all of us have a God of our understanding and the God within us. How we choose to communicate with that God is through the forms of religion, which is the language. So, looking at Allah, Buddha, or looking at orisas, deities ... for me, what's important is (hand gestures in a descending order), it's God, deities, ancestors, myself. That's how I look at it. That's how my crown works, how my head works. I look at God being that omnipresence, the God who is the creator of all things. Looking at the deities, the ones who've come. And then, our ancestors and me. So that's where I'm at right now, my understanding ... and still learning and carving it out.

[...] I think of God and I think about water and I think about my mom and all those, because water is the first way we're entered into this world. Water is what helps us cleanse. Most of our body is of water. I think about all of that. When I think about my mother and her capacity to fill my cup as a kid, to nurture me, to give me wisdom, to give me tools ... when I think of God and I think about spirituality, I have to go back to my mom. I think of my mothers and my grandmother and my aunts. The many women in my family.

Michael: When you read the Bible (which I did) and study different religions (which I had), I found it so difficult that we've been so manipulated in our society that, on the one hand, Christianity teaches love and greatness. But when you look at the organized religions of the world, there's a lot of hatred. It's such a contradiction as to what we are. I concluded that for me, religion is control.

Organized religion is a controlling force that controls society. And then you have to ask yourself, "Who benefits from that?" I concluded, it is the establishment [...] As a black person, I personally feel that religion has been the downfall of black Americans because the way that it was imposed upon us, and the writing of the rules, and making us more subservient in our attitude, and more importantly, telling us about the hereafter: "You're suffering now but there is, when you die, milk and honey and sweetness. But bear the burden now." I grew up with all the people telling you [...] as they say, "You must be at peace when you die." Why am I at peace when I die? Dammit, I'm just as mad as I was when I was alive. But it's part of the tradition.

In metaphysics, or this whole energy thing, you can have a great life *now* ... or bad life now. It's what you manifest and how your vibrations actually vibrate. As a gay man in America, those organized religions were not for me anyway. I was not accepted in them. I didn't want to be accepted into them. I wasn't looking for anything else. I believe in self. Part of metaphysics is the self-determination, the ability to do what you can do because you are the God Force. You are the Energy Force. You are everything. And you have to manifest that. You do not have to be accepted either way—for other people to accept you either way—because you are grounded in your own being and your own self. I'm not looking for approval from the outside. I get my approval from myself because I am part of the Energy Force of Nature or God or whatever the energy you may want to consider it to be. That's where I found myself over the years and it's worked for me.

Jé: The elders would say, "Come hell or high water." Come on! Right? That's what they would say. That would be those who understood how to make it *through*. They already understood, "Come hell or high water, we gon' be alright. We gon' hold together." There are those who were sanctified who would say, "I've come this far by faith," and I've extended that to be … (This is why I have to say I'm *culturally* Christian or *culturally* Pentecostal, because to claim it as a religion or faith of mine could be seen as sacrilegious. Jesus is not really someone I have beef with. If someone was to look at me and be like, "Oh, well, you're humanist, so you don't believe in Jesus?" No, no, no, it's not that. It's just I can't attach myself to a faith that most folks wouldn't even recognize me in.) I'm okay with saying "I've come this far by faith," knowing that I culturally came through the church. I'm culturally church. I'm culturally Pentecostal, but I don't go to a church. If I did attend one, I don't find the nourishment that I need in them. And I have not always been around folk who walk in—whether a ministerial formation or spiritual formation or theological formation—what has left me feeling in some way revived. In the time that we live in, I have accepted the fact that there is no place and possibly will not be one [for me]. As the old song would say, "Take me back to the hour from where I first believed." Well, when I go to that place, it is nothing recognizable to me in this time. And so, I got here because I've been lonely.

I've got here because the faith that I knew would no longer exist in the way that I knew it. I had to turn my faith into freedom. Once you get this far by faith, [then] what do you do with it?

[…] I got all the foundational stuff that I felt was necessary. I'm currently getting back into practicing Sikhism. That's very strange for some folks […] I think if I look at myself and I look at my journey—beyond struggle or aside from struggle (because I could talk about loneliness, depression, suicide, all the other parts of my life)—I've gotten this way because I've decided to be happy, for myself. And to be happy, for myself, was a lot harder than loving God.

Koach: I used to watch my grandfather. I was just fascinated with him and how he moved energy, both at church and in our family because our family was kind of like another church. There're a lot of people there. "They" had eight kids and "they" had a lot of kids so when we would get together for a reunion, we wouldn't have to go nowhere. We could just be in a hotel and have service together. I would just sit there and I would watch him. I would watch the way he moved his body, the way energy swept through the room, the way he knew what to say at a particular time, the way he would start a song. I watched how he moved energy. I didn't call it that back then, but I understood it when I was in Ferguson. I understood exactly what he was doing because I was channeling Reverend Jesse L. Peterson to be able to, like, "What are the words to say? Should I not say any words?" Because oftentimes he would say, "Don't talk over the Spirit." I learned to understand when the Spirit is here, so I don't talk over It. Or we allowed the drums to just do what they needed to do.

Alexis: I have been to queer churches and I recently went to a major revival in Durham, North Carolina, that was hosted by an amazing queer couple. And that was serious church ... serious church. My relationship with Christianity is, as I said, grounded in my grandmother's spiritual practice of religious practices. At the same time, I don't adhere to any religious institution that frames how you're going to live in certain ways. It's not just Christianity. It's Muslim religion. It's Judaism. It's anything that's codifying in ways that mean that people don't have the right to think for themselves. And wasn't it Karl Marx who said, "Religion is the [opium] of the people," something like that. It's dope. You know, it's like not *our* dope [as in, cool]. It's dope [drugs].

I'm not antagonistic because I think people believe what they want to believe, but I also want to believe what I want to believe. Those things should be able to coexist. I should be able to take from African spiritual practices what I need or what I understand my ancestors had available to them and remake those, reimagine those so that they work for me. My spouse is a practicing *Vodouisant,* so Vodou is her spiritual base and that's fine. She doesn't require of me to be that, and I don't require of her to practice a more syncretic kind of spiritual knowledge that I have.

[...] I used to have a much closer relationship with tarot than I do currently, but there's something that's calling me to integrate this knowledge with the other kinds of syncretic practices that I do now.

storäe: I started thinking about plant-based food as my medicine. I started cooking and then worrying about what else around me is toxic. All of these brought queries of like, "Oh my gosh, we live on Earth. She's alive, and I haven't paid any attention to her!"

When I went to Union [Theological Seminary], I took a class in eco-theology. [...] We had a teacher, Jea Sophia Oh, who was determined to get all of us to write [a proposal] and to turn it into [the American Academy of Religion]. I wrote about listening to Mother Earth and listening to black women because I saw black women as connected to Mother Earth. We get treated just like her. And we are also healers. We possess a lot of those healing qualities innately. It led me down this trail of seeking out other healers. Immediately, my mind went to Indigenous Peoples, and I started working with the Center for Earth Ethics. There, I had the opportunity to travel to Native American territories in South Dakota and in New Mexico.

I went to my first drum circles. I went to my first sweat lodge. I just did so many different things that exposed me. I got a chance, when I was in New Mexico, to actually speak and be with Native American elders for a whole ten days. Being with them and speaking with them and talking about things that reminded me of blackness in some ways. Like, one elder was talking about how they run on "Native American time"—when the Spirit's done movin' that's when you know you need to leave, but you stayed until the Spirit's done. Or, you know, time is different for them in very similar ways to how I think black time is different, "CP time" is different. Those experiences really exposed me to a lot of different things about spirituality, about Mother Earth, how we need to care for her, about things that are innately Indigenous to me. Practices that I was doing at home ... I didn't know where they came from, but they were also practices that our Indigenous elders did.

Finding spaces of connectivity, I truly believe, led me down this road of being open because all of those experiences happened the more I became open, the more I expanded myself. I know that if I had decided, "Nope, my family's Presbyterian. That's how I'm going to be. I'm going to stick to it," I would have never been exposed to all of that because we demonize it. Christians demonize a lot of that. But I had a different calling.

I thought I was going to Union to become a minister and I realized nope. I'm still a minister in some aspects. If you want to talk about ministry as a healer, it's through my art. And maybe it was, too, through me being an educator for all those years because I also played a lot of different roles. I was an art therapist. And so, I've always been seeking how to heal others and heal myself in the process. I'm just excited to see where it takes me. Now, it's taking me to film.

Olivia: [Maybe three years ago] I got deep into activism and social justice work. Then, I got burnt out of that because I noticed that there's a lot of fighting. There's a lot of interpersonal drama. I was observing how all these people are not listening to each other. They're talking over each other. They're fighting with each other while they're trying to fight this bigger thing. I just had a moment. I feel like, just from looking at these other people, I'm going to work on myself first and then get back to this because how are we going to do this—come together in relationship and resistance—if we don't even work on ourselves or know how to just listen to somebody? Active listening.

That's when I started looking for something, some type of spirituality. I went to a website and looked at the list of all the world religions they had to see what called me and none of them really called me. The only thing that was close was humanism. But, I felt it lacks spirituality a little. [...] My mom was having a conversation with her friend about New Orleans, and she was saying she doesn't like New Orleans because she doesn't like the energy from all the Voodoo. And I was in my head like, "Is it the Voodoo or is it all the racism What do *you* know about Voodoo?" And then I said, "What do *I* know about Voodoo?" I got online and I just got on Wikipedia and started looking up Voodoo and found out there was Haitian Vodou and New Orleans Voodoo. And then I got into Ifá and I saw the word "priestess." I didn't know what it meant, but that voice in the back of my head said, "I want to be a priestess." [...] That was my problem with Christianity or Western Christianity. I couldn't reconcile the fact that we became Christians as we became slaves. So yeah, I guess I put a lot of weight [on the idea of being a priestess]. I was thinking, I'm not going to just (and I was reading, you don't want to just) jump in. I didn't start calling on anyone or even reading about it. I was just sort of like, "If it's going to happen, it's going to happen." And this past year, I'm sitting in New York in front of an Ifá priestess and my reading says that I need to be initiated. Since then, my whole life has changed. My reading was about needing to live a spiritual life. At the time, I felt, "I don't know what that means, but let's do it." I've been listening since then [...] Yeah. Listening and waiting [...] listening for, I guess, just guidance. Trying to figure out what I'm here for.

Blackness and Queerness

Alexis: At the center of being black in this culture and being queer in this culture is difference. Blackness and queerness to me mesh in that way because both require one to know that one is different, one is not normative. And, who wants to be normative, right? Even the people who are normative don't really want that either. The critical idea here for me, the critical aesthetic, is difference, of really coming to terms with difference.

When you look in nature, difference abounds. It's just that humans have tried to determine that difference cannot coexist with other kinds of difference. If you look at whiteness, whiteness is different, too. But, because they've had the ball for so long, they've determined that whiteness is normative and everything else, particularly blackness, is in some ways inferior or not normative or different in a way that means that it has to be oppressed.

For me, blackness and queerness constitute dual ways of looking at difference. And that this should be okay. I mean, we should be able to, as human beings, embrace difference, but we have been living for however long humans have been around in ways that mean difference has been negotiated out of humanness.

storäe: I really do pull from rituals or songs or dances that I know are blackity-black. That's very important to me. My blackness is something I know I can never separate myself from even if I tried, because it's so embedded in me. My queerness has always been a part of me, too. I just didn't have a name for it. Thinking about the things that I used to wear or the things I used to do that were probably pretty fucking queer, but I didn't have a word for. I embrace that, as well. It's everything that I am. I say queerness in a way of being different from normative values, aesthetic, and now even in my lifestyle. Being a black queer woman in a [polyamorous] family, it definitely has an impact on the way that I live in the world and the way that I do ritual and the way that I think about spirituality.

Blackness and queerness, I think, are highly dangerous. We're living dangerously in a lot of ways. [Queerness is] less dangerous [here] than it would be other places in the world, and I'm grateful for that. I'm grateful to be able to live my truth, off-center, in the margins, in the public via social media, in the public via walking around New Orleans right now. And again, it's dangerous. It's nerve-racking because you don't know how people are going to respond to your queer, black self. But it's worth the risk.

Jé: You know the saints would say that "the Holy Ghost don't act unseemly" [...] as if the Spirit was regulated in some kind of way. [...] I agree with my dear brother, Dr. Tobias Wilson, when he says that he has come to the conclusion that "the spirit of homosexuality" and the Holy Ghost are one and the same. Beautiful quote. And I did play with that a bit one day, creating a [performance] piece exploring queer liberation as the Holy Spirit, turning on the [Instagram] filter where there are flames all around my body and I am lingering in the air, moving around sensually. And I think the reason why I bring this up is because in my practice and as a [black and queer] person it's that [my blackness and queerness] are not separate, they're not different. What they are most of all is the "interplay of things."

They are the interplay of things that allow for me to experience a full pour-in, a pour-in that is not just rooted in one cup, but, almost like, if you go to a banquet and you see the stacks of glasses. As soon as you pour one, that cup runneth over into the other cup and into the other cup and into the other cup. And it's so fascinating because all of the organizations and all of the things ... everything that I do is filled with layers of fulfillment. Even when I question, it's fulfilling. I am not interested in prophetic statements as much as I'm interested in prophetic questions. [...] Somebody asked me this recently, "Do you think of yourself as a prophet?" I said "Frankly, yes. I just don't have to have a closed ending." The question is open-ended for you to actualize your own agency and to fulfill the prophecy that you need within yourself. My job is to always keep the questions coming, to be markers to the journey. That has been what queerness has meant for me. That has been what it means to be black: new markers. That's what is meant to be polyamorous: new markers. What new markers are on the horizon? Yeah, I think every aspect of my queerness, my blackness, my poly-ness, my artistry, my humanism ... I am looking to these hills and realizing that every time they look like hills (one would suggest that "I look to the hills from which cometh my help") ... Now I'm realizing that I'm a help to those hills because I help climb them and make sure that they are never too tall to climb. Being queer is a call.

Michael: I know I stand on the shoulders of other Souls who have come before me [...] that Energy. Like, these chairs, this furniture, this house [was built in] 1868. A lot of people probably died in this house; I don't know. But think about it. It's not like it was built yesterday. I stand on all these Energy Forces, and I stand when a father and a mother or a child is saying, "I'm going to maybe be whipped today," or be separated from the family ... or the Civil Rights Movement when those men and women would leave home and say goodbye to their loved ones because they didn't know if they were going to come back. Read their profiles and hear their stories. They always said—and I tear up when I think about it—"I may not come back, but I'm doing this for the people who are coming after me." Not everybody does that. The movement could have been much larger. It was a small movement when you look at the population. Some of those people had a different kind of Energy Force. That *something* forced them to say, "I'm prepared to die so that people coming after me may live." Not everybody said that. Not everybody marched. Very few people really marched. So, what does that tell you about that Energy Force?

As a gay man or a queer person in America, what do you think about—and I get angry with closeted people about this, and maybe I shouldn't—but I think about after the Second World War, when they started cracking down on gays (prior to that, gays were acceptable in society and all that, but that's a different subject matter). But I think about all those people that got their head knocked in. Queer boys and girls didn't have to be queer [...] openly. They didn't have to march and fight openly, but they did. But not all of us did, because a lot of them were closeted [...] hiding, whatever it is. What was that Energy Force that brought this group together? Knowing "I'm losing my job, my life," whatever, "my livelihood ... " Whatever it is. "But I believe." They may not have even been conscious of—and this is the whole thing about metaphysics, the consciousness, the energies, the vibrations were connecting—And they were saying, "I will follow you. You will follow me. We will do this! It's only 10 of us, there's 1000 of [them], but it only took ten to make the movement." And many of them died. But they were bringing the Energy Forces from long time past—Spirit, God, Souls, whatever ... I don't think that way, but that Energy Force that was in them—And they said, "I'm going to do it."

And, coming back to the present, I have to honor that because somebody died for me to stand tall. Somebody died for me, as a black man who didn't have a chance. Why can I not honor them and stand proud for them? That's why people worship shrines. That's why they worship their ancestors. They do all this damn worshipping, but they don't do anything for the ancestors. They don't do anything for the present to take it to the future. They just talk about the past. [...] So we sit around, and we have these great conversations about all of this, but what do you *do*? And I don't blame them if they can't do because the Energy is not for them. Maybe they are the supporter behind the scenes, doing their thing. There are other warriors who actually go in and say, "I will sacrifice. I will do what I need to do." And I think for me, as a queer person, gay person, believing in the Energy Forces of the world, that's where I stand. As they say, if you're not prepared to die for something, what are you prepared to live for?

Olivia: Black people, queer people are just inherently—I feel—more spiritual ... Or at least, because of those identities, are pushed to become more spiritual, whether that's from the oppression that we face, the lack of access, the interpersonal problems we may have because of those identities. The history of being black, it's deeply spiritual and the history of being queer in many cultures, too. I just think it's inherent in our DNA, in our subconscious, in our memories. Memories we remember [or] don't. It's just in our bodies.

I think my identities—being black and queer—are what led me to a different type of spirituality. My identity—being black and being in activism—pushed me to think, "What is happening? What is this? And who's watching this? Who's watching this and thinking this is okay? Who's watching this and not intervening?" And then going to church and everyone's talking about "God is good all the time." And I'm just like, "Where, though?" How can you be black ... and ... I mean, I get it, but I couldn't be black and hold on to this idea that God is just good all the time. Or even the idea of God that you hear talked about in churches as [...] a very personified God. "He." It just didn't click.

Also, being in black churches and being queer, it just pushed me to find something else because queer people don't really fit into history that [well], especially in religion. For me, personally, being black and queer are the two things that definitely push me into spirituality, especially considering some of the most important people in my life who have pushed me toward spirituality are black and queer.

I just did a semester of theology school, and I was looking at the different ways people talk about God and the metaphors and everything. So, like, God is timeless. God is love. God is this. God is that. I was thinking about how queerness is kind of divine in that way, and blackness. Or, it's like God, queerness, and blackness are timeless because it does not fit in time. It changes in time because it's always rebelling [against] norms and [...] it's just like a continuous revolution. [...] It's like, as Catherine Keller [says], "on the way." It's kind of timeless.

Nala: When I take my blackness and my queerness and my transitions within life, all of those things I just feel were preparation for me. It can be frustrating. It is frustrating to know that blackness and queerness in the eyes of other folks can be received [...] in a way that is condemning. Blackness and queerness can be something that I need to protect, which then deepens my spiritual tools to protect it ... to protect that identity and the sacredness of it. And it's a place that I find liberation. I find myself in the intersection of feeling liberated for protecting that liberation because I understand that I can create it in the safety of my home. But when I walk outside into the other creation that other folks are allowed to create, it may not be as welcomed or honored or valued in the way that it should be.

[...] I went to South Africa. And it was in that moment where I was like I felt this sense of home. I didn't realize I was looking for home. I didn't know home was looking for me. Because we're told that home is where you are, what you make it. Yes, *and* ... there was something about being on the soil that I could feel the vibration go through the bottom of my feet to the top of my head. That was indescribable. It was emotional. It was this thing that I didn't know was taken away from me ... but I knew was taken away from me and I didn't understand why. I understood that I needed to be somewhere that was close to the soil of the continent of Africa. And that trip changed the trajectory of my life. It changed the trajectory of my relationship with God. Because when I came back, I was at a spiritual retreat with my church. And I said I wanted to do more where I was able to not only just go to the soil of Africa, but also, I wanted to know who my people were. Who were my people for my lineage? Also, who were my people for the intersections of queerness and transness? And how were they being loved? How were they experiencing love? How were they being filled up? I had all these questions now, and I wanted to be on the quest to find them.

Natasha: [Being black and queer] absolutely affirms my spiritual identity, my spiritual practices. You know, a lot of people will say, "I'm this tradition first." "I'm a Christian first." "I'm a Muslim first." "I'm a Buddhist first." And for me, that's not the case. You know, at my core, I'm a black, queer woman. And that shapes how I exist in this world. It shapes how I'm viewed in this world. It shapes my experiences and my thought processes, how I approach things. Without recognizing that part of myself, I'm doing myself a disservice. I've learned how to integrate those facets of my being, to co-create a spiritual practice or methodology, if you will, that works for me.

Charly: The multiplicity ... *that* is being queer. You're not one. You're not in a box. You're not just this. You're not just that. People like to label themselves, pigeonhole themselves into this one thing. When you're queer, you encompass so many different aspects of the [African] diaspora that you're coming in like an army, just yourself.

Benedictions

Alexis: I'm okay with saying that I'm still growing up. I'm still growing. I'm still trying to be new. Every day is the new, you know, and that's what I'm trying to be a part of. To that extent, what keeps me going or alive, if you will, is the acceptance of the spiritual as the new. As you wake up in the morning, whatever your plans are, it's a new day. Whatever you thought you were going to do when you went to sleep the night before, that morning, it's all new. So, you can toss all those things and do something else. Or you can continue going. But it's the everyday. It's the twenty-four hours that we get (if in fact we get the twenty-four, because we don't know). It's the everyday that I am learning and participating in and growing up in and I plan to grow up until I'm not here. You know what I'm saying? Until I'm physically not here, I'll grow up in some other kind of way. I hope.

Olivia: One thing that I've been understanding about spirituality … because when I first got my reading, she said, "You need to live a spiritual life." When I was asking about my next steps [after] graduating, she said, "Don't worry about money. Don't worry about anything." She's like, "Spiritual. Just go spiritual." And I was like, "Okay, that's easy." And I'm realizing that it's not easy at all. It's the hardest thing trying to be spiritual in a very materialistic world. At the time, I thought, "Oh, that's easy. Just meditate and shit." And I'm like, it's the hardest fucking thing. I'm trying to be nice to myself about it.

Michael: "You have hurt me today, Elyse." And you say, "Alright, Michael, I'm gonna go confess. God, I hurt Michael Johnson. Take it away from me." And the priest says, "Ok, you're now forgiven." So, you walk out there feeling fine. What does that do to the hurt that I have had? What does that do to the energy that you have put on me? You got the relief for yourself, but you haven't because it's contained in you. And it will evolve and show itself sometime in the future. You never know when it spurs up, because "as above, so below." You buried it for a moment but it's still brewing there. And then, all of a sudden, "Ahhhh!" and you don't know where the scream comes from. You've heard those people who have such a scream, that's guttural [...] such an earth-shattering scream. Like Mother Nature, like the hurricane when they scream. When they scream you are so paralyzed, that you [think], "Where did this come from?" It was brewing all along. Now it's time to release that energy. That volcano. It has nothing to do with pacifying it with a religious base because eventually it explodes.

In [metaphysical] belief and what we practice, you're not gonna allow it to explode because you're constantly evaluating it, you're constantly watching it, testing it, getting frustrated with it [...] and it's no difference in opportunities, being blessed or not. When you talk to people [they say], "I ain't had much opportunity." Okay, alright. But we all do every day. The key is, do you recognize it? Most people don't recognize it. It's not that blessing didn't come or that good faith didn't come or opportunity didn't come. You were just not physically or mentally ready to recognize it. It came and it left. You say it never happened. Happened many, many times. All of us. All the time. But our minds are such ... our energies say, "I can't recognize an opportunity."

"God, grant me the ability to see the opportunities that come before me, to recognize it as it comes before me."

Koach: One of the first prayers, kind of the seminal prayer of our three times a day prayer in the Jewish tradition, is the *Amidah*. And the first prayer that we say there is, "Blessed are You, God, the God of our ancestors, the God of Avraham, the God of Yitzhak, the God of Yaakov, and the God of Rivkah and Sarah and Le'ah and Rahel" and "Zilpah and Bilhah," which I've been adding, because those two were the mothers of the tribes. And that is essentially calling on the ancestors. Now, I need to be able to call on the God of somebody else, because "I know that my faith might not be as strong as theirs, but You worked with them. Work with me, too." I have an actual representation of that in our daily liturgy to say, call on the God of the people I know made it through. I can call on the God of my grandfather and the God of my grandmother. I can call on them very specifically. I'm using their relationship with God to help me, and also to call on them because I called on both my grandmothers often for the strength and courage that I knew that they had that I was trying to tap into, you know? It was kind of the both/and: the God of my ancestors and also asking the ancestors, "Please help us. Y'all been through some of this [injustice as we experienced in Ferguson] before. Y'all ain't been through this particular thing, but y'all been through some of this before." There're a couple of people that I call on most of the time. Their pictures are up here on my ancestor altar. But it's Fred Hampton. I call on Fred Hampton a lot as a co-journeyer of trying to do that work of coalition building, to let us build power together to be against the real enemy and not each other. And I call on the courage of Fred Hampton a lot because it took a lot of courage for him to do what he did, to walk into places he walked in. And also, Marsha P. Johnson. I call on her strength and courage and spirit of just like, being radically, unapologetically herself. You know what I mean, Like, "Mm-Mmm [no], you ain't going to tell me who I am. I'm gon tell you who I am." And those are two that I call on a lot. I call on their particular energies to help me.

Jé: I have literally attached and formulated in my mind a spiritual practice of liberation being like, "fuck it."[...] "Fuck it" deals with the fact that there is an actual property to inherently resist. As bell hooks would say, "I'm at odds with everything against me." That's the first part of queerness. I think attaching myself to that dialogue, [...] to say "fuck it" is my response to "Oh, that's so not Black" [or] "So not this" ... when someone already has insisted that it is "so not" because they do not have the imagination for it, it is the audacity to live out my inherent resistance because there's no space to imagine the un-Jé, the un-queerness, the un-blackness. When it becomes this "un" (as a prefix—to be removed from or loose from or set apart from something that is intrinsically me but not in alignment with the collective) ... there are moments that I have just gotten to a place where I'm like, "Liberation will always be attached to 'fuck it' because it unhinges." It respectfully and audaciously unhinges you from having to live out the status quo for the sake of your survival, for the sake of you being able to thrive, for the sake of you being able to even be and become. When we listen to the phrase just in the beginning, it's like you can add something to it: "Fuck it, I'll do it anyway." "Fuck it, let's go." Because there's always beyond after that. It's never just let it be. When I listen to a lot of my white counterparts who often say, "Well, it is what it is." It's a complicitness to it. But when you say, "Fuck it," there's a beyond-ness to it. [...] "Fuck it" implies an imagination that is a vehicle that can be used as resilience, resistance, and persistence.

storäe: I don't think at any point spirituality is finite. And, I don't want to say it as a thing of "levels" either because I don't believe that there is a hierarchy. Of course, you can learn more about something and focus on it. They got people out there that call themselves "masters" and things of that nature. I don't tend to believe in that. I tend to believe in, "We're ever evolving." We learn different things and explore different things. We become more intentional about certain aspects of our spirituality as we grow and as we need to. But there's no way you can ever master it. There're a lot of unknowns and a lot of not knowing. And there's some things that … not that I don't care to know, but I know that I could never understand and I'm okay with that. I've become okay with not knowing, with not understanding everything. Those things that I do get, and I do grab on and hold on to, I know that those are going to shift and change for me, too.

I believe that's the same thing for queerness. Queerness is not this finite thing where you've mastered who you are in your body as a queer person. It's always evolving, always changing, uncomfortable at some times because you are decentering the norm every time that you put your body out there and just dare to exist. I think spirituality, queerness, and blackness are things that are constantly evolving and beautiful and transformative. All I can think of is that old saying, "You stay true to the game, the game will stay true to you." You stay true to your queerness and your blackness and your spirituality, and it will stay true to you.

Conclusion

The oral histories and photographs featured within this chapter reflect the complexity and multiplicity of lived religion and moral imagination as articulated by those whose blackness and queerness inform their spiritual and/or religious selves. They are informed by and eschew formality. They speak to black queerness that is integrated with sex and sexuality in ways that cannot be disentangled. They reflect ways of being and doing that are distinctive and particular. Approaching this archive through the thematic headings—Origins in Religious and Spiritual Becoming, A Practice in Connecting, Cultivating Access, Queering Belief, Journeying Toward and Away/

Redefining, Blackness and Queerness, and Benedictions—signals embodied approaches to morality, religion, and spirituality that demonstrate the fecundity of blackqueer religious subjectivity and, subsequently, the ancient wisdom articulated in Christian sacred text: the spirit moves where it chooses.[10] In this chapter, we observe spirituality and religion in its various forms of embodiment through ritual, meditative practices, and religious devotion to create openings toward articulation of the spirit that moves in and through blackqueer bodies, to demonstrate the simultaneity of spirit/the religious with blackqueerness/es, to expand what is understood as religion, and to interrogate the limits of some religions in holding space for blackqueerness of spirit.[11] We move now to a constructive conversation between these resources—historical, ethical/theological, practical—that make up a living archive, the values and virtues toward a blackqueer ethics.

Notes

1 Ashon T. Crawley, *Blackpentecostal Breath: The Aesthetics of Possibility* (New York: Fordham University Press, 2017), 2.

2 Emilie M. Townes, *In a Blaze of Glory: Womanist Spirituality as Social Witness* (Nashville: Abingdon, 1995), 48.

3 See Chapter 1, note 45.

4 Thelathia N. Young and Shannon J. Miller, "Asé and Amen, Sister! Black Feminist Scholars Engage in Interdisciplinary, Dialogical, Transformative Ethical Praxis," *Journal of Religious Ethics* 43, no. 2 (April 2015): 297.

5 Young and Miller, "Asé and Amen, Sister!," 297.

6 E. Patrick Johnson, *Black. Queer. Southern. Women.: An Oral History* (Durham: UNC Press, 2018), 5.

7 Oral history interview with Gordon Parks, December 30, 1964, Archives of American Art, Smithsonian Institution. https://www.aaa.si.edu/collections/interviews/oral-history-interview-gordon-parks-11480#transcript.

8 Aesthetic intimacy refers specifically to ethically engaging art, particularly that of and from marginalized persons, in art criticism and in examining the social uses of art. "Aesthetic Intimacies: Reflections on Elle Pérez's Devotions at the BMA," BMoreArt,

September 26, 2022. https://bmoreart.com/2022/09/aesthetic-intimacies-reflections-on-elle-perezs-devotions.html.

9   See Tina M. Campt, *Listening to Images* (Durham: Duke University Press, 2017), 5–6. While Campt is working with images that serve a different function than those featured here, these photos share in the "quiet" she explores in that they are images of practices that tend to be personal, and layered with meaning for the blackqueer subjects and represent everyday acts (even if the actual image is stylized), but also carry a disruptive frequency. The potential exists for both experiences. They certainly carry a like function with Campt's photos, one of "rupture and refusal."

10 John 3:8a New Revised Standard Version (NRSV): The wind (spirit) blows where it chooses, and you hear the sound of it, but you do not know where it comes from or where it goes.

11 Josef Sorett, *Spirit in the Dark: A Religious History of Racial Aesthetics* (New York: Oxford University Press, 2016), 7.

4

Constructing a Blackqueer Sexual Ethics

In this final chapter, from the resources within a living blackqueer archive, I offer a transreligious, liberative, communal-sexual ethic built upon integrative values that move toward justice love: communal belonging, individual and collective becoming, goodness, inspirited bodies/embodied spirits, and shared thriving. Inspiring the integrative, relations-based values that could inform such an ethic, 1920s Harlem and the subversive, nonconformist spaces of blues environments, rent parties, and the Hamilton Lodge Balls expounded in Chapter 1 provided an archive of possibility and fodder for imagining the liberation that might be found among persons abjectified and challenged to shape a meaningful sense of self and community amid extra- and intra-communal oppressions. In Chapter 2, with an integrative, communal method of weaving a dialogue of blackqueering scholarship, I have offered a genealogy signaling those who have constructed, molded, prodded, deconstructed, reconstructed, and departed from Christian ethics and theology sexual discourse since the early 1990s and continue to contribute invaluably to liberative justice and community-centered ethical reflection rooted in black LGBTQ+ life and living. To locate a discursive grounding within the scholarship, I identified noteworthy themes: inclusion, subjectivity and identity, resistance and difference, embodiment, and power. Offering insight into the aliveness and aesthetics of a blackqueer archive, Chapter 3 features photographs and the immediate voices of nine persons living into the expansiveness of blackqueer moral imagination attentive to religion and spirituality, race, sexuality, and gender. They offer perspective to a blackqueer ethics that is transreligious and fluid, open-ended and in its aliveness, ever-changing.

In this chapter, I invite the reader to consider how the five aforementioned values may aid in welcoming justice love and wholeness for communities and individuals in thinking and doing sexual ethics. The momentary (perhaps, fleeting) nature of how these values may be embodied in community does not lessen their worth or usefulness. Rather, a realist perspective reminds us that we will always receive impermanent and incomplete glimpses of ethical ideals; still, they are worth living toward. As Mark D. Jordan accordingly argues, we ought not look to Christian ethics, or we could say any religious ethics, to finally "settle the question" of whatever we pose to it.[1] The five values highlighted here invite sitting with and continually returning to "the question" in discernment of steps in liberative communality that intentionally strives toward justice love. My intent in this chapter is not to provide universalizing prescriptive claims that can be applied in all times and in all places to yield integrative ends. While there are goods to consider, try on, and practice, it is important to note that this does not settle, and does not aim to settle, all questions posed to a sexual ethics, blackqueer or otherwise.

A blackqueer ethics is in process, continually becoming and, in this way, is more concerned with process than outcome. Because, as a liberative ethic, a blackqueer ethics depends upon communal reflection, universalizing would diminish the agency and moral wisdom of particular communities. This communal ethic of sexuality, that understands sexuality as impacting and impacted by our communal existence, invites sustained ethical reflection,[2] where communities may discern and grow into what they find to be the good. The ethic evolves as communities continue to engage and as they transform in their understandings of and relationship to themselves, the sacred, all that exists, and the good. Through a blackqueer ethics, we consider how the five values—communal belonging, individual and collective becoming, goodness, embodied spirits/inspired bodies, and shared thriving—will be enacted differently in each community and individual and offer entry into varying processes with different outcomes.

Because (sexual) ethics are always communal and subsequently relational, one could also examine what these values might look like beyond solely sexual ethics. A blackqueer ethics, in its integrative, relational quality, has implications and applicability beyond sexuality and sex acts. Such malleability is a demonstration that sexuality is not a fragmentable, disintegrated part of the self that requires special rules and ought to be reserved only for the private, but that it is and ought to be integrated into our self- and communal-understandings. The integrative is a persistent calling to be in relationship with, and more specifically, in right relationship with.

Before examining these five blackqueer ethical values in-depth, a brief discussion of justice love—the grounds for right-relatedness—is warranted. As articulated by liberative Christian ethicist Marvin M. Ellison, justice love may be described as "a strong commitment to the dignity and well-being of persons, a fair sharing of power and pleasure, concern for each person's safety and health, and a mutual pledge to foster respect and care for each other and to invest, as well, in the vitality of our wider communities."[3] To do justice love is to pursue right relationships that reflect wholeness through individuals in communities with the aim of impacting society.[4] This is sexual ethics as social ethics. My understanding of justice love likewise honors pleasure, well-being, and just power, while also fostering a commitment to creating and cultivating the spaces in which collective thriving—specifically of communities impacted by anti-black racial, gender, and sexuality-based injustice and equipped with practices that have sustained survival, joy, and healing—can take place.

Justice love is not primarily an end but is a reflection of the processes communities enact as they live into ethics, as well as a posture within living an ethical life. In justice love there is not only (human) interpersonal relationality, but right relating with oneself, God, one's community, nature, and Earth.[5] For some, a relationship to nature and Earth may appear to have no role in sexual ethics. Yet, in fostering this blackqueer sexual ethic, the individual and communal human body honors nonhuman, living bodies by which we also receive pleasure, well-being, sustenance, and with whom humanity is becoming. Justice love in a blackqueer ethics demands a politically integrative approach that refuses the anti-black racial, sexual, gender hegemony that attempts to hinder collective (human and beyond) well-being alongside a refusal of individualism and anthropocentrism that thwarts the comprehensive reach of the integrative.

Further, though I utilize the term "blackqueer," a blackqueer ethic's approach to justice love is akin to the quaring of justice utilized by Jennifer S. Leath, which is centered in an integrative approach to justice for all people—a justice that does not ignore race/is anti-racist:

> To 'quare' justice, normatively speaking, is to awaken visions and expressions of justice that insert off-kilter blue notes, troubling epistemological and ontological certainties or arrogances with primary perspectival regard for the subjectivity of LGBTQ persons of color who love other people and appreciate Black culture or community. And it means to do this in a way that is holistically committed to the struggle against all oppression, in a way that reflects the connection between gender, sexuality, and race, and in a form that engages situations deeply instead of 'throwing shade'.[6]

My emphasis, with Leath, infuses a blackqueer ethics with a broader outlook on justice that is not an abstraction, but is located in material realities for black LGBTQ+ bodies and subsequently all marginalized bodies.[7] This approach to liberative sexual ethics serves as a response to the experiences that have been erased in Christian sexual ethics and as a contribution to the body of liberative ethical scholarship that confronts the disciplines' anti-blackness.

The love within justice love is political. It is anti-racist, gender expansive, sexually liberative, socioeconomically equitable. That love is enacted through and with justice and informs any relationship that integrates communal right-relatedness as its practice. The power of such love is found in the radical, undergirding expression of it in the work of living into justice—affirming and seeking the fullness of life for those enduring oppressions and those who self-deleteriously uphold oppressions. Justice when coupled with love brings us to a core question of this blackqueer ethic: *How* are we toward one another? Continually assessing and reassessing the answers to this question, reflecting on whether communities are indeed espousing the values they seek or claim to hold, challenging our ethics to answer the invitation to justice love break down the holds that shame and legalism possess in sexual ethics marred by traditionalism as well as the whiteness, heterocentrism, and cis-centrism in some sexual ethics.

We turn now to a constructive sexual ethics through a blackqueer lens, one of many possibilities toward doing liberative, integrative ethics and disrupting the normativizing and hegemonic logics of traditionalism's sexual ethics.

Integrative Values of a Blackqueer Ethics

I begin now with an exploration of each of the five values that I identified at the beginning of this chapter: communal belonging, individual and collective becoming, goodness, inspirited bodies/embodied spirits, and shared thriving. Under each heading, we will draw upon the elements of the archive that inspire each value and I will expand on the significance of each to a blackqueer ethics. In determining each heading, the themes from black LGBTQ+-focused discourse in ethics and theology that I identified in the previous chapter served as a springboard: inclusion, subjectivity and identity, resistance and difference, embodiment, and power. I asked what it might look like to think these themes through an integrative lens and with the living archive. Through this process, inclusion's locus of power was disrupted and became communal belonging. Subjectivity and identity leaned into instability and became individual and collective becoming. Resistance and difference expanded beyond the logics of oppression and homogeneity to become goodness. Embodiment's comprehensive nature became more explicit as embodied spirits/inspirited bodies. And attentiveness to the notion that power, albeit in varying, inequitable measures, is nevertheless possessed by everyone yielded shared thriving.

The five values should not be understood as ethical ideals or values that are to be, or that could be, reached in a complete way. Therefore, I have chosen to begin each heading with the word "toward." This reflects process, rather than ends, and continuous change that yields right practice. As named throughout this book, the work of communities is to continually revisit and rework their praxes of ethics. The ethical is found in the daily, persistent striving toward, rather than having arrived.

I have named these values collectively as integrative. While integrative can mean wholeness, completeness, or harmony, it does not reflect perfection. The doing of ethics, and likewise a blackqueer ethics, is messy. Within the archive, we also find contradiction, disorderliness, questionable practices, in-betweenness, and openness; this is akin to what Martin F. Manalansan IV frames, in his analysis of queer immigrant archives, as "queer as mess" wherein the "material and affective disarray and the narratives spun from them" shape archive, as well as queer stories.[8] He further defines this symbiosis between queerness and mess as an "analytical stance that negates, deflects, if not resists the 'cleaning up' function of the normative."[9] Traditionalism—a rigid morality rooted in imperialist white supremacist capitalist heteropatriarchy—and various normativizing impulses within sexual ethics are what make them disintegrative; the willingness to sit with messiness and locate fecundity within the mess, where there is space for error and questioning and fluidity is the realm of the integrative. The messiness of ethical decision-making enlivens integrative values by allowing them the spaciousness to be worked out in community. Like the example of 1920s gender and sexual conformists of Harlem demonstrates, purist utopias are not needed for a generative and flourishing moral imagination. For a contemporarily lived example, as the practitioners model, messiness via trial and error, as named by Natasha, in her oral history, as well as experimentation and liminality, shared by Charly, can make for a meaningful moral and religious/spiritual life. Ultimately, through the blackqueer lens offered here toward the integrative, messiness is a virtue.

My method in this chapter, mirroring that of Chapter 2, is what black feminist Christian social ethicist Traci C. West calls a dialogical method, that is, one that enables conversation among resources and "maintains a fluid interaction between text and context, theory and practice, religion and particular social conditions."[10] Constructing a blackqueer ethics from the contents of a living archive—the communal experiences of blackqueer Harlemites of the 1920s, blackqueering LGBTQ+-focused discourse, and the narratives of practitioners of blackqueer moral imagination—I draw from varied theoretical and practical sources of moral wisdom and subsequently, challenge the racial superiority—and I would add the heteronormative superiority—that has so long determined the delineations of prevalent Christian sexual ethics.[11] As named in the previous chapter, in particular with the oral histories, my aim is not to theorize their narratives; but the stories are offered for the ways they have sparked my thinking expansively and with possibility and open-endedness about these values. Allowing these resources and approaches to converge with one another as a methodological strategy creates space for an evolving, dynamic ethic, a model that can further aid in yielding a dialogical approach to living into ethics. The constructive collaboration that I generate between these archival elements is a practice of integrative communality and justice love in a blackqueer ethics.

Toward Communal Belonging

Communal belonging serves as an integrative value for our consideration in a blackqueer ethics because it is not contingent; it is innate. Access to inclusion comes by conferral of this "gift" by persons in power; therefore, inclusion is not a practice I find morally fecund. As noted by Ellison, inclusion is "an insufficient change strategy" (though he argues for it as a good).[12] Inclusion assumes hegemonic power, which in the United States and disciplinary context buttresses whiteness and heteropatriarchy (as well as able-bodiedness and economic privilege) and is meant to maintain or force conformity. Subsequently, the concept of inclusion is counter to right relationship.

As outsiders, blackqueer Harlemites created ways of belonging to/with one another within the spaces that they constructed for a celebration of what was deemed abject—their black sexual and gender nonconforming selves. Ostracized by much of Harlem's black bourgeoisie hopefuls' understandings of upstanding company, the blackqueer people of Harlem established communality rooted in self-determination and chosen connectedness. Within such counterpublics, "members of subordinated social groups invent and circulate counterdiscourses, which in turn permit them to formulate oppositional interpretations of their identities, interests, and needs."[13] They ascribe alternative meaning to their reality. This can be empowering for a community because it has the capacity, in some instances, to reduce the harms caused by exclusion from the public[14] and, particularly in this instance, to shift the locus of power from the dominant public.

Blues environments, rent parties, and the Hamilton Lodge Balls conjured belonging by fostering permission of expression: as sexual beings, as people resisting the restricting binds of gender, as people embracing their desire and pleasure. Visions of queer futures could be grasped through the liberating gender and sexual performance of blues women who modeled possibility to their listeners,[15] and as their songs offered the articulation of and reprieve from troubles (e.g., racial, economic, relational) that cultural productions often provide. As historian Lawrence Levine affirms, "Although blues songs were individual expression they were meant to be shared, they were meant to evoke experiences common to the group, they were meant to provide relief and release for all involved."[16] The rent parties fostered communal belonging by developing community, establishing cultural solidarity, and demonstrating interdependence.[17] They existed as places where new-comers could go to become acquainted with others, and the light atmosphere accompanied a sense of welcome in the "overlay of camaraderie, sex, and music."[18] The economic disparities in New York City gave rise to the need for such gatherings, yet in the assembling of themselves, sexual and gender nonconformists in some instances were able to create deeper community rooted in authenticity, risk, joyfulness, song, dance, food-connectedness. The Hamilton Lodge Balls uniquely offered what newspapers of the time framed as a suspension from the color prejudice ordinarily experienced day-to-day in New York City. While the reach and veracity of such a claim cannot be confirmed, the flourishing of a blackqueer aesthetic on their "home turf" in the heart of Harlem refuted the hegemony and burden of white supremacy found outside of the Balls. The Balls invite the possibility for imagining, creating, and playing (even at times in drag) together.

The black LGBTQ+-focused ethical and theological critique of exclusion and calls for inclusion expand existing disciplinary and communal space to include blackqueer, including trans, existence. They also create openings to alternative blackqueer spaces of autonomy and self-sufficiency. Such critique offers the opportunity to grapple with and potentially rectify the diminishment of communality through erasure of blackqueer/LGBTQ+ persons and to strategize new ways of being together. Frequently, persons impacted by HIV/AIDS have been erased, and continue to be. Too often the insights and adaptations of transgender and gender nonconforming people have been erased from narratives of history and theology by either exclusion of their experiences or the marginalization of their stories and continue to be.[19] As Tourmaline, a transgender artist, activist and filmmaker, argues, historical and consistent erasure of transgender communities' legacies and work toward justice and thriving is a form of violence.[20] Because these erasures are violence, a restorative move is needed. In confronting the violence of erasure and honoring one another's stories, particularly those who have been disinherited, the foundations for community may become increasingly liberative and perhaps, those erased may again find desire to belong in a community that has practiced restoration.

The struggle for inclusion, discussed in depth in Chapter 2, offers helpful insights for reflection on belonging. Because within the blackqueering discourse inclusion of LGBTQ+ persons was contingent upon a powerful people bestowing the opportunity to be included or through heterosexual people being transformed by learning from black gay and lesbian people's stories, particularly in churches, it depends on heterosexual benevolence for the inclusion of queer sexualities to take place.[21] As examined in Chapter 3, black communities' and the discipline's exclusionary reasoning lies in heterosexism, homophobia, embarrassment by association, HIV/AIDS stigma, heteronormative biblical interpretation, and commitments to right-wing conservative agendas. Conversely, black LGBTQ+-focused discourse provides inroads to upholding that difference should be affirmed without the need for narrow, hegemonic relational norms. Ibrahim Abdurrahman Farajajé's in-the-life theology and Pamela R. Lightsey's queer womanist theology, as well as Roger A. Sneed's ethic of openness offer a counter to exclusion by each theology's connectivity with all persons surviving and thriving under oppressions and the ethic's unwillingness to exclude.

Communal belonging was present in the oral histories as Charly, a child growing up under the spiritual tutelage of women in the community, found connection and later the capacity to critique his community as he practiced ritual with them. Additionally, seeking a space that could hold a fuller presentation of Tasha's evolving and distinctively black and queer self led her to find belonging in an affirming African-centered Christian ministry and with spiritual practices from varying traditions, a far cry from her Church of God in Christ upbringing and young adulthood. storäe located a temporary belonging during a brief but resonant journey with Indigenous elders that catapulted them into new religious and spiritual directions. Finally, Alexis, with her partner, creates an interpersonal belonging (with implications for their communal life), honoring each of their paths—namely, her partner being a *Vodouisant* while Alexis does not adhere to Vodou, but both maintain an altar to a lwa, Erzulie Freda.

As signaled in 1920s Harlem and among the narratives, communities can practice values that create environments for the belonging of fuller selves as each lives into their becoming by fostering an ethos of embodiment without the burdens of striving for prescribed notions of "normalcy" and respectability. Communal belonging upholds consent, accountability, forgiveness, vulnerability, and acknowledgment of others' belonging, even those with whom one may disagree, in openness and in holy curiosity. Communities create environments of belonging through enabling and supporting exploration and becoming. Such communal belonging may grant persons the courage they need to take the bold steps toward living in blackqueer (as in, unconventional, "off-kilter") ways, to include, but also beyond sexual orientation.

Further, as a member of a community, belonging connotes a sense of one's own realization of having value as part of a body, of a participatory hold on the dignity of mattering. To belong within community is to have space for the self-in-truth and that of others—living into selves as they know themselves to be in the moment, without shame.[22] Belonging within a community is more than a matter of affiliation by invitation, proximity, or homogeneity. Instead, belonging is an opening to knowing and being known without a compulsion toward unity. Belonging is a choice that each member of a community decides to live into. Community is built upon an innate sense of belonging, a outgrowth springing from aliveness.[23]

I am; therefore, I belong. You are; therefore, you belong. We are; therefore, we belong.[24] Recognizing integration, this belonging is true in all of nature. Innate belonging signals the expectation of communal belonging that may exist within or outside of institutional religious space if the space is developed enough to affirm the belonging of persons. Belonging means that no one possesses the ability to say who does and who does not belong. In this way, belonging is more than a utopic vision; it is the messy and continuous work of choosing to be in community and the ongoing epistemological effort of being present with the knowledge that one's belonging and that of others is undebatable, and that belongings of selves-in-truth—living and distinct as they are—may clash in hurtful and sometimes harmful ways.

Communal belonging does not discount that harm is a possibility when there is an encounter, and it requires responses oriented toward restorative justice love. In the practices of communal belonging that are nurtured through a blackqueer ethics, accountability is paramount. Accountability demands responsibility for harm done but does not sanction communal harm of the perpetrator that leads to denying their basic human worth and dignity. Justice love and integrative commitments equate to neither reconciliation nor forgiveness. It allows space and time for grief, anger, distance, and for processes of individual and communal healing.

Communality reflects the power of people to practice communal belonging where institutions, as structures maintained by systematizing the status quo, have not. It is sometimes the case that persons find that they misalign with the communities, often housed within institutions, in which they find themselves. In this instance, belonging remains noncontingent, but community members must demonstrate agency regarding their belonging that reflects their ideas of the good. Where the situation demands (e.g., in spaces where there is a consistent commitment to disintegrative values), the practice of communal belonging can always be implemented elsewhere.

Assertion of belonging, in some instances, may demand new ethical and theological frameworks that better serve justice love. Sneed's ethic of openness is instructive in its "deep appreciation for difference," its affirmation of the innate worthiness of humanity, and its practices of vulnerability.[25] Sneed finds that a God of love and liberation, often invoked in pro-LGBTQ+ discourse, is not sufficient to battle Christianity's long-standing anti-LGBTQ+ rhetoric. Subsequently, an ethic of openness takes a humanist orientation in a desire to shift black intellectual discourse away from conventional, inflexible theological articulations and toward examining the actions of humans toward other humans, which also affirms human sacredness.[26] With Sneed, I assert the futility of seeking to sway the opinions of those in communities who believe in a God-ordained "heteronormative social order"[27]—as was found in 1920s black Harlem and currently in various traditionalism-centered Christian (and other religious) spaces—a blackqueer ethics is not an apologetic to convince anyone of the worth of people who are lesbian, gay, bisexual, transgender, queer, nonbinary, two-spirit, intersex, asexual, questioning, or any other sexual or gender nonconformists. It is rooted in the belief that queer worth is not debatable and the practice of communal belonging ought to create space for all sexualities and the persons who enliven them.

Toward Individual and Collective Becoming

From many ethicists and theologians foregrounding LGBTQ+ discourse comes the call to reclaim and name the collective as creative, resilient, complex, and unapologetically queer, rather than solely as victim(ized).[28] Telling their own stories and formulating their own theories is a start, but not if the outcome will be flattened characterizations of blackqueer people as either heroes or "the oppressed." As a matter of strategy and the development of the academic and activist discourse, perhaps an essentialist take on identity once served a needful end.[29] Yet, a blackqueer ethics is an invitation to complicated becoming and unpredictable ways of being. Instead of a hindrance, such inexactitude can be utilized toward communal creativity and imagination in the process of becoming.[30]

The historical example of black sexual and gender nonconformists in Harlem inspires the value of individual and collective becoming through the community's commitment to its developing embodied existence and expression. As a subaltern counterpublic, their spaces serve as examples of not only queer realities, but of potentiality. In reference to New York City's "amusement districts" like Greenwich Village and Harlem, George Chauncey argues:

> Part of the attraction [...] was that it constituted a liminal space where visitors were encouraged to disregard some of the social injunctions that normally constrained their behavior, where they could observe and vicariously experience behavior that in other settings—particularly their own neighborhoods—they might consider objectionable enough to suppress.[31]

The space for the blackqueer body to move more freely, to live more deeply into its desired expression, and to counter hegemonic norms of suppression and constriction fostered diverse imaginings of being, and subsequently becoming. As "transgender Latinx public scholar" Roberto Che Espinoza argues, "combining disparate strands of thinking and being (and becoming) and finding a particular style of relationality in the in/betweenness of difference [...] allows for becoming to materialize."[32] Inching toward the value of becoming, though incremental, provided generative spaces for difference. They became for one another reflections of a liberation that was not present in the legal, social, economic, and religious customs of much of Harlem, New York City, and most of the nation.

The social and political freedom reflected in the space of rent parties contrasted the legalized discrimination and criminalization of gender and sexual subversion so prevalent throughout the city.[33] The arts, in the form of the blues environments, and the Hamilton Lodge Balls that Harlem's sexual and gender nonconformists inhabited inspired becoming through imagination and through emboldened embodiment, including performance. According to performance theorist James F. Wilson, the (primarily) supportive space of rent parties aided in the development of talents of attendees, particularly musicians, and even cultivated the skills of such soon-to-be-renowned artists as Thomas "Fatts" Waller.[34] The communality of such supportive and life-shaping attitudes points toward an integrative affirmation of personhood and offers space for fostering vulnerability needed for relational mutuality and becoming.

An emphasis on subjectivity and identity, as examined in the blackqueering discourse, reflects the aims of individual and collective becoming. These ethicists and theologians write about the particularity of being both black and LGBTQ+, centering this subjectivity within theological, ethical, and ecclesial settings and destabilizing whiteness- and hetero-centric religious discourses of sexuality and gender. By disrupting the orientation, aims, and values of the discourse, they likewise disrupt the technologies of normalization, as black queer ethicist Thelathia "Nikki" Young notes, to invite becoming both within academia and in community.[35] The liminality that accompanies becoming creates space for expansive expressions and embrace of difference. As explored by Leath, having an identity so closely connected with alterity and deviance lends itself to becoming because the otherness can be utilized as a tool of discerning potentialities when utilized strategically. Leath's black sexual ethic "dares to develop a distinctive discourse on sexuality, that is, a discourse that engages the normative potential of sexuality without stipulations of respectability and without rejecting the latent morality of deviance."[36] Through becoming, unlikely sites of moral reflection provide openings to unfettered and shameless, though community-conscious, searches for possibility.

Each of the interviewees from the oral histories shared their evolving understanding of themselves in their journey and the communities to which they belong/ed with the capacity to hold space for them, or not, as they changed. Whether it was Olivia's listening for purpose and next steps in their journey to priestesshood, Nala's becoming by way of her many spatial, dream-world and ancestor-led transitions, or Charly's declarations, "I am very queer because I'm multiplicities. I am many different things. I'm many different existences as Charly and I'm aware of that," they inspire further thinking about the openness that creates space for greater moral imagination, not only in one's worlds but toward themselves and their own self-making.

Becoming is a process wherein realities are continually transforming and being organized anew.[37] To conceive of becoming within a collective, it is important to consider the ways that the sexualities of subjects (and all other aspects of them) exist together and subsequently influence one another's becoming. Such becoming is facilitated by "intra-action" between agents. Drawing from feminist theorist Karen Barad, Espinoza utilizes "intra-action" to indicate the mutual entanglement of agencies that relate to one another when bodies are in relationships of difference and multiplicity toward becoming.[38] Barad defines intra-action "in contrast to the usual 'interaction'," that recognizes "distinct agencies do not precede, but rather emerge through, their intra-action." What communities become is because of their intra-action with one another. The intra-action also reminds us that selves who recognize their entanglement with others build stronger, more compassionate communities, and that mutuality in recognition of this entanglement can sharpen communities' moral reflection toward the goods they seek.

Creating communities that enable the exploration of who they can become and how they become challenges the notion of a static, purist community of sexual and gender beings. Becoming holds chaotic potential and requires diligence in tending its unfolding. If there is to be authenticity and vulnerability through communities opening space for becoming, it is likely that community members will clash. This clashing, which when sat with can lead to reworking, is a necessary component of generative processes of failure wherein we find "alternative ways of knowing and being that are not unduly optimistic, but nor are they mired in nihilistic critical dead ends."[39] While many seek a fully safe space where nurture and learning can take place, this is frequently unrealistic, and at times, it is not helpful. A community must prod itself in discomforting ways in order to grow, explore, risk power, forgive, correct, and confront for the sake of a fuller manifestation of individual and collective becoming.

Toward Goodness

Engaging processes of communal moral and ethical reflection assumes that the good is not always readily knowable, even if tradition, scripture, experience, or reason have persistently affirmed a particular idea of the good even for centuries. This requires humility—that is, the capacity to sit with the discomfort of the unknown. Humility is consistently open to revisiting, reforming, imagining, and reimagining.

The alternative understandings about communal ways of being together that blackqueer Harlem provided composed of less social scripts and allowed for the assertion of self-worth and expression. Among one another, Harlem's black sexual and gender nonconformists "danced, drank, saw their friends, and claimed stature and respect in a cultural zone governed by their own social codes rather than those of white employers of the black bourgeoisie."[40] To the chagrin of some members of the black middle-class invested in social welfare through moral conformity, blackqueer folks took an anti-respectability stance, rejecting the notion of being exceptionally "good." While this may have been more circumstantial than strategic—Chauncey notes, some (namely, men perceived to be feminine) "had no hope of respectability"[41]—it allowed for a differing set of values, new definitions and common language, and communal supports to emerge in their counterpublic which at times glimpsed liberative, integrative practices like authenticity, freedom, disruption of hegemony, pleasure, lightheartedness, and mutuality. Ultimately, blackqueer Harlemites defied established notions of the good forwarded by black powerbrokers and generated goods that reflected their communality.

Blackqueering critical thought takes on the task of countering dominant discourses that diminish and marginalize LGBTQ+ persons by providing a counternarrative to immorality, suffering, and shame. Though some of the scholarship relates to and perpetuates a narrative of suffering and shame, it also presents a fuller picture of black LGBTQ+ life and points of inquiry concerned with black LGBTQ+ subjectivity. Through their resistance and embrace of the difference embodied by LGBTQ+ people, they transformed the theological and ethical understandings of queer faith and communal moral reflection. Their resistance included unseating established sources of authority (e.g., the Bible, black liberationist exclusionary thought); loving body, pleasure, and stories; re-constructing the meanings of family; and reclaiming dignity and integrity in otherness. While deconstructing, building upon, and acknowledging the value in their resistance, they look to queer epistemologies and experiences to offer constructive resources and to assert the goodness of blackqueerness without qualification. As mentioned in Chapter 3, Young aptly argues that it is resistance that is a crucial first step in communities' exploration toward goods.[42] Blackqueering discourse offers to a blackqueer ethics the import of resistance and difference, but also the need to thrive beyond that which needs to be resisted and that from which one is differentiated.[43]

Moral practices like those mentioned above—authenticity, freedom, disruption of hegemony, pleasure, lightheartedness, and mutuality, to name a few—contribute to the stories of communities and scholars striving toward some sense of the good. A blackqueer ethics argues not about prescribing the specific goods that communities should espouse, but rather, what is good is that communities come to their determination of what is good in a process and in togetherness. In such a process, it is fecund to hold moral diversity. As defined by Ellison, "moral diversity arises when we recognize that responsible people differ in their moral judgments and can offer good, even compelling reasons for their positions, and we must figure out where we stand, and why."[44] Diversity may seem easy when persons function primarily from an individualist position (and there are ethical choices to be made by individuals, while considering communal right-relatedness). However, in community, plurality in ethical judgments serves to destabilize the "either-or" approaches to sexual ethics that have fragmented individuals, families, communities, and societies, and allows for particularity to have a role in shaping communal goods.

Communal reflection on the good requires deep listening. For example, Renee L. Hill, Horace L. Griffin, Lightsey, Sneed, and Young included in their own theological and ethical reflection the narratives and experiences of black LGBTQ+ people. More than the disruptive quality of decentering whiteness and heteropatriarchy, the value of sharing these stories lies in the opportunity it presents to LGBTQ+ communities to know LGBTQ+ communities in their own language and values. In this practice toward knowing, ethics can be formulated based upon compassion and practicability, rather than the normativizing impulse. Lastly, engaging the process of formulating ethics in community requires vulnerability, which lies at the center of relationality. I have consistently utilized the term "community" in examining the process of formulating ethics as opposed to church (as indicative of an institution), the Black Church, or other institutional powers. I conceive of community alongside belonging, which relies upon choice and connectivity with persons who honor one another's dignity and their own integrity. Vulnerability can be practiced where there is community, that is, where there is a grounding willingness to center relationality. A practice of vulnerability within community softens the heart, in opening to others and in receiving, which supports communities as they strive toward fuller becoming and fosters an environment of belonging, nonduality, and thriving.

The oral histories invite a consideration of multiple paths to and conceptions of the good. The good may show up as cultivating beauty and gratitude, as in Alexis's case. Or, it can be, as in storäe's, changing their eating habits and being attentive to Earth care as a means of establishing right relationship in harmony with nature. The good can also come by way of hardship and discernment through the lens of one's own experience, as Natasha shows in their severing ties with those aspects of their traditions that alienate her from herself and departing from her long-time faith after feeling "bamboozled." Michael's concept of tempering, concentrating with intentionality in order to "find the lesson," can prompt one to consider that the good is a practice and a pursuit. The "fuck it" with which Jé intertwines liberation, the capacity to refuse and create something else outside of limiting logics and systems, further speaks to a kind of goodness that is not necessarily oppositional, but is its own path toward liberation.

At times what is most needed is a willingness to revisit what is considered good, especially when individuals, communities, or societies believe they have the "right answer." This speaks to the opportunity for creative possibility in liminality and becoming. Communities must also be attentive to create the space, as Christian ethicist Kate M. Ott posits, "For individuals to discover and define their sexuality in a way that is most consistent with whom they know themselves to be as God's beloved."[45] Goodness that is established and intentional on an individual level can then contribute to a more just and loving approach to sexuality within the community and in society.

Toward Inspirited Bodies/Embodied Spirits

Black LGBTQ+-focused scholarship responds to the disintegration of being blackqueer in black spaces and blackqueer in queer spaces, as well as the internal dissonance that accompanies the command to hold abjectification in the flesh. In this in-betweenness, ethicists like Victor Anderson, Sneed, and Leath de-problematized the bodies of blackqueer persons by centering the meanings they have formulated for themselves in their generativity, in their liminality, and in their quare-ness, respectively. What is rejected and outside of the framing of normativity necessarily makes its own meaning. And there is the possibility. The possibility is in inspirited bodies/embodied spirits.[46]

Blackqueerness with embodiment reflects integration by holding inseparable black and queer, body and spirit, and, subsequently, a pursuit of (in)spirit(edness) despite rejection of finding community despite pressures to disregard one's blackqueerness and its expressions. Embodied spirits/inspirited bodies are a value that reflects the equity of and entanglement of body and spirit through lived experience, and namely through sexuality; for "the body is the self, [...] the mind is a part of that body, and [...] emotions, too, emerge from the bodyself"; one could summatively say, spirit is of the bodyself.[47]

Blackqueer Harlem's counterpublics in part developed out a response to dire physical and social need. Early on, rent parties were a response to economic impoverishment, but also built community among many who were migrants from the south and from the

Caribbean. In the spaces they created, blackqueer Harlemites had a rare opportunity for the integration that eluded them in the racist segregation of New York City and the gender and sexual middle-class sensibilities espoused in black Harlem. Daily they faced the obstacle of needing to negotiate their full blackqueer presence in the Harlem public,[48] a fragmenting hierarchy of the self often experienced by persons who are both black and queer and marginalized peoples whose bodies have been vilified in heteronormative spaces. Yet, in their bodies they carried their resistance: the expression of gender through sartorial fluidity; the use of the body for personal pleasure where it had only come to recently know autonomy in its departure from the New South; the exploration of sexuality in communality that the civil society would punish with jail and the local society by ostracism. They were labeled as "part of an undesirable and all-too-visible black 'lowlife' that brought disrepute to the neighborhood and 'the race'."[49] Despite the backlash, they continued to live toward an integrative existence that enabled a fuller expression of the self. As both black feminist theorist Angela Y. Davis and historian David Levering Lewis affirmed, particularly their blues environments facilitated this reclamation of the body and its freeing from sexually repressive norms, while also going deeper into "sacred consciousness," providing a holistic experience of transcendence, albeit brief and circumstantial, yet frequently denied them in religious spaces that disparaged gender and sexual subversion.[50]

Within blackqueering critique, the body has undergone a process of transformation from a body framed as a site of trouble, fragmentation, and dissension to a body of a complex subjectivity and potentiality. Understanding the blackqueer body as a black body, stereotyped and stigmatized through subjection to anti-black ideology, blackqueering scholarship contends with its hypervisibility in scholarship and society, as well as its peculiar absence.[51] Further, it deals with/attends to the shame internalized by black LGBTQ+ people who have been taught to alienate themselves from their bodies. Yet, alongside the imposed hypersexualization and vulnerability of blackqueer bodies is potentiality and, as Emilie M. Townes notes, the holy.[52]

The oral histories, with their accompanying photographs of bodies engaging the sacred, mirror this value of embodied spirits/inspired bodies. Koach's drumming, inspired by ancestors known and unknown, reflects the embodiment of spirit in the world, even its capacity to shift the social space and individual sense of wellness, as in the case of their healing work at the Ferguson protests. Both Olivia and Alexis spoke to how one's positionality as a blackqueer person and black person informs an engagement with spirituality. In speaking to its exceptional quality, they cause me to consider, alongside womanists, what particularity in thinking of whole people might do to shape ethics. I think of storäe's approach to fashion, their sartorial ritual, as a means of integrating body and spirit, as well as both their and Charly's affirmation that art as ritual merges their physical, mental, spiritual, emotional, social selves. Finally, Charly's willingness to receive the spasms and "awkward" manifestations of Spirit connotes the ways spirit and body and the borders between them in relationship to others can be blurred or illusory, further situating the interconnectedness of integrativeness and justice love within an ethic.

As a part of a sexual ethic, there must be an embrace of the is-ness of all bodies, whatever the state of those bodies, and the spirit that inhabits them.[53] That spirit is of and in all, equitable in its accessibility, whatever the identity or practices of the beholder. Because we share human experience as inspirited bodies/embodied spirits, as a "unified whole'[54] (which we strive toward both individually and communally), we are able with effort to be more mindful of these truths when engaging one another—mindful of one another's suffering, mindful to not objectify but to create space for folks" subjectivity, mindful that our bodies are subject to a variety of conditions (e.g., illness, disability, aging) as time goes on and this will demand evolving just responses from individuals, communities, and society.[55]

Attentiveness to the intersection of gender and sexuality with race is much needed if an ethic is to be attentive to the inspirited bodies/embodied spirits of black people. As social theorist and religious ethicist Elias Ortega-Aponte notes, "For those committed to the Christian faith it is imperative to decry the sinful transubstantiation of black living bodies into dead flesh."[56] More specifically, the violence enacted against the embodied spirits/inspirited bodies of Black transgender women most frequently, but also trans people, must be addressed. Black transgender women experience multiple forms of violence in a trans-antagonistic society.[57] The violence frequently occurs in secrecy, without anyone witnessing it or willing to stop it, and disappears quickly without media coverage, sometimes with open-and-shut trials written off with the use of the "trans panic defense."[58] Egregiously, the violence is largely overlooked by religious communities and even those affirming the mattering of black lives, causing even greater specificity to come about in activist circles proclaiming, "all black lives matter" and "black trans lives matter."[59] H. Richard Niebuhr's ethic of response, as employed by Ortega-Aponte, finds resonance in upholding the value of inspired bodies/embodied spirits amidst bodily violence based on sexuality or gender, wherein communities may respond to the actions upon marginalized bodies, interpret the meanings and potential responses to the event, practice accountability, and offer social solidarity to affected community members.[60]

Toward Shared Thriving

Power has played a role in discourses of blackqueerness in theological and ethical scholarship from its beginnings. As examined in Chapter 2, both scholarly and community spaces have retained the power to construct family and community in exclusive terms, in ways that view blackqueer people as a perversion, a threat, a sin (e.g., as in the case of the ethicist Cheryl J. Sanders and Protestant denominations like the United Methodist Church). The power to direct the dialogue about a particular people (especially a marginalized people) and to take up space that crowds out their voices and power leads to a hyper(in)vis/audibility that maintains the positionality of "other" for black LGBTQ+ people.[61] In other cases, it leads to a focus on HIV/AIDS and homophobia (which are vital, though not sole, aspects of blackqueer experience), without attention to the ways blackqueer people create communal bonds, their strategies of thriving, their resistances and goodnesses, and the cultural productions of blackqueer people that can enable living into freer futures. Blackqueering theorists relocate power from traditionalism's relational framings and methodological constrictions toward expansiveness, deconstruction and reconstruction, interdependence, vulnerability, process, and change—more integrative values.

The settings fostered by Harlem's black sexual and gender nonconformists for the participation in communality of people of varying sexual orientations and gender expressions served to offer an alternative experience than what was available in more "respectable" parts of Harlem and of New York City. Arguably, as mentioned in Chapter 2, it is deviance that gives an alternative public its power, and that invites a disruption of heteronormativity, namely its gender and sexual roles and body politics.[62] People were welcomed from around the country and world to experience the communal spaces which blackqueer Harlem played a major role in creating. This flocking to the blues environments, the Hamilton Lodge Balls, and the rent parties should not be brushed off as merely "culture vulture" tourism, though it is certain the entertainment and the cultural burst of energy in Harlem were a draw to those outside of the neighborhood. I contend it was the openness and accessibility, the sharing of blackqueer Harlem, that made for a unique sense of engagement for those who were not a part of the neighborhood.

A counterpublic's power also lies in its ability to shape the public and to influence it toward some desired end, according to Nancy Fraser.[63] While the scope of this project does not enumerate the specific impact of blackqueer Harlem on their public, it is clear that it's disruption to the status quo was a force to be reckoned with—not because it had the power to forcibly change the society around it, but because in its being and becoming, it offered a counter-reality in which others from New York City and beyond could participate. Even the bohemians of Greenwich Village, the country's premiere gay enclave, came uptown to Harlem to experience the livelier, less exclusive gay life.[64]

The sounds of blackqueer Harlem, through the blues, presented disruptive and imaginative possibilities rooted in turning power on its head.[65] The rent parties were more than just parties. In a space and place where marginalization is the everyday experience, communality is political. The filled apartment and the elevated platforms of the Hamilton Lodge created openings to explorations of sexuality and gender that challenged the power of society's ability to dictate what is and what could be not only for blackqueer Harlem, but for black people. blackqueer Harlem in its openness to others and individual member's agency in exploring their personal power (sexual, gender, bodily) inspired the value of finding joy in one's and one's communities' power without the systematic hegemonizing of that power in the lives of others—shared thriving.

In blackqueering scholarship, a critique of power necessarily includes power redistribution. For example, Irene Monroe and Lightsey admonish the Black Church/es for forfeiting their power in the interest of whiteness and right-wing fundamentalist aims and in power grabs that sacrifice black LGBTQ+ people and even black communities' interests.[66] This critique is not exclusive to black Christian institutions and could be applied to the institutions of people of color and various black religions that support these same aims. The indictment of the struggle for relevancy that runs roughshod over black LGBTQ+ people in the process is an example of an unwillingness to interrogate one's own limiting relationship to power and an aversion to sharing power with those who are typically marginalized. A redistribution of power makes space for "everyone's moral potential" while supporting communities in doing communosexual ethics more justly.[67]

Alexis's realization of her planethood inspires me to think of power differently, and with shared thriving in relationship to her questions:

> What if we all understood that we were stars and planets? What if we all kind of *got* that? How would we then treat each other? How would we then respect each other? How would we then give each other the room to revolve and rotate, all at once? Would we have a different relationship to each other if we understood life is more cosmic than we do?

In an ethic, what might space for one another's power look like? Additionally, Michael's rejection of the designation of being blessed, because of its inequitable conferral, can create openings to what it may mean to eschew more power than one is entitled to so that power's reach may be more impactful for the collective good. Lastly, Nala's sense of shared thriving is reflected through her experience of having visited South Africa and creating her organization, "a trans-led grassroots project invested in advancing the social and economic well-being of African Descendants, with an urgent focus on queer, same-gender loving, transgender, and non-binary people, and ultimately the entire community."[68]

Shared thriving is enacted through equitable power relations. It retains power that does not seek to be power over. It evolves out of shared power. Thriving means having and wielding enough power. For some, because of the harms of oppression, power is perceived as a liability and a source of corruption. Its abuse does lead to corruption. However, power is possessed by everyone as a tool of self-determination, not of other-subjugation. Within shared thriving, power is a good toward communal vitality and social wellness.

Shared thriving helps us understand that there is no virtue in surrendering power to one's own detriment. Rather, shared power in the interest of shared thriving is an empowering posture rooted in communal belonging and a commitment to collective becoming for the good. When one person's power meets another, a choice (intentionally or habitually) is made to engage equitably, to assert dominating power, or to surrender one's power. The aim of the engagement of powers is not to create a new center, a new possessor of "the" power. Drawing from Young's ethical approach to power, which marked a move away from the self-sufficient autonomous self of queer theory (in tandem with Muñoz, to center a relationality rooted in mutuality), a blackqueer ethic seeks the shared thriving only found in relationality in order to practice mutuality and reciprocity in the opportunities for equitable power engagement that humans encounter each day.[69]

It is also necessary to include a critique of how race informs the use of power in communal notions of shared thriving. Racism has consistently functioned within Christian and United States sexual discourse to limit the thriving of people of color, especially black people in its anti-blackness and myth of white supremacy. West explains the ways anti-queer Christian teachings and white racism work together:

> The racial status of white people constitutes an abiding cultural norm and centre [sic] as black and brown people are consigned to a marginal racial status perpetually lacking in human worth and high-level human capacities. Sometimes, in a supposedly less harsh Christian narrative of white supremacy, black and brown people are regarded as occupying a perpetually pitiful human identity in need of ongoing, paternal, white Christian assistance. In both secular and Christian religious constructions of how moral worth is racially and sexually marked in society, insiders are indelibly divided from outsiders in a social arrangement that maintains hierarchical understandings of how we value one another in our communal lives.[70]

Such hierarchical understandings cause communities to neglect sexual and gender injustice with more lives being lost in the process. They stigmatize. They disintegrate community. Essentially, hierarchies that devaluate community members cause inequity in power that prompts erasure and produces a false sense of thriving for the few. Under this weight, everyone suffers.

West likewise forwards the rejection of claims upholding heterosexual supremacy, and instead finds value in a fluid power balance between heterosexuality, "same-sex desire and the gendering of sexuality."[71] This fluidity is the work of queering, more specifically black bisexual queering. It is often rigidity that keeps communities beholden to sexual ethics that do not serve communal right-relatedness. Embracing the expansion that black bisexual queering offers to a blackqueer ethics may enable communities to assess their relationships to power and their fears of the scarcity of power. Fluidity evokes abundance because nothing belongs in just one hand of power. Subsequently, breaking the binaries—of powerholder and oppressed, white and black, heterosexual and queer, cisgender and transgender—evokes abundance. Black bisexual queering utilized in the service of shared thriving promotes a disruption of the status quo as it relates to power: power does not have to be power-over in order to be powerful.

Conclusion

The five integrative values of a blackqueer ethic—communal belonging, individual and collective becoming, goodness, embodied spirits/inspirited bodies, and shared thriving—can offer communities a basis for sexual ethics that values people over the perception of piety. Rules-based sexual ethics, and even liberative sexual ethics that center whiteness, cis-gender, and heteropatriarchy, fragment communities and society, while limiting the capacity for individuals to show up as their fullest self-in-truth for the doing of community together. A blackqueer ethic posits that *how* we are to one another, our relations, is what determines the capacity of communities to thrive or to die. Disrupting the normativizing discourse by asserting blackqueer moral value—as found in certain integrative values in 1920s Harlem, with blackqueering ethical and theological scholarship, and blackqueer practitioners—challenges universalizing ideals that ignore or fracture particularity and diminish the experiences of those deemed "other." When blackqueer experiences can matter enough to communities to shape our sexual ethics, all experiences will matter. As long as sexual ethics centers whiteness, patriarchy, heteronormativity, homonormativity, cisgender experiences, and Christianity, they will be hypocritical, limited, and subsequently, unusable ethics. The mattering of blackqueer people—as makers of new meaning, establishers of communal worth and value, and resisters of abjectification—is at the heart of a blackqueer communal-sexual ethic that strives toward justice love so that all may be whole.

Notes

1   Mark D. Jordan, *The Ethics of Sex* (Malden, MA: Blackwell Publishers, 2002), 7.
2   Lisa Sowle Cahill, *Between the Sexes: Foundations for a Christian Ethics of Sexuality* (Philadelphia: Fortress Press, 1985), 152.
3   Marvin M. Ellison, *Making Love Just: Sexual Ethics for Perplexing Times* (Minneapolis: Fortress Press, 2012), 58.
4   Marvin Ellison, *Erotic Justice: A Liberating Ethic of Sexuality* (Louisville, KY: Westminster John Knox Press, 1996), 115.
5   Ellison, *Erotic Justice,* 114.
6   Jennifer S. Leath, "Is Queer the New Black?" *Harvard Divinity Bulletin* 43, nos. 3 and 4 (Summer/Autumn 2015), https://bulletin.hds.harvard.edu/articles/summerautumn2015/queer-new-black.
7   Leath, "Is Queer the New Black?"
8   Martin F. Manalansan IV, "The 'Stuff' of Archives: Mess, Migration, and Queer Lives," *Radical History Review* 120 (2014): 95.
9   Martin F. Manalansan IV, "The Messy Itineraries of Queerness," *Fieldsights* (July 21, 2015), accessed October 16, 2022, https://culanth.org/fieldsights/the-messy-itineraries-of-queerness.
10 Traci C. West, "Constructing Ethics: Reinhold Niebuhr and Harlem Women Activists," *Journal of the Society of Christian Ethics* 24, no. 1 (2004): 29.
11 Traci C. West, "Constructing Ethics: Reinhold Niebuhr and Harlem Women Activists," *Journal of the Society of Christian Ethics* 24, no. 1 (2004): 37, 46.
12 Ellison, *Making Love Just*, 68.

13   Fraser speaks more specifically to subaltern counterpublics. Nancy Fraser, "Rethinking the Public Sphere: A Contribution to the Critique of Actually Existing Democracy," *Social Text* 25, no. 26 (1990): 67.
14   Fraser, "Rethinking the Public Sphere" *Social Text* 25, no. 26 (1990): 67.
15   Angela Y. Davis, *Blues Legacies and Black Feminism: Gertrude "Ma" Rainey, Bessie Smith, and Billie Holiday* (New York: Random House, 1999), 41.
16   Lawrence W. Levine, *Black Culture and Black Consciousness: Afro-American Folk Thought from Slavery to Freedom* (New York: Oxford University Press, 1977), 237.
17   James F. Wilson, *Bulldaggers, Pansies, and Chocolate Babies: Performance, Race, and Sexuality in the Harlem Renaissance* (Ann Arbor: University of Michigan Press, 2010), 12.
18   David Levering Lewis, *When Harlem Was in Vogue* (New York: Oxford University Press, 1979), 107–8.
19   C. Riley Snorton makes a comprehensive argument for the ways that blackness and transness are "inextricably linked" with "transness [as] a racial narrative" and as "blackness finds its articulation within transness," though the two are also "irreconcilable." This is evidenced, for instance, in the mutability of gender that was practiced during chattel enslavement of black people (as also explicated by Hortense Spillers). See C. Riley Snorton, *Black on Both Sides: A Racial History of Trans Identity* (Minneapolis: University of Minnesota Press, 2017), 8, 57. I argue, building upon the intervention of Naomi Simmons-Thorne, for "interrupt[ing] the logic of biological determinism and the constraints of cissexism operating historically" in the life of trans figures. See Naomi Simmons-Thorne, "Pauli Murray and the Pronominal Problem: A De-essentialist Trans Historiography," *The Activist History Review*, May 30, 2019.
20   "Reina Gossett: Historical Erasure as Violence," interview by Hope Dector and Dean Spade, Barnard Center for Research on Women, Queer Dreams and Nonprofit Blues Conference at Columbia Law School, October 4–5, 2013. https://vimeo.com/144135575
21   Sneed, *Representations of Homosexuality*, 9.
22   It is tempting to refer to an "authentic self" but there are key distinctions to the self-in-truth. While an authentic self may speak to a static sense of identity or an essential self, the self-in-truth is ever evolving and tied to the environment of which it is a part; it is a fluid sense of self that shape-shifts in the moment based on the truth as

understood in that moment. Each moment invites a changing, though no less true, expression of the self.

23 Aliveness is not a juxtaposition of death. Ancestors, who have died, for instance, express aliveness though they are dead. A compost pile, full of decomposing things, expresses aliveness. A physically living person who is limited in their imagination limits aliveness. For more on aliveness despite and rethought in relationship to death, see Kevin Quashie, *Black Aliveness, or A Poetics of Being* (Durham: Duke University Press, 2021). There is also healing to be found in relation to and with the dead. For more on this, namely in light of queer death, see Laurel C. Schneider and Thelathia Nikki Young, "Talking to the Dead," in *Queer Soul and Queer Theology Ethics and Redemption in Real Life* (New York: Routledge, 2021). 17–33.

24 This is inspired by the southern African philosophy of Ubuntu.

25 Sneed, *Representations of Homosexuality*, 179, 192.

26 Sneed, *Representations of Homosexuality*, 179, 180. According to Sneed, a humanist ethic of openness recognizes ethics as a human endeavor, appreciates human worth, value, and action, and centers human being and agency. Much like a humanist ethic, a transreligious ethic evades theology-based or religion-based limitations by centering communality, including communal reflection. However, I contend that a human-centric emphasis can create a binary relationship with humans and the whole of nature and concede that theocentric interest can diminish the fervor of human agency out of dependence on the action of an unknowable God. I affirm a post-humanist understanding as forwarded by Roberto Che Espinoza: "By post-humanism, I do not mean after humanity or beyond humanity. I mean to point toward a radically material entanglement that unites or braids together all matter of life, which is vibrant in its becoming." Robyn Henderson-Espinoza, "Difference, Becoming, and Interrelatedness: A Material Resistance Becoming," *Cross Currents* 66, no. 2 (July 2016): 286.

27 Roger A. Sneed, *Representations of Homosexuality: Black Liberation Theology and Cultural Criticism* (New York: Palgrave Macmillan, 2010), 179.

28 Roger A. Sneed, "Like Fire Shut Up in Our Bones: Religion and Spirituality in Black Gay Men's Literature," *Black Theology* 6, no. 2 (2008): 242.

29 For insight into strategic essentialism, see Gayatri Chakravorty Spivak, "Subaltern Studies: Deconstructing Historiography," in *The Spivak Reader*, ed. Donna Landry and Gerald MacLean (London: Routledge, [1985] 1996), 203–36.

30 Roger A. Sneed, "Dark Matter: Liminality and Black Queer Bodies," in *Ain't I a Womanist Too?: Third Wave Womanist Religious Thought*, ed. Monica A. Coleman (Minneapolis: Fortress 2013), 142.

31 George Chauncey, *Gay New York: Gender, Urban Culture, and the Making of the Gay Male World 1890–1940* (New York: Basic 1994), 236.

32 "Robyn Henderson-Espinoza: Biography," SpeakOut—The Institute for Democratic Education and Culture, accessed May 17, 2019, https://www.speakoutnow.org/speaker/henderson-espinoza-robyn. Espinoza, "Difference, Becoming," 283. The process that Espinoza is explaining, diffraction, is from Karen Barad, *Meeting the University Halfway: Quantum Physics and the Entanglement of Matter and Meaning* (Durham: Duke University Press, 2007).

33 Wilson, *Bulldaggers, Pansies, and Chocolate Babies*, 18.

34 Wilson, *Bulldaggers, Pansies, and Chocolate Babies*, 20–1.

35 Thelathia "Nikki" Young, *Black Queer Ethics, Family, and Philosophical Imagination* (New York: Palgrave MacMillan, 2016), 59.

36 Jennifer S. Leath, "Revising Jezebel Politics: Toward a New Black Sexual Ethic," in *Black Intersectionalities: A Critique for the 21st Century*, ed. Monica Michlin and Jean-Paul Rocchi (Liverpool: Liverpool University Press, 2013), 196.

37 Henderson-Espinoza, "Difference, Becoming, and Interrelatedness," 286. Espinoza's description of becoming builds upon philosophers Gilles Deleuze and Félix Guattari's argument that becoming changes and continually renews the function of the element, which is, in this case, community. For Espinoza, this becoming takes place in the borderlands (á la Gloria Anzaldúa), the in-between, liminal space. As the body is also continually in a process of becoming, the discourse of the body continues to unfold to reflect the values espoused within a community and to articulate new values.

38 Henderson-Espinoza, "Difference, Becoming, and Interrelatedness," 284, 286.

39 Jack Halberstam, *The Queer Art of Failure* (Durham: Duke University Press, 2011), 24.

40 Chauncey, *Gay New York*, 248.

41 Chauncey, *Gay New York*, 15–16. The quote reads, "While the 'faggots' who were highly visible in the neighborhood's streets and nightspots might earn a degree of grudging respect from others, they had no hope of respectability. Most middle-class gay Harlemites

struggled to keep news of their homosexuality from spreading, lest it cause their social downfall." For clarification, Chauncey explains use of the term "faggot," which was used more frequently by black people than white people in New York City to refer to men "who dressed or behaved in what they considered to be an effeminate manner."

42 Young, *Black Queer Ethics*, 195.
43 Victor Anderson, *Beyond Ontological Blackness* (New York: Continuum, 1995), 16. As Victor Anderson argues regarding black theology and its liberationist construction that he claims does not create space for transcendence beyond its oppressed-oppressor paradigm, blackqueering centering in resistance can create a similar paradigm built around hegemony that needs imagination to envision blackqueer futures (and present) beyond (or even powerfully alongside) struggle.
44 Ellison, *Making Love Just*, 2.
45 Kate M. Ott, "Sexuality, Health, and Integrity," in *Professional Sexual Ethics: A Holistic Ministry Approach*, ed. Patricia Beattie Jung and Darryl W. Stephens (Minneapolis: Fortress 2013), 14.
46 The use of "embodied spirits" and "inspirited bodies," as well as their reversal so as to not place either term in a position of primacy is from Margaret Farley, "Sexuality and Its Meanings," in *Just Love: A Framework for Christian Ethics* (New York: Contiuum 2006), 109–73. I focus on this framing for the ways it is exacerbated by religiosity grounded in traditionalism and with the understanding that other immaterial factors that make up the internal self may be included in "spirit." "Spirits"/ "inspirited" conceived here connotes that which animates and gives life, but not necessarily in theistic terms.
47 Christine E. Gudorf, *Body, Sex, and Pleasure: Reconstructing Christian Sexual Ethics* (Cleveland: Pilgrim 1994), 160.
48 Chauncey, *Gay New York*, 248.
49 Chauncey, *Gay New York*, 253. According to Chauncey, they were labeled along "with prostitutes, salacious entertainers, and 'uncultured' rural migrants" by "many middle-class and churchgoing African Americans."
50 Davis, *Blues Legacies and Black Feminism*, 8–9.
51 See Pamela R. Lightsey, "Inner Dictum: A Womanist Reflection from the Queer Realm," *Black Theology* 10, no. 3 (November 2011): 248. See also Pamela R. Lightsey, *Our Lives Matter: A Womanist Queer Theology* (Eugene, OR: Wipf and Stock, 2015), 7.

52 Emilie M. Townes, "The Dancing Mind: Queer Black Bodies and Activism in Academy and Church" (Gilberto Castañeda Lecture, Chicago Theological Seminary, Chicago, IL, April 28, 2011).

53 The embrace of a body's is-ness rests on the presupposition that the bodies are not innately evil, and do not require a moral valuation of "good" in order to be honored. A blackqueer ethics honors the complexity of bodies for people whose bodies do not align with their understanding of themselves and people with disabilities, bodies that sometimes act in opposition to the mind or spirit of the embodied. See Jackie Leach Scully, "When Embodiment Isn't Good," *Theology & Sexuality* 9 (1998): 10–28. See also Krzysztof Bujnowski, "Through the Wilderness," in *Trans/Formations*, ed. Lisa Isherwood and Marcella Althaus-Reid (London: SCM Press, 2009), 59–69. Also, Elizabeth Stuart, "Disruptive Bodies: Disability, Embodiment, and Sexuality," in *Sexuality and the Sacred: Sources for Theological Reflection*, Second Edition, ed. Marvin M. Ellison and Kelly Brown Douglas (Louisville: Westminster John Knox Press, 2010), 322–37. For insight into one perspective of the gifts offered by transgender people in religious community, see Virginia Ramey Mollenkott, "We Come Bearing Gifts: Seven Lessons Religious Congregations Can Learn from Transpeople," in *Trans/Formations*, ed. Lisa Isherwood and Marcella Althaus-Reid (London: SCM 2009), 46–58.

54 Farley, *Just Love*, 120.

55 Farley, *Just Love*, 120.

56 Elias Ortega-Aponte, "The Haunting of Lynching Spectacles: An Ethic of Response," in *Anti-Blackness and Christian Ethics*, ed. Vincent W. Lloyd and Andrew Prevot (Maryknoll: Orbis Books, 2017), 112.

57 "Violence against the Transgender Community in 2019," The Human Rights Campaign, accessed April 28, 2019, https://www.hrc.org/resources/violence-against-the—transgender-community-in-2019.

58 According to The National LGBT Bar Association and Foundation, "The gay and trans 'panic' defense is a legal strategy which asks a jury to find that a victim's sexual orientation or gender identity is to blame for the defendant's violent reaction, including murder. It is not a freestanding defense to criminal liability, but rather a legal tactic which is used to bolster other defenses." The National LGBTBar Association and Foundation, "Gay/Trans Panic Defense," accessed May 1, 2019, https://lgbtbar.org/programs/advocacy/gay-trans-panic-defense/.

59 I accept the necropolitical critique that could be fielded regarding my inclusion of black trans death and the generativity this may create for

this portion of my book. At the same time, I hold the complexity of what it means to retain silence as it relates to the mattering of black trans lives and deaths with so few national stories that reflect a level of care from among religious realms. See C. Riley Snorton and Jin Haritaworn, "Trans Necropolitics: A Transnational Reflection on Violence, Death, and the Trans of Color Afterlife," in *Transgender Studies Reader 2*, ed. Susan Stryker and Aren Aizura (New York: Routledge, 2013), 66–76.

60 Ortega-Aponte, "The Haunting of Lynching Spectacles," 118.
61 Leath, "Is Queer the New Black?".
62 See Cathy J. Cohen, "Deviance as Resistance: A New Research Agenda for the Study of Black Politics," *DuBois Review* 1, no. 1 (2004), 27–45.
63 Fraser, "Rethinking the Public Sphere," 71.
64 Chauncey, *Gay New York*, 244.
65 Daphne Duval Harrison, *Black Pearls: Blues Queens of the 1920s* (New Brunswick: Rutgers University Press, 1988), 111.
66 Lightsey, "Inner Dictum," 345. Irene Monroe, "Between a Rock and a Hard Place," in *Out of the Shadows, Into the Light: Christianity and Homosexuality*, ed. Miguel A. De La Torre (Danvers: Chalice Press, 2009), 44–51.
67 Young, *Black Queer Ethics*, 182.
68 Reuniting of African Descendants, "Mission & Vision," accessed December 16, 2022, https://theroadproject.org/our-vision.
69 Young, *Black Queer Ethics*, 168–70.
70 Traci C. West, "Black Bisexual Queering of Anti-Violence Christian Ethics," *Modern Believing* 60, no. 1 (2019): 16.
71 West, "Black Bisexual Queering," 20.

EPILOGUE

Living archives are for those who dream themselves possible: in the now, in the past, in futures. *A Blackqueer Sexual Ethics* and its sources for ethical reflection are a hopeful representation of the possibility one can be fortunate to encounter in a living archive. It was a transformative experience for me to examine and curate these stories and images of blackqueerness and spirit in the service of blackqueer and trans futures—their here/there-ness, now/always-ness, already/not yet-ness—that I know will be and will be glorious.

This work is not intended to be a neat, refined presentation of blackqueerness (and in the spirit of blackqueerness, it should not be), but an opening. To otherwise. To opacities. To mysteries and unknowns. Black feminist futuring prompts one toward living into a future that ought to be, "a future that should be right now," as forwarded by black feminist theorist Tina Campt.[1] A blackqueer ethics offers a consideration into "the should, the ought," which is an opening for an ethical claim. And this is where my moral inquiry began: what should's and ought's do blackqueerness prompt us toward in thinking ethics? In what sources would such claims and values and virtues lie? Where, within a blackqueer canon—which is always a "loose canon"—might one locate moral subjectivity and a vision that counters the hegemonic power that makes abject the black, the queer, the trans, the femme?

As I named in the introduction, I do not think queerness—and more specifically, blackqueerness—apart from transness. Still, I have space to develop further in my enacting this enmeshment disciplinarily (or, more accurately, beyond disciplinary bounds), and subsequently, personally. I understand transness warrants its own deep and situated exploration in the disciplines of ethics and sexual ethics. And that transness and queerness are distinct, though at times overlapping. While more than half of the subjects in Chapter 3 identify as nonbinary or transgender along with expressions growing out of gender nonconformity in 1920s Harlem, I am aware that this project is limited in its exploration of trans experiences. However, it is my hope that it speaks to the kinds of spaces in which trans people have thrived and can thrive.

I am also curious about what a deepening into the transreligious might mean for religious ethics. Will it create the famed "slippery slope" that purportedly appears when discourse is destabilized, a discourse where anything goes? I doubt it. I believe in communities' moral reflectivity a bit more than this, that what is disintegrative, with a shift, can become integrative. This is what it means to be in process. Could it become a universalizing of "love" and a co-opting of Eastern and Global South traditions, as so often happens in the Western world? Likely. Still, as noted in my final chapter, fluidity makes space for mistakes and messiness. This, too, is what it means to be in process, living into and often stumbling toward the integrative, the liberative, right relationship.

A blackqueer ethics posits that *how* we are to one another in our doing of the actions we choose is what determines the capacity of communities to thrive, or for them to suffer through their abuses of power and limiting norms. Disrupting normativizing logics by asserting blackqueer moral fecundity, as affirmed in this living archive, challenges universalizing ideals that ignore or fracture particularity and diminish the experiences of those deemed "other." As previously mentioned, when blackqueer experience matters enough to shape our ethics, then all experiences will matter, and the discourse may more robustly reflect a liberative relationality. If ethics (sexual or otherwise) center whiteness, patriarchy, heteronormativity, homonormativity, and cis-centricism and accompanying hegemonic logics and is bound by Western Christianity, they will be impotent, and subsequently, unusable ethics. The mattering of blackqueer people—as makers of new meaning, establishers of communal worth and value, resisters of abjectification, and as simply blackqueer folks—is at the heart of a blackqueer communal-sexual ethic that strives toward justice love so that all may be liberated through seeking new, old, revolutionary, deviant, and radically imaginative ways of relating that are not "straight and narrow" but are as blackqueerly crooked as they are wide.

Note

1 Tina Campt, "Black Feminist Futures and the Practice of Fugitivity," Barnard College Center for Research on Women, October 7, 2014, accessed October 16, 2022, https://www.youtube.com/watch?v=2ozhqw840PU.

BIBLIOGRAPHY

"A Rent Party Tragedy." In *The New York Age*. New York, NY, December 11, 1926.

Agard-Jones, Vanessa. "What the Sands Remember." *GLQ: A Journal of Lesbian and Gay Studies* 18, nos. 2–3 (June 1, 2012): 325–46.

Ambrose, Elyse. "Aesthetic Intimacies: Reflections on Elle Pérez's Devotions at the BMA." BMoreArt, September 26, 2022. Accessed October 16, 2022. https://bmoreart.com/2022/09/aesthetic-intimacies-reflections-on-elle-perezs-devotions.html.

Anderson, Jervis. *This Was Harlem: A Cultural Portrait, 1900–1950*. New York: Farrar, Straus, Giroux, 1981.

Anderson, Victor. *Beyond Ontological Blackness*. New York: Continuum 1995.

Anderson, Victor. "The Black Church and the Curious Body of the Black Homosexual." In *Loving the Body: Black Religious Studies and the Erotic*, edited by Anthony Pinn and Dwight Hopkins, 297–314. New York: Palgrave Macmillan, 2004.

Armstrong, Amaryah Shaye. "Thinking Practice: Method, Pedagogy, Power and the Question of a Black Queer Theology." *Modern Believing* 60, no. 1 (2019): 5–14.

Barad, Karen. *Meeting the University Halfway: Quantum Physics and the Entanglement of Matter and Meaning*. Durham: Duke University Press, 2007.

Barnet, Andrea. *All-Night Party: The Women of Bohemian Greenwich Village and Harlem, 1913–1930*. Chapel Hill: Algonquin Books of Chapel Hill, 2004.

Beam, Joseph. "Making Ourselves from Scratch." In *Brother to Brother: New Writings by Black Gay Men*, edited by Essex Hemphill, conceived by Joseph Beam. Boston: Alyson 1991.

Best, Wallace D. *Langston's Salvation: American Religion and the Bard of Harlem*. New York: New York University 2017.

Bidwell, Duane R. *When One Religion Isn't Enough: The Lives of Spiritually Fluid People*. Boston: Beacon 2018.

"Bishop Yvette Flunder." City of Refuge UCC. Accessed April 27, 2019. http://www.sfrefuge.org/bishop-yvette-flunder.

Bujnowski, Krzysztof. "Through the Wilderness." In *Trans/Formations*, edited by Lisa Isherwood and Marcella Althaus-Reid, 59–69. London: SCM 2009.

Cahill, Lisa Sowle. *Between the Sexes: Foundations for a Christian Ethics of Sexuality*. Minneapolis: Fortress Press, 1985.

Cahill, Lisa Sowle. *Sex, Gender, and Christian Ethics*. Cambridge: Cambridge University Press, 1996.

Campt, Tina M. *Listening to Images*. Durham: Duke University Press, 2017.

Campt, Tina. "Black Feminist Futures and the Practice of Fugitivity." *Barnard College Center for Research on Women*, October 7, 2014. Accessed October 16, 2022, https://www.youtube.com/watch?v=2ozhqw840PU

Cannon, Katie G. "Sexing Black Women: Liberation from the Prisonhouse of Anatomical Authority." In *Loving the Body: Black Religious Studies and the Erotic*, edited by Dwight N. Hopkins and Anthony B. Pinn. New York: Palgrave Macmillan, 2007.

Chauncey, George. *Gay New York: Gender, Urban Culture, and the Making of the Gay Male World 1890–1940*. New York: Basic 1994.

Cheng, Patrick. *Rainbow Theology: Bridging Race, Sexuality, and Spirit*. New York: Seabury 2013.

Cohen, Cathy. "Deviance as Resistance: A New Research Agenda for the Study of Black Politics." *Du Bois Review* 1, no. 1 (2004): 27–45.

Cone, James H. *The Spirituals and the Blues: An Interpretation*. Maryknoll: Orbis Books, 1992.

Copeland, M. Shawn. *Enfleshing Freedom: Body, Race and Being*. Minneapolis: Fortress 2009.

Crawley, Ashon T. *Blackpentecostal Breath: The Aesthetics of Possibility*. New York: Fordham University Press, 2017.

Crawley, Ashon T. "Blackqueer Aesthesis: Sexuality and the Rumor and Gossip of Black Gospel." In *Race and Displacement Nation, Migration, and Identity in the Twenty-First Century*, edited by Maha Marouan and Merinda Simmons, 27–42. Tuscaloosa: University of Alabama Press, 2013.

Cvetkovich, Ann. *An Archive of Feelings: Trauma, Sexuality, and Lesbian Public Cultures (Series Q)*. Illustrated. Durham: Duke University Press 2003.

Davis, Angela Y. *Blues Legacies and Black Feminism: Gertrude "Ma" Rainey, Bessie Smith, and Billie Holiday*. New York: Vintage 1999.

De La Torre, Miguel A. *A Lily Among the Thorns: Imagining a New Christian Sexuality*. 1st ed. San Francisco: Jossey-Bass, 2007.

De La Torre, Miguel A. *Liberating Sexuality: Justice between the Sheets*. St. Louis: Chalice 2016.

Dorsey, Bruce. "'Making Men What They Should Be': Male Same-Sex Intimacy and Evangelical Religion in Early Nineteenth-Century New England." *Journal of the History of Sexuality* 24, no. 3 (September 2015): 345–77.

Douglas, Kelly Brown. *Black Bodies and the Black Church: A Blues Slant*. New York: Palgrave Macmillan, 2014.

Douglas, Kelly Brown. *Sexuality and the Black Church: A Womanist Perspective*. Maryknoll: Orbis Press, 1999.

"Dr. A. C. Powell Scores Pulpit Evils." In *The New York Age*. New York, NY, November 16, 1929.

"Dr. Powell's Crusade against Abnormal Vice Is Approved: Pastors and Laity Endorse Dr. Powell's Denunciation of Degeneracy in the Pulpit: Chorus of Commendation Is Heard as Eminent Men Express Approval and Give Promises of Their Support." In *The New York Age*. New York, NY, November 23, 1929.

Duggan, Lisa. *The Twilight of Equality?: Neoliberalism, Cultural Politics, and the Attack on Democracy*. Boston: Beacon 2003.

Ellison, Marvin M. *Erotic Justice: A Liberating Ethic of Sexuality*. Louisville: Westminster John Knox Press, 1996.

Ellison, Marvin M. *Making Love Just: Sexual Ethics for Perplexing Times*. Minneapolis: Fortress 2012.

"Fact Sheet on LGBT Youth." Religious Institute. Accessed May 8, 2019. http://religiousinstitute.org/resources/fact-sheet-lgbt-youth/.

Farajajé-Jones, Elias (Ibrahim Abdurrahman Farajajé). "Breaking the Silence: Towards an In-the-Life Theology." In *Black Theology: A Documentary History (Volume Two: 1980–1992)*, edited by James H. Cone and Gayraud S. Wilmore, 139–59. Maryknoll: Orbis 1993.

Farber, Roland. *The Ocean of God: On the Transreligious Future of Religions*. London: Anthem 2019.

Farley, Margaret A. *Personal Commitments: Beginning, Keeping, Changing*. New York: Harper & Row 1986.

Farley, Margaret A. *Just Love: A Framework for Christian Sexual Ethics*. New York: Continuum 2006.

Feinstein, Elaine. *Bessie Smith: Empress of the Blues*. New York: Penguin 1985.

Fell, John L. and Terkild Vinding. *Stride! Fats, Jimmy, Lion, Lamb, and All the Other Ticklers*. Lanham: Scarecrow 1999.

The Flying Cavelier. "Carrying the Torch." In *The New York Age*. New York, NY, March 4, 1933.

Fraser, Nancy. "Rethinking the Public Sphere: A Contribution to the Critique of Actually Existing Democracy." *Social Text* 25, no. 26 (1990): 56–80.

Gallagher, Julie A. *Black Women and Politics in New York City*. Urbana: University of Illinois Press, 2012.
Garber, Eric. "A Spectacle in Color: The Lesbian and Gay Subculture of Jazz Age Harlem." In *Hidden from History: Reclaiming the Gay and Lesbian Past*, edited by Martin B. Duberman, Martha Vicinus and George Chauncey, 318–31. New York: Penguin 1989.
Glaude, Eddie. "The History That James Baldwin Wanted America to See." *The New Yorker*, June 19, 2020.
Gold, Roberta S. "The Black Jews of Harlem: Representation, Identity, and Race, 1920–1939." *American Quarterly* 55, no. 2 (June 2003): 179–225.
Gossett, Reina (Tourmaline). Interview by Hope Dector and Dean Spade, Barnard Center for Research on Women. Queer Dreams and Nonprofit Blues Conference at Columbia Law School, October 4–5, 2013.
Griffin, Horace L. "Giving New Birth: Lesbians, Gays, and "The Family": A Pastoral Care Perspective." *Journal of Pastoral Theology* 3, no. 84 (1993): 88–98.
Griffin, Horace L. "Revisioning Christian Ethical Discourse on Homosexuality: A Challenge for Pastoral Care in the 21st Century." *Journal of Pastoral Care* 53, no. 2 (June 1999): 209–19.
Griffin, Horace L. *Their Own Receive Them Not: African American Lesbians and Gays in Black Churches*. Cleveland: Pilgrim 2006.
Griffin, Horace L. "Toward a True Black Liberation Theology: Affirming Homoeroticism, Black Gay Christians, and Their Love Relationships." In *Loving the Body: Black Religious Studies and the Erotic*, edited by Anthony Pinn and Dwight Hopkins, 133–56. New York: Palgrave Macmillan, 2004.
Gumbs, Alexis Pauline. *M Archives: After the End of the World*. Durham: Duke University Press, 2018.
Gudorf, Christine E. *Body, Sex, and Pleasure: Reconstructing Christian Sexual Ethics*. Cleveland: Pilgrim 1994.
Halberstam, Jack. *The Queer Art of Failure*. Durham: Duke University Press, 2011.
"Hamilton Lodge Ball an Unusual Spectacle." In *The New York Age*. New York, NY, March 6, 1926.
"Hamilton Lodge, No. 710 in Annual Masquerade and Civic Ball." In *The New York Age*. New York, NY, March 5, 1927.
Harris, Frederick C. "The Rise of Respectability Politics." *Dissent* 61, no. 1 (Winter 2014): 33–7.
Harrison, Beverly Wildung. "Doing Christian Ethics." In *Justice in the Making: Feminist Social Ethics*, edited by Elizabeth Bounds, Pamela

Brubaker, Jane E. Hicks, Marilyn J. Legge, Rebecca Todd Peters, and Traci C. West, 30–7. Louisville: Westminster John Knox Press, 2004.

Harrison, Daphne Duval. *Black Pearls: Blues Queens of the 1920s*. New Brunswick: Rutgers University Press, 1988.

Hartman, Saidiya. "Venus in Two Acts." *Small Axe: A Caribbean Journal of Criticism* 26 (May 31, 2008): 1–14.

Hartman, Saidiya. *Wayward Lives, Beautiful Experiments: Intimate Histories of Social Upheaval*. London: W. W. Norton 2019.

Harvey, Jennifer. "Disrupting the Normal: Queer Family Life as Sacred Work." In *Queer Christianities: Lived Religion in Transgressive Forms*, edited by Kathleen T. Talvacchia, Michael F. Pettinger, and Mark Larrimore, 103–14. New York: New York University Press, 2015.

Henderson-Espinoza, Robyn (Roberto Che Espinoza). "Difference, Becoming, and Interrelatedness: A Material Resistance Becoming." *Cross Currents* 66, no. 2 (July 2016): 281–9.

Henry, Dorinda G. "'I, Too, Sing Songs of Freedom': A Theo-Sociological Praxis toward an Emancipatory Ethic for the Black Church and Its Trans-Same-and-Both-Gender-Loving Members." In *The Black Church Studies Reader*, edited by Alton B., Pollard III, and Carol B. Duncan, 279–90. New York: Palgrave Macmillan, 2016.

Higginbotham, Evelyn Brooks. *Righteous Discontent: The Women's Movement in the Black Baptist Church, 1880–1920*. Cambridge: Harvard University Press, 1994.

Hill, Renee L. "Who Are We for Each Other?: Sexism, Sexuality, and Womanist Theology." In *Black Theology: A Documentary History (Volume Two: 1980–1992)*, edited by James H. Cone and Gayraud S. Wilmore, 345–54. Maryknoll: Orbis 1993.

Hill, Renee L. "Human Sexuality: The Rest of the Story." In *Walk Together Children: Black and Womanist Theologies, Church and Theological Education*, edited by Dwight N. Hopkins and Linda E. Thomas, 183–92. Eugene: Cascade 2010.

hooks, bell. *Belonging: A Culture of Place*. New York: Routledge, 2009.

The HRC Foundation. "Violence against the Transgender Community in 2019." The Human Rights Campaign. Accessed April 28, 2019. https://www.hrc.org/resources/violence-against-the-transgender-community-in-2019.

Hull, Gloria T. and Akasha Gloria Hull. *Soul Talk: The New Spirituality of African American Women*. Rochester: Inner Traditions/Bear & Co, 2001.

Imarisha, Walidah, adrienne maree brown, and Sheree Renee Thomas, eds. *Octavia's Brood: Science Fiction Stories from Social Justice Movements*. Oakland: AK/IAS, 2015.

Jakobsen, Janet and Ann Pellegrini. "Not Born That Way." In *Love the Sin: Sexual Regulation and the Limits of Religious Tolerance*. Boston: Beacon Press, 2004.

Johnson, Charles Spurgeon. "The Negro Frontage on American Life." In *The New Negro*, edited by Alain Locke, 279–99. New York: Touchstone, 1992.

Johnson, E. Patrick. *Black. Queer. Southern. Women: An Oral History*. Durham: UNC Press, 2018.

Johnson, E. Patrick. *Honeypot: Black Southern Women Who Love Women*. Durham: Duke University Press, 2019.

Johnson, E. Patrick. "'Quare' Studies, or (Almost) Everything I Know about Queer Studies I Learned from My Grandmother." *Text and Performance Quarterly* 21, no. 1 (January 2001): 1–25.

Johnson, E. Patrick. *Sweet Tea: Black Gay Men of the South*. University of North Carolina Press, 2011.

Johnson, James Weldon. *Black Manhattan*. New York: Da Capo Press, Inc., 1930.

Johnson, James Weldon. "Harlem: The Culture Capital." In *Double Take: A Revisionist Harlem Renaissance Anthology*. New Brunswick: Rutgers University Press, 2001.

Jordan, Mark D. *The Ethics of Sex*. Malden: Blackwell Publishers, 2002.

Karera, Axelle. "Black Feminist Philosophy and the Politics of Refusal," In *The Oxford Handbook of Feminist Philosophy*, edited by Ásta and Kim Q. Hall, 109–119. New York: Oxford University Press, 2021.

King, Shannon. *Whose Harlem Is This, Anyway?: Community Politics and Grassroots Activism during the New Negro Era*. New York: New York University Press, 2015.

Leath, Jennifer. "Is Queer the New Black?" *Harvard Divinity Bulletin* 43, nos. 3 and 4 (Summer/Autumn 2015).

Leath, Jennifer S. "(Out of) Places, Please! Demystifying Opposition to Procreative Choice in Afro-Diasporic Communities in the United States." *Journal of Feminist Studies in Religion* 30, no. 1 (Spring 2014): 156–65.

Leath, Jennifer S. "Revising Jezebel Politics: Toward a New Black Sexual Ethic." In *Black Intersectionalities: A Critique for the 21st Century*, edited by Monica Michlin and Jean-Paul Rocchi, 195–210. Liverpool: Liverpool University Press, 2013.

Levine, Lawrence W. *Black Culture and Black Consciousness: Afro-American Folk Thought from Slavery to Freedom*. New York: Oxford University Press, 1977.

Lewis, David Levering. *When Harlem Was in Vogue*. New York: Oxford University Press, 1979.

Lightsey, Pamela R. "Inner Dictum: A Womanist Reflection from the Queer Realm." *Black Theology* 10, no. 3 (November 2011): 339–49.

Lightsey, Pamela R. *Our Lives Matter: A Womanist Queer Theology.* Eugene, OR: Wipf and Stock, 2015.
Locke, Alain. *The Negro and His Music.* New York: J.B. Lyon Press, 1936.
Manalansan IV, Martin F. "The 'Stuff' of Archives: Mess, Migration, and Queer Lives." *Radical History Review,* no. 120 (2014): 94–107.
Manalansan IV, Martin F. 2015. "The Messy Itineraries of Queerness." Theorizing the Contemporary, *Fieldsights,* July 21. Accessed December 30, 2022. https://culanth.org/fieldsights/the-messy-itineraries-of-queerness.
Martin, Jerry L., ed. *Theology without Walls: The Transreligious Imperative.* London: Routledge, 2020.
michele, storäe. "Freedom-making as Praxis." Accessed March 1, 2021. https://www.practicefreedommaking.com/.
Mollenkott, Virginia Ramey. "We Come Bearing Gifts: Seven Lessons Religious Congregations Can Learn from Transpeople." In *Trans/Formations,* edited by Lisa Isherwood and Marcella Althaus-Reid, 46–58. London: SCM Press, 2009.
Monroe, Irene. "Between a Rock and a Hard Place." In *Out of the Shadows, Into the Light: Christianity and Homosexuality,* edited by Miguel A. De La Torre, 39–58. Danvers: Chalice Press, 2009.
Monroe, Irene. "When and Where I Enter, then the Whole Race Enters with Me: Que(e)rying Exodus." In *Loving the Body: Black Religious Studies and the Erotic,* edited by Anthony Pinn and Dwight Hopkins, 121–31. New York: Palgrave Macmillan, 2004.
Moore, Darnell L. *No Ashes in the Fire: Coming of Age Black and Free in America.* New York: Bold Type Books, 2018.
Moultrie, Monique. *Passionate and Pious: Religious Media and Black Women's Sexuality.* Durham: Duke University Press, 2017.
Muñoz, José Esteban. *Cruising Utopia: The Then and There of Queer Futurity.* New York: New York University Press, 2009.
Murray, Pauli. "Black Theology and Feminist Theology." In *Black Theology: A Documentary History (Volume One: 1966–1979),* edited by James H. Cone and Gayraud S. Wilmore. Maryknoll: Orbis Books, 1993.
Naison, Mark D. *Communists in Harlem during the Depression.* Champaign: University of Illinois Press, 2004.
National Action Network. "Sharpton Entertainment to Hold 'My Brother's Keeper' Panel Focusing on LGBT Rights Saturday at National Action Network After Violence Claims the Life of Community Transgender Woman Islan Nettles." Accessed May 3, 2019. http://nationalactionnetwork.net/press/sharpton-entertainment-to-hold-my-brothers-keeper-panel-focusing-on-lgbt-rights-saturday-at-

national-action-network-after-violence-claims-the-life-of-community-transgender-woman-islan-nettles/.
The National LGBT Bar Association and Foundation. "Gay/Trans Panic Defense." Accessed May 1, 2019. https://lgbtbar.org/programs/advocacy/gay-trans-panic-defense/.
Nelson, James B. *Embodiment: An Approach to Sexuality and Christian Theology*. Minneapolis: Fortress Press, 1978.
Nestle, Joan. "'I Lift My Eyes to the Hill': The Life of Mabel Hampton as Told by a White Woman." In *A Fragile Union: New and Selected Writings by Joan Nestle*. San Francisco: Cleiss Press, 1998.
Oakley, Giles. *The Devil's Music: A History of the Blues*. Cambridge: DaCapo Press, 1983.
Ortega-Aponte, Elias. "The Haunting of Lynching Spectacles: An Ethic of Response." In *Anti-Blackness and Christian Ethics*, edited by Vincent W. Lloyd and Andrew Prevot, 111–29. Maryknoll: Orbis Books, 2017.
Osofsky, Gilbert. *Harlem: The Making of a Ghetto; Negro New York, 1890–1930*. New York: Harper & Row, 1971.
Ott, Kate M. "Sexuality, Health, and Integrity." In *Professional Sexual Ethics: A Holistic Ministry Approach*, edited by Patricia Beattie Jung and Darryl W. Stephens, 11–22. Minneapolis: Fortress Press, 2013.
Ott, Kate. *Sex, Tech, and Faith: Ethics for a Digital Age*. Grand Rapids: Eerdmans, 2022.
Parks, Gordon (oral history interview). December 30, 1964. Archives of American Art. Smithsonian Institution. https://www.aaa.si.edu/collections/interviews/oral-history-interview-gordon-parks-11480#transcript
Patton, Venetria K. and Maureen Honey. *Double-Take: A Revisionist Harlem Renaissance Anthology*. New Brunswick: Rutgers University Press, 2001.
"Pentecostal Faith Church Closes Revival Campaign." In *The New York Age*, September 17, 1932.
Quashie, Kevin. *Black Aliveness, or A Poetics of Being*. Durham: Duke University Press, 2021.
"Race Riot in New York." In *Springville Journal*. July 20, 1905.
Rainey, Gertrude "Ma." In *Double Take: A Revisionist Harlem Renaissance Anthology*, edited by Venetria K. Patton and Maureen Honey. New Brunswick: Rutgers University Press, 2001.
Ray, Ebenezer. "Fifteen Arrested by Police as 'Fairies' Turn 'Em On: Oops My Dear, Fairies Stomp at Rockland." In *The New York Age*. New York, NY, March 5, 1938.

Reuniting of African Descendants. "Mission & Vision." Accessed December 16, 2022. https://theroadproject.org/our-vision.

Rhodes, Tamara. "A Living, Breathing Revolution: How Libraries Can Use 'Living Archives' to Support, Engage, and Document Social Movements." *IFLA Journal* 40, no. 1 (2014): 5–11.

Robertson, Stephen, Shane White, Stephen Garton, and Graham White. "Disorderly Houses: Residences, Privacy, and the Surveillance of Sexuality in 1920s Harlem." *Journal of the History of Sexuality* 21, no. 3 (September 2012): 443–66.

Romo, Vanessa. "Georgia's Governor Signs 'Fetal Heartbeat' Abortion Law." National Public Radio. Accessed May 7, 2019. https://www.npr.org/2019/05/07/721028329/georgias-governor-signs-fetal-heartbeat-law.

Sanders, Cheryl J. "Sexual Orientation and Human Rights Discourse in the African American Churches." In *Sexual Orientation and Human Rights in African American Discourse*, edited by Saul Olyan and Martha C. Nussbaum, 178–84. New York: Oxford University Press, 1998.

Sanders, Cheryl J., Cheryl Townsend Gilkes, Katie G. Cannon, Emilie M. Townes, M. Shawn Copeland, and bell hooks. "Roundtable Discussion: Christian Ethics and Theology in Womanist Perspective." *Journal of Feminist Studies in Religion* 5, no. 2 (1989): 83–112.

Schneider, Laurel C. "What if It Is a Choice?: Some Implications for the Homosexuality Debates for Theology." In *Sexuality and the Sacred: Sources for Theological Reflection*, Second Edition, edited by Marvin M. Ellison and Kelly Brown Douglas, 297–304. Louisville: Westminster John Knox Press, 2010.

Schneider, Laurel C. and Thelathia Nikki Young. "Talking to the Dead." In *Queer Soul and Queer Theology Ethics and Redemption in Real Life*. London: Routledge, 2021.

Scully, Jackie Leach. "When Embodiment Isn't Good." *Theology & Sexuality* 9 (1998): 10–28.

Simmons-Thorne, Naomi. "Pauli Murray and the Pronominal Problem: A De-essentialist Trans Historiography." *The Activist History Review*. May 30, 2019. Accessed December 30, 2022. https://activisthistory.com/2019/05/30/pauli-murray-and-the-pronominal-problem-a-de-essentialist-trans-historiography/.

Sneed, Roger A. "Dark Matter: Liminality and Black Queer Bodies." In *Ain't I a Womanist Too?: Third Wave Womanist Religious Thought*, edited by Monica A. Coleman, 138–48. Minneapolis: Fortress Press, 2013.

Sneed, Roger A. "Like Fire Shut Up in Our Bones: Religion and Spirituality in Black Gay Men's Literature." *Black Theology* 6, no. 2 (2008): 241–61.

Sneed, Roger A. *Representations of Homosexuality: Black Liberation Theology and Cultural Criticism*. New York: Palgrave Macmillan, 2010.
Snelson, Floyd G. "Strange 'Third' Sex Flooding Nation, Writer Reveals." *Pittsburgh Courier*. March 19, 1932.
Snorton, C. Riley. *Black on Both Sides: A Racial History of Trans Identity*. Minneapolis: University of Minnesota Press, 2017.
Snorton, C. Riley and Jin Haritaworn. "Trans Necropolitics: A Transnational Reflection on Violence, Death, and the Trans of Color Afterlife." In *Transgender Studies Reader 2*, edited by Susan Stryker and Aren Aizura, 66–76. New York: Routledge, 2013.
Sorett, Josef. *Spirit in the Dark: A Religious History of Racial Aesthetics*. New York: Oxford University Press, 2016.
Spencer, Jon Michael. "The Black Church and the Harlem Renaissance." *African American Review* 30, no. 3 (Autumn, 1996): 453–60.
Spivak, Gayatri Chakravorty. "Subaltern Studies: Deconstructing Historiography." In *The Spivak Reader*, edited by Donna Landry and Gerlad MacLean, 203–36. London: Routledge, 1996.
Stringfellow, Roland. "Soul Work: Developing a Black LGBT Liberation Theology." In *Queer Religion: Volume I*, edited by Donald L. Boisvert and Jay Emerson Johnson, 113–25. Santa Barbara: Praeger, 2012.
Stuart, Elizabeth. "Disruptive Bodies: Disability, Embodiment, and Sexuality." In *Sexuality and the Sacred: Sources for Theological Reflection, Second Edition*, edited by Marvin M. Ellison and Kelly Brown Douglas, 322–37. Louisville: Westminster John Knox Press, 2010.
Stuart, Elizabeth. "Third Sex Hold Sway at Rockland When Hamilton Lodge Holds 65th Masquerade Ball and Dance; Police Arrest Two." In *The New York Age*. New York, NY, March 4, 1933.
The Human Rights Campaign. "Violence against the Transgender Community in 2019." Accessed April 28, 2019. https://www.hrc.org/resources/violence-against-the—transgender-community-in-2019.
Thurman, Wallace. *Negro Life in New York's Harlem: A Lively Picture of a Popular and Interesting Section*. Girard: Haldeman-Julius Publications, 1927.
Townes, Emilie M. "The Dancing Mind: Queer Black Bodies and Activism in Academy and Church." 2011 Gilberto Castañeda Lecture. Chicago Theological Seminary (April 28, 2011).
Townes, Emilie M. *In a Blaze of Glory: Womanist Spirituality as Social Witness*. Nashville: Abingdon Press, 1995.
Townes, Emilie M. *Womanist Ethics and the Cultural Production of Evil*. New York: Palgrave Macmillan, 2006.

Vogel, Shane. *The Scene of Harlem Cabaret: Race, Sexuality, Performance.* Chicago: University of Chicago Press, 2009.
Warner, Michael. *The Trouble with Normal: Sex, Politics, and the Ethics of Queer Life.* Cambridge: Harvard University Press, 1999.
Warner, Michael. "Publics and Counterpublics (abbreviated version)." *Quarterly Journal of Speech* 88, no. 4 (November 2002): 413–25.
Watts, Jill. *God, Harlem, USA: The Father Divine Story.* Berkeley: University of California Press, 1995.
Weisbrot, Robert. *Father Divine and the Struggle for Racial Equality.* Champaign: University of Illinois Press, 1983.
Weisenfeld, Judith. *African American Women and Christian Activism: New York's Black YWCA, 1905–1945.* Cambridge: Harvard University Press, 1997.
Weisenfeld, Judith. "Real True Buds: Celibacy and Same-Sex Desire across the Color Line in Father Divine's Peace Mission Movement." In *Devotions and Desires: Histories of Sexuality and Religion in the Twentieth-Century United States*, edited by Gillian Frank, Bethany Moreton, and Heather R. White. Chapel Hill: UNC Press, 2018.
West, Traci C. "Black Bisexual Queering of Anti-Violence Christian Ethics." *Modern Believing* 60, no. 1 (2019): 15–28.
West, Traci C. "Constructing Ethics: Reinhold Niebuhr and Harlem Women Activists." *Journal of the Society of Christian Ethics* 24, no. 1 (Spring/Summer 2004): 29–49.
West, Traci C. *Disruptive Christian Ethics: When Racism and Women's Lives Matter.* Louisville: Westminster John Knox Press, 2006.
West, Traci C. "Visions of Womanhood: Beyond Idolizing Heteropatriarchy." *Union Seminary Quarterly Review* 58, nos. 3 and 4 (2004): 128–39.
Wilcox, Melissa M. *Queer Religiosities: An Introduction to Queer and Transgender Studies in Religion.* New York: Rowman & Littlefield, 2021.
Wilkerson, Isabel. "The Kinder Mistress." In *The Warmth of Other Suns: The Epic Story of America's Great Migration.* New York: Vintage Books, 2010.
Williams, Alwyn. "Jazz and the New Negro: Harlem's Intellectuals Wrestle with the Art of the Age." *Australasian Journal of American Studies* 21, no. 1 (July 2002): 1–18.
Williams, Delores. *Sisters in the Wilderness: The Challenges of Womanist God-Talk.* New York: Orbis Books, 1993.
Wilson, James F. *Bulldaggers, Pansies, and Chocolate Babies: Performance, Race, and Sexuality in the Harlem Renaissance.* Ann Arbor: University of Michigan Press, 2011.

Wilson, James F. "Woman Sues Church over Gay Marriage." Interview by Soledad O'Brien. CNN Religion, June 24, 2010. Accessed April 27, 2019. http://religion.blogs.cnn.com/2010/06/24/gay-marriage-splits-african-american-church/.

Yetunde, Pamela Ayo. "Black Lesbians to the Rescue! A Brief Correction with Implications for Womanist Christian Theology and Womanist Buddhology," *Religions* 8, no. 9 (2017): 175.

Yetunde, Pamela Ayo. "Young People and the History of the Ryan White HIV/AIDS Program." Health Resources and Services Administration: Ryan White and Global HIV/AIDS Programs. Accessed April 14, 2019. https://hab.hrsa.gov/livinghistory/issues/youth_1.htm.

Young, Thelathia "Nikki." In *Black Queer Ethics, Family, and Philosophical Imagination*. New York: Palgrave Macmillan, 2016.

Young, Thelathia "Nikki" and Shannon J. Miller. "Asé and Amen, Sister!: Black Feminist Scholars Engage in Interdisciplinary, Dialogical, Transformative Ethical Praxis." *Journal of Religious Ethics* 43, no. 2 (2015): 289–316.

INDEX

African Traditional Religion (ATR) 119
  Ifá 117, 119, 130, 138, 147–8
Anderson, Victor 69–71, 82–3, 86, 178
anti-blackness 18, 41, 83, 86, 184
Armstrong, Amaryah Shaye 5

Beam, Joseph 66–7
Best, Wallace D. 34
"bhomophobia" 9, 72, 95 n.35
Black Church 15, 34–5, 40, 152
  and leadership 69, 86
  power and 89, 182–3
Black Jews and Black Hebrews 35
blackness and queerness 148–53
blackqueer 3, 9–10, 20 n.1, 28, 70, 78–9, 85–6
blackqueer ethics 1–4, 162. *See also* sexuality/sexual ethics
  communal belonging 167–72
  communality 4, 63
  creating communities 174–5
  goodness 175–8
  identities 78
  individual and collective becoming 172–5
  inspirited bodies/embodied spirits and embodied spirits/inspirited bodies 178–81
  integrative values of 27, 165–7
  justice love in 163–5, 167
  messiness and 166
  moral practices 176–7
  narrative in 102–5
  right relationship 3
  sexual ethics 18–19, 63
  shared thriving 181–5
blackqueering 63–4
  Bible authority 79
  in ethics and theology 64–5
  LGBTQ+ experience 64–5
  power 85–9
  subjectivity and identity 72–3, 77–8
  transformation of body 82–3, 85, 125, 179
blackqueerness 1–2
  in Harlem 28–30 (*see also* Harlem)
  in histories (*see* oral histories)
  with immateriality 10
  integrative values 161 (*see also* integrative)
  living archive of 2–3, 5
  moral imagination 101
  spirituality and religion 103–5
blues (music) 36–7, 40–1
blues environments 7, 29, 38–45, 173, 182
  musical performance 41–5
  religious sphere 39–40
  "the Devil's music" 39
buffet flats 33, 45–6

Cannon, Katie G. 67, 82
Cheng, Patrick S. 16–17
Christian ethics/Christian sexual ethics 2, 5–7, 10, 161–3, 166
  disintegrative 13–14

gender and sexuality 14
heteronormative characteristics 69
imago Dei 74–5
LGBTQ+ life and living 161
racism 6, 16
theological perspectives 14–15
whiteness and anti-blackness in 18
clobber texts 18, 72, 79
Cohen, Cathy J. 29, 82
communal belonging 167–72
communal-sexual ethics 5–6, 11, 27
community(ies) 2, 10–11, 23 n.25, 51. *See also* integrative
integrative/disintegrative practices 12–13
Cone, James H. 39–40
Corey, Dorian 76
counterpublics 36–8, 51, 53 n.8, 167, 178–9
power and 182

Davis, Angela Y. 38, 40–1, 179
De La Torre, Miguel, A. 16–18
dialogical method 166
disintegrative 4, 10–14, 166
    Christian tradition 13–14
    communities 12
    sexuality/sexual ethics 11–12
Douglas, Kelly Brown 15, 39, 40
Du Bois, W. E. B. 1, 40–1

Ellison, Marvin M. 4, 16, 22 n.6, 163, 167, 176
embodiment 82–5, 158, 178, 180. *See also* inspirited bodies/embodied spirits
Espinoza, Roberto Che 173–4, 188 n.25

Farajajé, Ibrahim Abdurrahman (Elias Farajajé-Jones) 15, 66–8, 73, 76, 87, 91 n.5, 96 n.46

Ferguson, Roderick 78
Fraser, Nancy 53 n.8, 182

gay 15–16, 29, 46–8. *See also* LGBTQ+
alterity and 73
Black Churches and 69–70
imago Dei 74–5
visibility is survival 81–2
goodness 7–8, 50, 90, 165, 175–8
Griffin, Horace L. 15, 66, 68, 70, 74, 80, 83, 86–8, 92 n.18
Gumbs, Alexis Pauline 3

Hamilton Lodge Balls 7, 29, 36–7, 48–51, 173, 182
communal belonging 168
Hammonds, Evelyn M. 82
Harlem 2, 6
    Black Jews and Black Hebrews 35
    Black Mecca 30–6, 54 n.13
    blackqueerness in 28–30, 167
    churches 34–5
    as counterpublics 36–8, 51, 53 n.8, 178–9
    individual and collective becoming 172–3
    integrative values 27–30
    microhistories 36–7
    migration of Black people 31–2, 37
    moral inquiry 28
    "Negro 'invasion'" 32
    organizations 33
    quare 77
    racism and economic disparity 36
    sexual and gender nonconformity 28–30, 33, 36, 53 n.5, 77, 167–8, 172, 175, 182
Harlem Renaissance 19, 30, 37, 40
Harrison, Beverly 16, 28

Hartman, Saidiya 3, 6, 58 n.45
heteronormativity 13, 24 n.30, 36–7, 69, 182
heterosexism 8–9, 15, 37, 46, 67–8, 77, 87
Hill, Renée L. 14–15, 66–8, 75, 84–6
homonormativity 13, 24 n.29, 94 n.26
homophobia 8–9, 67, 87, 181–2
homosexuality 47, 69, 71–2
   convincing heterosexuals of worth 80
   love-relationships 74
   power and 87
   scriptures and 79
humanist ethic of openness 72, 82, 188 n.25

identity 9, 35, 46, 68, 72–8
imago Dei 74–5
inclusion 65–72, 167
individual and collective becoming 13, 172–5
inspirited bodies/embodied spirits 178–81, 190 n.45
integrative 2–4, 10–14, 166
   blackqueer ethics 165–7
   Christian traditions 13
   communal belonging 167–72
   communal-sexual ethic 27
   communities 13
   embodiment and 178–81
   goodness 175–8
   individual and collective becoming 172–5
   individuals 12–13
   inspirited bodies/embodied spirits 178–81
   sexuality/sexual ethics 11–12
   shared thriving 181–5
   traditionalism 166

Johnson, E. Patrick 76, 78
Johnson, James Weldon, *Negro Americans, What Now?* 34–5
Jordan, Mark D. 162
Judaism 109, 118, 119, 128–9, 141, 155
justice love 4, 13, 22 n.6
   blackqueer ethics and 163–5, 167

Leath, Jennifer S. 8–9, 73, 76–8, 81–3, 164, 178
lesbian 15–16, 29, 46–8. *See also* LGBTQ+
Levine, Lawrence W. 40, 168
Lewis, David Levering 35, 179
LGBTQ+ 7–8
   Black men's experience 73
   Christians' experience 69–70, 73–4
   embodiment 82–5
   HIV/AIDS persons 65, 71, 81, 92 n.18, 169, 181
   inclusion 65–72
   life in ethics and theology 64–7
   resistance and difference 78–82
   self-love 79
   self-naming 76
   subjectivity and identity 72–8
liberation theologies 5, 66, 74, 94 n.26
Lightsey, Pamela R. 8–9, 71, 73, 76–7, 80–1, 85, 92 n.18, 183
living archive 2–3, 22 n.5, 105–16. *See also* oral histories
   visuals in 106–16

Manalansan IV, Martin F. 166
marginalization 15–16, 168–9, 182–3
migration of Black people 31–2, 37, 45. *See also* Harlem

Monroe, Irene 79, 89, 99 n.101, 182–3
moral imagination 1–2, 6, 9–10, 20, 64, 86, 101–4, 157, 161
moral practices 6, 176–7
multiplicity 1, 17, 36, 64, 68, 82, 115, 128, 135, 153

Nelson, James B. 11

oral histories 6, 9, 102–6, 174. *See also* spirituality/religion
  benedictions 154–7
  blackness and queerness 148–53
  connecting spirituality 128–37
  goodness 177–8
  photographs 108–10, 113–15, 179–80
  queering belief 137–48
  religious and spiritual becoming 117–28
  visual representations of 106–16
Ortega-Aponte, Elias 181
orthoeros 17

possibility 1, 4–5, 29–30, 50, 101, 161, 168, 178
Powell, Adam Clayton, Sr. 33
power 85–9, 181–3. *See also* communal belonging
  counterpublics 182
  redistribution of 183
  shared thriving and 184

quare 8, 76–7
queer
  immigrant archives 166
  Queer Asian Pacific American (QAPA) 17
  queering belief 137–42
  radicals 3
  theory 8–9, 18, 30, 77

racism 6, 16, 18, 32, 35–7, 89, 184
religious ethics 6, 101–4, 166. *See also* spirituality/religion
rent parties 29, 36–7, 45–8, 168, 178, 182
  communal belonging 168
  social and political freedom 173
resistance and difference 78–82. *See also* goodness
right-relatedness/right relationship/right-relating 2
  and communality 4
  inclusion and 167
  and justice love 163
  in sexual ethics 16, 27

sexuality/sexual ethics 1–2, 63, 162–3, 176–7, 186
  as communal ethics 4–5, 102 (*see also* communal-sexual ethics)
  integrative/disintegrative 11–12, 165–6
  liberative 164
  moral imagination 10
  religious and social imagination 15
  right-relatedness in 16, 185
  silences 87, 89
  transreligious approach to 2
shared thriving 181–5
Sneed, Roger A. 6, 15, 69–70, 72–4, 81, 84, 94 n.26, 96 n.46, 100 n.113, 171–2, 178
Social Gospel Movement 34–5
spirituality/religion 103–7, 113
  aliveness and 124, 188 n.23
  as artistry 113, 115, 132
  astrology and ancient practices 134
  beauty 108

benedictions 154–8
blackness and queerness 148–53
body transformation 124–5
connecting to God 124–6
cultural diffusion 117
cultural experience 120–1
embodiment 108, 158, 165, 178
faith tradition 119
freedom of 108
identities and expressions 112
knowledge and wisdom 124
meditation and 131, 134
metaphysical conception of 117, 119–20, 128
multilayered voices 124
multiplicity and 135, 138
music and dance 118, 137
self-determination and 121
self-reflection and 127
Universe speaking 123
storäe michele 3
Stringfellow, Roland 75
subjectivity and identity 72–8. *See also* individual and collective

Tourmaline 168–9
Townes, Emilie M. 18, 37, 80–1, 83, 101
traditionalism 2, 4, 16, 51, 101, 164–6, 181
trans 6, 81, 85, 103, 108, 192 n.58. *See also* LGBTQ+
transdisciplinary approach 5
transness 187 n.19, 193
transreligious 2, 6, 11, 18, 20, 103, 188 n.25

violence 11, 55 n.15, 75, 169, 181
visuals in archive 106–16
vodou/voodoo 117, 146–7, 170
Vogel, Shane 29, 52

Walker, Alice 67, 76, 86–7
West, Traci C. 7, 9, 92 n.11, 166, 184
Wilcox, Melissa M. 23 n.13
Wilson, James F. 33, 45–6, 49–50, 173
womanism 67, 76, 86, 94 n.26
womanist theologies 66–7, 71

Yetunde, Pamela Ayo 6, 85–6
Young, Thelathia "Nikki" 2, 6, 8, 27, 69, 74, 77–80, 86, 184